# Five-Star
# Service Solutions

*Winning Ideas for Achieving*
*Exceptional Service*
*in Today's Financial Institutions*

## Barbara Sanfilippo

FINANCIAL SOURCEBOOKS
NAPERVILLE, ILLINOIS

For further information or additional copies, please contact the publisher: **Financial Sourcebooks**
A Division of Sourcebooks, Inc.
P.O. Box 313
Naperville, Illinois 60566
(708) 961-2161

Cover design: Creative Mind Services/Concialdi Design
Editorial: Patricia K. Kummer
Proofreading: Joyce Petersen
Design and Production: Monica Paxson

 **KENDALL/HUNT PUBLISHING COMPANY**
2460 Kerper Boulevard  P.O. Box 539  Dubuque, Iowa 52004-0539          0-8403-6373-7

This publication is designed to provide accurate and authoritative information in regard to the subject matter covered. It is sold with the understanding that the publisher is not engaged in rendering legal, accounting, or other professional service. If legal advice or other expert assistance is required, the services of a competent professional person should be sought.

*From a Declaration of Principles Jointly Adopted by a Committee of the American Bar Association and a Committee of Publishers and Associations*

---

**Library of Congress Cataloging-in-Publication Data**

Sanfilippo, Barbara, 1951-
 Five-star service solutions : winning ideas for achieving
exceptional service in today's financial institutions / Barbara
Sanfilippo.
  p.   cm.
 ISBN 0-942061-07-1
 1. Banks and banking--Customer services.  2. Savings and loan
associations--Customer services.  3. Credit unions--Customer
services.  4. Financial institutions--Customer services.     I. Title.
HG1616.C87S27  1990
332.1'068'5--dc20

                                                          90-46551
                                                           CIP

---

Printed and bound in the United States of America.
10  9  8  7  6  5  4  3  2

# Table of Contents

## Chapter 1

Sometimes management demands service, but does not serve as a role model to inspire it. Chapter 1 offers ideas on how management can act as service champions, as well as how to communicate the mission statement throughout the organization.

## Chapter 2

Quality service can only be delivered to our customers and members if our own internal departments are delivering quality service to fellow employees. Chapter 2 opens with a discussion of why internal service is important and goes on to offer several tips for heightening employee awareness and for improving and monitoring internal service.

## Chapter 3

> In order to be responsive to our customers and members, we must empower our employees to make decisions and give them the necessary authority for carrying them out. Chapter 3 offers practical ideas for pushing decision making down the line.

## Chapter 4

> Many organizations are more concerned with attracting new customers than retaining existing customers. Chapter 4 outlines several exciting ideas for retaining customers, such as thank you note contests, customer appreciation weeks, advisory boards, customer luncheons, and service guarantees. Also discussed are methods for determining customers' and members' expectations, such as opinion surveys and focus groups.

## Chapter 5

> If we want good service, we must expect it. Whether it be smiling, answering the telephones, or improving accuracy and turnaround time, we must establish clear standards for all employees. Chapter 5 gives examples of standards utilized by actual companies and tips on how to develop standards.

## Chapter 6

> Chapter 6 discusses the benefits of offering customer service training, as well as sales and service leadership training. Specific strategies are outlined for basic training, management retreats, product knowledge certification and testing programs, and utilizing customers and guests from other industries.

### Chapter 7

Developing service standards does not by itself guarantee service performance. We must be able to measure success and provide feedback to our people. Every time a customer complains is an opportunity to keep that customer. Yet many of our customers and members don't complain at all—they just leave and go to our competitors. Chapter 7 offers specific strategies for measuring service and for allowing complaints to surface easily, such as closed account and annual surveys, comment cards, customer service windows, and mystery shoppers.

### Chapter 8

Many organizations ask employees to deliver good service. However, if they deliver poor service, there are no consequences whatsoever. Chapter 8 offers tips on how to hold people accountable for service, such as including service and product knowledge goals in their performance appraisals and other practical strategies.

### Chapter 9

Rewarding and recognizing service efforts is critical to reinforce and sustain a service culture for the long term. Chapter 9 gives many easy ideas on how to do this, such as service clubs, special trips, on-the-spot rewards, and customer involvement programs.

### Chapter 10

Personal service is delivered each day by our employees. They are without question the key to achieving service excellence. How we hire and introduce new employees to our existing culture directly affects the results we get. Chapter 10 offers valuable suggestions on orienting new employees, personality assessment tools, and hiring from other industries.

## Chapter 11

Happy employees tend to automatically deliver good customer service. If we are obsessed with profits and with
customer and member satisfaction but ignore employee
dissatisfaction, our overall level of service can suffer. Chapter
11 discusses several fun ideas for creating a happy, productive team, such as employee appreciation days, employee
surveys, and special perks.

## Chapter 12

Today's branch manager, much like a "store" manager, is
seeking to develop a high performing sales and service
team. Chapter 12 outlines a sample blueprint for service
that a branch manager can use to implement some of the
practical ideas in the previous chapters.

## Chapter 13

Many of our service programs fail because we use the quick-
fix approach. Quality service does not happen overnight. It
requires a well-conceived implementation plan that includes
the total organization. Chapter 13 outlines strategies for a
long-term service action plan that will get results.

# Introduction

On August 5, 1989, my husband, Bob, and I excitedly approached the British Airways ticket counter at San Francisco International Airport. The reservation agent checked her computer, looked up, smiled at us, and said, "Oh, you're the honeymoon couple. Congratulations! Enjoy your honeymoon in Greece." Bob and I looked at each other and broke out in a smile. How did she know? we wondered.

Several weeks later, after visiting the Greek islands, we returned to the Athens airport for the long journey home. On checking in at the ticket counter, the reservations agent looked at us and asked, "How did you enjoy your honeymoon?" Again, Bob and I were stunned and thought to ourselves, How did she know? We boarded the long flight home and changed planes in London. At the London airport, another British Airways employee asked us, "What was your favorite island in Greece?" At this point, Bob and I were totally impressed with the level of care shown by these employees.

We then boarded the last leg of our flight from London to San Francisco. In the middle of the flight, we were approached by a flight attendant who presented us with a silver tray upon which were a bottle of champagne, two crystal glasses, and a card signed by the entire British Airways flight crew. The card congratulated us on our marriage and wished us success. Needless to say, Bob and I were extremely touched by the overwhelming service of the British Airways staff.

If British Airways with thousands of employees worldwide can instill such an incredibly strong service culture, why is it so difficult for us to create that same service ethic throughout our own organizations? The answer lies in our corporate culture. Corporate culture can be defined by the thoughts, feelings, actions, and beliefs that are shared by our employees (Butler and Dynan, 1988). If the majority of our people believe that service quality and customer satisfaction is the number one priority, we have a foundation for success.

Why do so many financial institutions talk about the importance of service quality and then not make it a priority? According to a survey by Raymond Ketchledge, president of the Sandy Corporation (*Western Banker*, April 1989), "Most leaders of the service industry still do not see a clear connection between the level of customer satisfaction and profit," despite the serious associated costs. Customer satisfaction costs the average service company 10.6 percent of annual revenue. Banks estimate an average customer loss of 5 percent annually. This amounts to a large financial loss per customer. The average cost to attract one new bank customer or member, if the institution is a credit union, can be as high as $100. It can cost five times more to acquire a new customer than to keep an existing one.

Instead of focusing our efforts on drumming up new business, it makes more sense to invest our resources in satisfying our loyal customers or members. Yet according to the Sandy survey, 42 percent of all companies perform no customer surveys, 70 percent have no customer service or public affairs departments, 83 percent have no 800 number or customer hotline, and 19 percent employ no customer monitoring at all.

In the December 1988 *Retail Banking Strategist*, David Bennett shared some interesting comments from a senior bank executive:

As fast as we were opening an account at the front counter, one of our tellers or customer service representatives would be closing an account at the back counter. We were selling wonderfully, but we weren't doing anything about keeping customers in-house. We've done some numeric studies on what we call "account turning," and it's amazing that many branches were richly rewarded for opening 600 accounts in a month, even though their actual position was only a net increase of six accounts.

This executive lamented that it would be better to open half the number of new accounts and use the extra time to provide better customer service. "We would have had a better chance to cross-sell more services, enhance the profitability of each relationship and have a far more profitable bank."

In the same article, Stanley J. Calderon, president and CEO of **Bank One** in Lafayette, Indiana, was quoted as saying, "We believe nearly one-third of a typical financial institution's non-interest expenses are attributable to the absence of quality or the correction of errors and/ or exceptions. By paying more attention to doing things right the first time and thereby making even modest improvements in error rates, significant cost reduction will result."

What causes an organization to deliver mediocre service as opposed to excellent service? The most common reasons are (Moore, August 1987):

★ Lack of management's commitment to adopting a quality service program

★ Organizational obstacles to achieving service quality

★ Unawareness of how to focus and meet customer expectations

★ Lack of knowledge and skills necessary to address service quality

Just think of how much it can cost us to not improve our service. Customer turnover and loss can be very expensive, not to mention the cost of having our employees making the same mistakes over and over. Consider all the time it takes our staffs to respond to complaints and to research problems. In addition, let's not forget all those dissatisfied customers who are telling their friends about their negative experiences with our bank or credit union. This damages our reputation and our business. While a service program might involve some increased cash outlay—perhaps for training and monitoring—there is no question that, in the long run, it can substantially lower overall costs by increasing customer or member retention, reducing mistakes and complaint handling, and improving productivity.

Please take a moment to have your management team and employees rate your organization on its level of service. You can make copies of "How Well Do You Score on Service Quality?" in Exhibit I.1 for this purpose.

Now take a look at First National Bank of Clarion's "Rules for Bank Customers." As you can see, those of us in the financial industry have come a long way since 1894 in providing service. However, the journey has just begun and the road is difficult.

## Rules for Bank Customers

The following rules are respectfully recommended to the attention of those who do business at the Banks. They will be the means of saving a great deal of time and annoyance.—viz:

1st. If you have any business with a Bank *do not* put it off until 3 o'clock.

2d. In depositing money do not get it upside down and wrong end foremost, but nice and straight, like it should be.

3d. If a check or draft is payable to your order or requires your name, be careful and endorse same.

4th. Always keep a record when your notes fall due.

5th. Never date your checks ahead. (You may never live to see that date)

6th. Always keep a correct record of your checks, and in *no* case overdraw your account, as this Bank will refuse to pay them.

A strict observation of the foregoing rules will make your account desirable for any bank.

We are very respectfully,

First National Bank

## Exhibit I.1

## How Well Do You Score on Service Quality?
### Edward T. Cannie
### Vice President
### Learning Dynamics, Inc.
### Needham, Massachusetts

| | | | | | |
|---|---|---|---|---|---|
| **Customer Orientation** | | | | | |
| We have a formal process in place to determine our customers' wants, needs, and expectations, now and for the future. | 1 | 2 | 3 | 4 | 5 |
| We encourage all employees to listen carefully to customer needs through informal feedback systems, and to act on this information. | 1 | 2 | 3 | 4 | 5 |
| Our repeat business exceeds the industry average. | 1 | 2 | 3 | 4 | 5 |
| When we lose a customer we know why. Or we find out. | 1 | 2 | 3 | 4 | 5 |
| **Management Climate** | | | | | |
| Managers give workers the responsibility and authority to take care of customers. | 1 | 2 | 3 | 4 | 5 |
| The predominant attitude around here is risk-taking rather than defensive; solving problems rather than laying blame. | 1 | 2 | 3 | 4 | 5 |
| We see ourselves as customers and suppliers in work relationships with one another. | 1 | 2 | 3 | 4 | 5 |
| **Cooperation/Integration** | | | | | |
| Our systems make clear who has responsibility for tasks. | 1 | 2 | 3 | 4 | 5 |
| Supervisors and managers in different departments work well together. | 1 | 2 | 3 | 4 | 5 |
| Very few things fall through the cracks because the left hand doesn't know what the right hand is doing. | 1 | 2 | 3 | 4 | 5 |
| We have clear measures and tracking systems to tell us how we are meeting our customers' requirements in every department. | 1 | 2 | 3 | 4 | 5 |
| **Attitudes and Skills** | | | | | |
| What happens in the organization really matters to all our people, executives and workers alike. | 1 | 2 | 3 | 4 | 5 |
| People feel responsible, needed, and empowered to do what needs to be done and take care of customers and keep them satisfied. | 1 | 2 | 3 | 4 | 5 |
| Managers and supervisors have the skills to influence others, communicate effectively, and motivate and lead subordinates. | 1 | 2 | 3 | 4 | 5 |
| **Costs-Prevention/Results** | | | | | |
| Our focus is on preventing problems rather than fixing them after the fact. | 1 | 2 | 3 | 4 | 5 |
| We concentrate on exceptional customer care, rather than cost-cutting, to increase earnings and profits. | 1 | 2 | 3 | 4 | 5 |

**Scoring and Interpretation**

| SCORE | INTERPRETATION |
|---|---|
| 68–80 | Your corporate culture seems very customer-oriented. |
| 48–67 | You seem personally committed to service excellence, but you need to get your systems in line. |
| 23–47 | You may need to recognize the importance of customers, but your organization doesn't seem to be acting this way. |
| 16–22 | You and your organization seem to be interested in other things instead of service excellence. |

I'm sure by now you realize that improving service quality is hard work and there are no quick answers or magic solutions. There are many excellent books on the market dealing with the whys and hows of quality service. *Five-Star Service Solutions* is an assortment of practical, tried-and-true ideas that many banks and credit unions throughout the United States have utilized.

Financial organizations mentioned in this book are included because they, like so many of you, are creatively pursuing service excellence. It does not mean, however, that they have achieved service perfection. Whenever possible, I have identified the originator of an idea. Many of the tips that I have included have been picked up indirectly over the years, and I could no longer track down the organizations that created them. I apologize to those organizations who might recognize an idea as theirs.

This book is simple, basic, and user friendly. The chapters are set up according to the key components necessary to develop a quality service program. If you're the type who hates to read books cover-to-cover, just flip to any chapter of interest and enjoy the list of ideas. The last two chapters are worthy of special mention. Chapter 12 is designed specifically to assist branch managers to develop a branch, quality service plan. The final chapter, How to Develop a Comprehensive Service Plan, offers a step-by-step outline for those who are beginning, or fine-tuning, their service program. I have included examples of surveys and forms whenever possible.

I would like to thank all of those who contributed to this book and all of my clients and associates who supported me to make this book possible. Special thanks to: my publisher, Dominique Raccah, for her incredible enthusiasm and belief in me and this book; my assistant, Kathy Balint, for her patience and terrific organizational skills; and my husband and cheerleader, Bob Romano, for his unconditional love and constant support. Most of all, thank you God for your guiding light and once again making my dream come true.

# Chapter 1

## Leading by Example

A big "kickoff meeting" is held to announce a new service excellence program. All employees are asked to smile, be friendly and courteous, and support the customer bill of rights. Everyone is given a printed card stating the new philosophy.

I'm sure you've seen this before. Then what? Usually, that is the last that employees hear about the new program. Although the CEO and his team periodically "talk" about service, the lack of funding, resources, time, and commitment send out a signal that, "service is not a priority." Without follow-up and management support, the program quietly fades away.

The role of the CEO is to heighten awareness and lead the service quality crusade. At American Express Company, Chairman James D. Robinson likes to say the company has four major objectives: quality, quality, quality and quality (Lateef, March 1988). This strategy has paid off handsomely for American Express in customer loyalty and the ability to command premium prices for premium products and services.

According to an October 1987 article in *Management Review* by Robert L. Desatnick, a committed CEO can:

★ Instill service as one of the most, if not *the* most, important value in an organization

★ Incorporate service as an important part of the organization's mission statement, strategic plan, and total marketing effort

The idea is to create and maintain a corporate sense of total customer awareness of customers or members in everything you do—in every daily activity of every employee.

In a March 1988 *Bank Marketing* article, Barbara Duncan, manager of Disney University in Anaheim, California, said, "We insist that our management team experience our product firsthand through something we call the Disneyland Guest Experience. Each summer, management must spend at least one 'day off' at the park with their families. Every member of management is involved, and sees the facilities from the guest perspective."

For any quality service program to succeed, management's commitment and support is absolutely essential. How many of us try to solve our service problems by asking our tellers to be more friendly? What good does that do if a member or customer had to wait in line for 10 minutes? No teller can hold a smile long enough to make that person happy! In that case, the problem is not the employee, but management. Unless the CEO is standing by, shouting "charge," and enthusiastically leading the way, the battle is lost. The rest of this chapter presents several simple but effective steps that senior management can take to provide a role model for quality service.

## *Management Retreats and Strategic Planning Sessions*

If you want your entire organization focused on service quality, hold a special retreat or make service a key agenda item at your annual strategic planning meeting. To avoid interruptions and encourage everyone to open up in a team spirit, it is best to hold these sessions off-site, in an informal and relaxed manner. All senior management should be required to attend. Get yourself a good note taker or tape the sessions. After the retreat, draft an action plan and distribute it to all attendees for their final approval. This document then becomes your guide to involve every single unit in the company.

The following are two examples of how credit unions used management retreats to improve service quality. **Monterey Federal Credit Union,** Monterey, California, for example, wanted to focus on enhancing its level of service performance. Stewart Fuller, the president, arranged for a one-day retreat for his senior management team in a comfortable and lovely setting. I facilitated an active dialogue with the senior management team, and we openly exchanged ideas on the key elements that needed to be addressed. By having an open and honest discussion and using small work groups, we were able to draft not only broad objectives, but also specific steps to implement in all departments. This meeting provided the impetus for the service action plan that Monterey Federal is persistently pursuing today. It is also a key agenda item at management meetings.

**North Island Federal Credit Union** in San Diego also holds an annual management retreat to review past performance and to plan for the coming year. Service quality is the number one priority at North Island's planning meetings. Mike Maslak, the CEO, invited me to facilitate part of this program on building a sales and service culture. I can assure you that if you worked for Mike, you would get caught up in his obsession with, and enthusiasm for, service excellence and his commitment to his employees.

## Fifty Dollars on the Spot

I sat waiting to be introduced as the guest speaker at **Olympic Bank** in Los Angeles. Kent Johnson, president of this dynamic little bank, was standing in front of his employees waving a $50 bill. "Who would like to try this month?" he asked. I thought to myself, What is this all about? One employee nervously raised his hand, stood up, and recited word for word the mission statement and service philosophy statement of the bank. As a reward, Kent handed the employee the $50 bill

3

and then challenged the remainder of the staff to also get their money. He then proceeded to honor service heroes and to get input from his staff. When the evening was over, I asked him, "How long have you been doing this and why?" Kent responded, "I began about six months ago. I want every single employee here to be aware of my vision and mission. I can't do it alone."

Many organizations distribute beautiful flyers about their mission and philosophy statements. However, when you walk up to an employee and ask, "What is the philosophy or mission of your bank or credit union?" they cannot respond. The example of Kent Johnson and his employees is a simple but powerful tip that senior executives can utilize to create awareness of their service mission.

## Senior Management and Headquarters' Staff Field Days

Some time ago, I read in *USA Today* that the Hyatt Corporation closed its headquarters one day to give all the senior management and support staff an opportunity to work in the field and get close to their customers. The president even filled in as a doorman!

I cannot think of a more powerful way for senior management to demonstrate its commitment both to customers and to staff than to "walk in their shoes" for a day. Think of the fun you can have planning this day and announcing it to your staff. The key is to get all senior management totally involved, regardless of their responsibilities. The implicit message to senior management is that no matter what their positions, they all work directly or indirectly for the customers or members.

## Adopt-a-Branch

**Connecticut Trust and Savings Bank** in Bridgeport, Connecticut, and Radio Shack have something in common. Each of these organizations has implemented a program that is guaranteed to get senior management out in the field, waving the service flag. This program is simple to implement. Ask each of your senior executives to adopt a branch or an internal department that they do not manage. For example, suppose I am the manager of the Data Processing Department, and I have adopted the Main Street branch and the Haven Street branch. This means that I agree to visit those branches at least once a month, sit in at their meetings, find out who their top performers are, share the service vision, and shake hands and greet customers while I am there.

Here is another way to implement this program. Support and operational departments can buddy up with a senior executive who is a user of their services. For example, suppose the head of the branch network adopts the Data Processing or the Customer Service department. Connecticut Trust commented that while this program was highly successful it takes top-down managing and scheduling to make it happen. The advantage of "Adopt-a-Branch" is that it mobilizes your senior management team to focus on customer or member satisfaction and to become a service champion in the trenches. To keep the momentum going, your CEO should ask managers to report monthly on how their on-site visits are going and what they hear in the field.

According to Karl Albrecht and Ron Zemke in *Service America*, when Jan Carlzon attempted his amazing turnaround of SAS, he realized that changing the attitudes and culture of this massive organization could take a long time. To speed up the process, he decided to personally take his message to the people. He also expected his executive team to become service champions. This implementation team, led by an energetic Jan Carlzon, personally visited frontline people throughout the SAS system, spreading the vision of finding a better way through service and creativity.

Why not turn your management team into service champions? Begin your "Adopt-a-Branch," or department, program today. Make sure to include your support and operational senior managers.

## *Service:   A Priority Item on Meeting Agendas*

The president of a small community bank in California is without question a service evangelist. He starts his senior management meetings by reviewing complaint letters. This sends out a very strong signal to his senior management team about what the priorities really are. He also comments on the service scores achieved, including internal service scores between departments in the bank.

How are senior management meetings conducted in your bank or credit union? What is the first thing discussed on the agenda? Is measuring service and sales results and monitoring complaints included on every single agenda? If not, you could be demanding quality service but sending out messages that say, "Quality service is really not important." Make sure service quality is a regular agenda item at your executive management meetings.

## Service Excellence Council

**Society Corporation**, Cleveland, Ohio, has a comprehensive service program called the Service Excellence Council, which involves all departments and employees. Rob Maddox, vice president of sales and service development, explained how this special council works:

The Service Excellence Council is a committee comprised of senior and mid-level managers, representing a cross-section of the organization's functions. The council focuses on service quality issues as they relate to:

★  Policy and Procedure

★  Human Resources

★  Communication/Awareness

★  Measurement/Tracking

★  Recognition and Rewards

The council membership meets monthly or as necessary to identify broader, cross-functional service quality issues and brings together those required to implement a change process. When needed, we utilize subgroups responsible for a specific area/issue. Each subgroup reviews and prioritizes the issue they must address and then puts together and administers a team to facilitate the improvement. Subgroups measure and track their improvement efforts and regularly report results back to the Service Excellence Council.

Each member of the council is responsible for promoting service quality awareness. By working with other areas represented on the council, we can cut through many of the barriers preventing us from delivering superior service quality. The council is an effective forum to bring about change in the organization.

The mission and efforts of the Service Excellence Council are given the highest priority. Without the active, visible support of executive management, council initiatives will not gain the awareness and support required to bring change. The council is committed to serving the mission of the Corporation but must have continuous support to make it happen.

The mission of the Service Excellence Council is to champion and insure the establishment of a service quality mind-set throughout the organization that positions Society Corporation as the premier provider of quality service in the financial services industry.

Our Service Excellence Council objectives are as follows:

1. Serve as the focal point for quality initiatives throughout the Corporation.
   * ★ Identify quality improvement projects
   * ★ Initiate plans of action to improve and enhance quality
   * ★ Develop ongoing monitoring of quality programs
   * ★ Communicate quality programs and initiatives

2. Assign and administer corporate subcommittees, as needed, to recommend and implement service quality improvements for issues identified in the following areas:
   * ★ Policy and Procedures
   * ★ Human Resources
   * ★ Measurement
   * ★ Recognition
   * ★ Communication

3. Assure [that] each employee exhibits a commitment to quality consistent with Society's objective of being a superior financial services provider.

   ★ Develop our human resources

   ★ Recognize and reward quality efforts

   ★ Communicate accomplishments and successes

4. Measure the Five Dimensions of Service Performance. Service quality specifications must be defined by the customer's expectations.

   ★ Tangibles—The seeable part of the service offer

   ★ Reliability—Keeping the service promise

   ★ Responsiveness—The readiness and willingness to serve promptly and efficiently

   ★ Assurance—Courtesy and competence of service

   ★ Empathy—Commitment, understanding, and caring

Rob told me that the council has the active support and involvement of executive, senior, and midlevel management from every department in the bank. As a result, the message that quality service is a major focus is rapidly spreading throughout the organization.

## Management Filling In for Staff

If you want your frontline employees to take you seriously about service quality, consider having your senior management staff fill in for them when they need to attend special meetings or training sessions. For example, when I visited **Olympic Bank** in Los Angeles, Kent Johnson, the president, and his senior management team filled in for the tellers so they could attend my customer service workshop. Not only did the employees feel important because management would cover for them, but the customers were extremely impressed with the support of the management for the development of the staff.

Typically in a small bank or credit union, it is difficult to get employees together for meetings or training sessions. Often the comment is, "We

8

have to have a session on a Saturday or simply not at all; it's impossible during the week." Kent did not want to ask his staff to work on Saturday. He felt so strongly about having his staff get the skills they needed that he gladly volunteered to cover for the tellers. Kent leads by example.

David Glass, president and CEO of Wal-Mart, commented in an October 1987 article in *Bank Marketing:*

> When we have long lines at the checkouts, a member of senior management will go behind the checkouts and will work with those customers. And they'll do things like pre-approve the checks, visit with the customers, answer questions, give candy to the kids, along with Cokes and coffee for the adults. You'd be amazed at how tolerant, patient, and appreciative customers are when they know that you at least recognize their plight, are attentive to it, and want to do something about it.

## *Infusion of a Mission Statement*

Creating a corporate mission statement that clearly defines your vision and commitment is a key element of your service culture. Ideally, this statement addresses the importance of your customers or members, as well as your employees, and serves as a motivating force throughout your organization. Talking about the "bottom line" alone rarely inspires employee loyalty.

The mission statement sets forth the theme of striving for excellence in operating efficiency and image. It expresses your commitment to helping your employees achieve personal development through training and advancement, as well as rewarding them with recognition and incentives. The mission statement is your chance to rally the troops. It should be posted in highly visible areas.

The mission statement of many banks and credit unions says: We will deliver the best service available. But what does this mean specifically if I am a bookkeeper or a loan processor? For a mission statement to be effective and meaningful, it must be broken down into specific, measurable behaviors and then communicated to each employee.

**Sun Bank** in Orlando, Florida, is a bank obsessed with achieving the highest level of service quality. To do this, it embarked on a very comprehensive service program. A key part of this program was the development of a specific statement about the bank's service mission and philosophy. This statement, with its specific objectives, was printed and distributed to the entire staff.

Next, to bring this statement to life, each department developed its own mission statement. Unfortunately, many internal operational and support departments in banks and credit unions have no clear idea of how they contribute to the overall picture. Therefore, the development of department mission statements is an effective way of including the support groups. For example, a Data Processing Department might declare: Our mission is to turn around all requests by our internal customers within 48 hours and deliver friendly, responsive, and accurate service.

Sun Bank was not satisfied with just an overall mission statement and department mission statements. Individual pledges were also requested of every single employee. Each employee was asked to develop one measurable commitment to quality service that he or she could implement that year. These pledges were collected and reviewed by every department's senior manager. A teller might pledge, "I commit to thanking all customers for their business and asking them to return." A customer service representative might make a commitment to standing and shaking hands with each customer.

As a result of a sales and service leadership session that I facilitated with **Alameda First National Bank** in Alameda, California, the following department mission statements were developed by the managers with input from their staffs:

Submitted by: William H. Bailey, vice president and branch manager, Harbor Bay Isle Branch

> "Caring is our business—bankwise are our customers. The employees of Harbor Bay Isle strive for excellence in providing ensured satisfied customer service. We pride ourselves in acknowledging our cus-

tomers by name and with a friendly smile and responding to their needs with enthusiasm and promptness."

Submitted by: Peggy Monahan, assistant vice president and manager, Proof Department

"Our mission: To promote awareness throughout our banking system of the correct way to organize work so quality control can more quickly and accurately process transactions and so we can meet our deadlines."

Submitted by: James Sasaki, auditor

"The Audit Department's mission is to independently evaluate the adequacy, effectiveness, and efficiency of the controls within the organization and the quality of ongoing operations ensuring that the bank's assets and shareholders' investments are protected from fraud, misconduct, and negligence."

Submitted by: Chris Hamilton, assistant vice president and personnel director

"Mission Statement of the Personnel Department: To provide superior service to all personnel of Alameda Bancorporation, Inc., through personalized and innovative services and through the administration of salary, benefits, and educational and career enhancement programs; and to provide equitable resolutions to job-related problems."

If you have a mission statement, is it alive and thriving, or is it dead? To infuse your mission throughout your organization, consider developing a clear mission statement with input from employees at all levels within your organization. Next, ask each department to develop its own mission statement. Finally, have each employee develop his or her own pledge as well. Sun Bank feels that this comprehensive approach will pay off in the long run, and I totally agree. Every single staff member must clearly understand the direction of the organization, of his or her department, and of his or her own individual contribution.

## *Visits by CEOs to Branches, Departments, and with Customers*

CEOs should try to be accessible to employees and customers. Presidents or CEOs of financial institutions should spend at least 20 percent to 50 percent of their time visiting with their employees and customers.

Leonard Berry and George Rieder mention in an *American Banker* article (December 24, 1985) that before Bill Marriott slowed down his pace, he travelled over 200,000 miles a year visiting his Marriott properties. Likewise, Sam Walton, founder of Wal-Mart Stores, also devotes considerable time and energy visiting his stores. In the same article, Bob Onstead of Randall's Food Markets is quoted as saying, "I can't sit in my office reading computer printouts all day and not know what's going on. How in the world can you get your employees to be interested in customers, if you are not interested in employees." If Bill Marriott, Sam Walton, and Bob Onstead can find the time to visit their many locations, our senior bank and credit union executives should be able to find the time to visit a handful of offices.

When **Penn Savings Bank**, Wyomissing, Pennsylvania, had their customer service kickoff day in June 1989, senior officers went to each branch to greet customers and hand out pencils with a "Customers Are #1" slogan on them (Naugle, January, 1990).

Bob Mariano of **Chase Bank** in Scottsdale, Arizona, is an accessible CEO. One of his commercial loan officers told me that once when he had a hot prospect, he needed Bob to go on a sales call with him. He picked up the phone and Bob was eager to be of assistance. At Chase, if employees have special requests from customers and cannot get through to their manager, they feel comfortable picking up the phone and calling Bob's office.

## *President's Column in Employee Newsletters*

I read many excellent employee newsletters. However, I am surprised that many of these newsletters do not include a column from the CEO or president. This is an ideal opportunity for a president or CEO to share his or her vision and philosophy, to highlight sales and service success stories, and to recognize those individuals who contribute to fulfilling the organization's mission.

## Greeting Employees like Customers or Members

A president once complained to me that his employees were not outgoing and friendly when greeting customers. This same president arrives in the morning and ignores his employees. At a reward function for his staff, rather than mingling, greeting them by name, and smiling, he stood off in a corner talking with managers.

It warms my heart, however, when I remember the time I spoke at a bank and was chatting with the president at a large cocktail reception to recognize and reward his employees. He turned to me and said, "Excuse me, Barbara. I want to visit with the staff." I watched this executive as he went from table to table. He knew most of his employees' names; he shook their hands; he was warm, friendly, and demonstrated the behavior he was asking for.

When **Penn Savings Bank** launched a major customer service program, senior management was actively involved. On the first day of the program, each support employee in the operational departments was personally greeted with a handshake by one of the bank's executive officers and given a "Customers Are #1" T-shirt to wear during the program. Helium-filled balloons were handed out with the same message. In the branches, the manager was the morning greeter. As these employees arrived, the greeting was "Welcome to Penn Savings Bank. I'm glad you're here."

According to a January 1990 article in *Bank Marketing* by Joni Naugle, director of marketing at Penn Savings, "This was to make a point that everyone is a customer or helps a customer at some point in the day. Bank management was showing employees appreciation for being with Penn—the same type of appreciation that should be shown to customers every day."

If you want excellent service, treat your employees the way you would treat a customer or member. Ask your managers to greet employees each day, circulate at social events, and split up and sit with the troops at banquets.

13

### *Jump for the Telephone*

We all agree that the telephone is an essential customer service tool. Many banks and credit unions have developed telephone standards and introduced phone etiquette training for their staffs. Yet, sometimes senior managers are allowed to ignore ringing phones. Employees get the message that there are two sets of standards, one for them (employees) and one for senior managers.

Since we are service organizations, it is imperative that our senior managers literally jump for a telephone when it is ringing. Our employees will then see that management is not just giving lip service to telephone standards. An easily instituted telephone standard is to have the person closest to a ringing phone answer within three rings.

### *Fireside Chats*

Mike Maslak, CEO of **North Island Federal Credit Union** in San Diego, is a vibrant man with a burning service mission. Both to keep his vision alive and to listen to his staff's ideas, he introduced "fireside chats."

On a quarterly basis, Mike visits each branch and department to communicate how the service culture is developing and where the credit union is going, as well as to listen to his staff's ideas. The meetings last about 45 minutes and are held in the morning or evening. The staff looks forward to his visits and creates themes to make them fun. For example, one department called it a "poolside chat" and used beach towels, chairs, and sunglasses to get into the spirit. Another branch made a mock fire and got rocking chairs for his fireside chat.

Most top service leaders recognize that communicating top-down and bottom up is essential to keep everyone focused and on track. In *Service Quality* (Berry, Bennett, and Brown), Paul Limbert, general manager of the outstanding Park Hyatt Hotel in Washington, D.C., is quoted as saying, "We listen to the staff, they are the ones who give us the customer feedback that enables us to improve." Like Mike Maslak, Limbert chairs monthly "Hyatt talks," to encourage upward communication.

14

This all sounds so simple. Yet, often directors of marketing tell me they practically have to beg their CEOs to take the time to make a commitment to programs like these. Leadership is a verbal, high-touch process; it is not memo driven. Start your monthly forums now.

Your managers and employees probably believe they don't have enough time to do all that is expected of them, let alone deliver a high level of service. Unless you show them that quality service is the number one priority, nothing will happen. Leading by example requires you to demonstrate the importance of quality service to employees every chance you get. By utilizing the simple ideas in this chapter, you will be well on your way to demonstrating to your team—senior management and employees—that you're really committed to service.

# Chapter 2

## Improving Internal Service

The basic premise of a sales and service organization is that everyone has a customer to serve. While everyone does not necessarily deal with customers or members directly, it is true that everyone has somebody to please, either internally or externally. In a December 1986 article in *Mortgage Banking*, James C. Pratt and James L. Hennessy, Jr., commented that "senior management's customer is ownership, middle management's customers are senior managers, processors service agents, loan officers, borrowers, and underwriters. Receptionists serve everyone, including other employees."

Eric R. Blume, in the September 1988 issue of *Training and Development* presented an interesting piece on TRW. At TRW's Information Services Division in Orange, California, the approach to improving customer service is to work from the inside out. "We're saying that we can't provide the best service possible to our customer until we provide the best service internally," said Devon Scheef, manager of sales and marketing training. One of TRW's internal support departments, Information Processing Organization, surveyed its key internal customers by asking how they would define good service and what IPO could do to meet their standards. "It's the best thing we've done throughout the entire process," said Scheef. "They started talking to other people and realized, hey, they really are mad at us, we really could improve."

The quality of the work delivered by support and administrative employees is far more crucial than most people realize. As Jan Carlzon points out in his book, *Moments of Truth*, these employees also have an opportunity to serve a customer or member internally or externally. So what can we do to bring our internal service to a superior level of performance?

## *Climate Survey of Organizational Readiness*

"If you haven't done an assessment of the internal climate of your business, this is your first step. You have to discover whether or not the organization is ready for a major cultural change." I couldn't agree more with this statement from Albrecht and Bradford's *The Service Advantage*. Internal problems simmering under the surface can sabotage even the best quality service program.

The first step in improving internal service is to take a climate survey. A climate survey is typically a questionnaire that all managers and employees complete anonymously. Questions are asked about every aspect of the organization to determine how employees view the present culture and how they believe it should be. Some common areas addressed in a climate survey are:

★ Responsibility: Do employees feel a personal responsibility for work? Are they encouraged to take increased responsibility and risks? Is their individual judgement trusted? Do they have a sense of autonomy?

★ Recognition: Are employees recognized and rewarded for doing good work, or are they just criticized for poor performance?

★ Teamwork: Do employees feel they belong to a nurturing organization? Is there mutual warmth and support; trust and pride; a feeling of personal loyalty, and trust and respect for others?

★ Clarity: Do employees understand the organization's goals and policies? Are they clear about their job? Are plans and activities organized and run smoothly? Do they understand what is expected of them? Is there a smooth flow of information?

★ Commitment: Are employees involved in goal setting? Do they take part in regular goal-setting and review meetings? Do they make a personal commitment to achieve goals? Do they feel that goals are realistic?

★ Standards: How do employees feel about the emphasis that management puts on setting high standards of performance? Does management provide coaching to improve performance? Do employees take pride in doing a good job? Do employees feel that standards are clear and tied to performance reviews?

★ Service and Sales: How do employees feel about management making the building of a sales and service culture a strategic priority? Does the organization have an obsession with monitoring service? Is sales viewed as a key service element? Is product knowledge reinforced? Is sales leadership strong?

Each employee responds to questions from the preceding areas with responses ranging from *strongly agree* to *strongly disagree*. The final survey can be used to determine your organization's weaknesses, employee resistance, and overall organizational readiness for your service program. Without the entire organization's support, it is difficult to implement a major service program and achieve long-term success.

We offer a climate survey to our clients, and together we use it as a diagnostic tool to determine any potential obstacles, as well as to insure success. Before you start a service program, survey your staff to get an honest picture of the existing state of affairs at your institution.

## Include Support and Operational Departments in Your Service Plan

Sometimes banks and credit unions embark on a service program aimed only at their frontline staff (Blume, September 1988). Because the support and operational departments are typically not included in the initial planning stages, problems arise later. How well your operations department delivers its services substantially affects the service quality perceived by your customers or members. To gain support and commitment early on, it is important to include support departments in the strategic planning process. Ask your senior managers how they feel their unit can deliver excellent service to users throughout your organization. How can the loan processing area better serve the branches? How can the data processing area better serve all departments?

The managers can then go back to their staffs and ask them for ideas on how they can contribute to the service mission. What standards can they use to deliver excellent service? How should standards be measured? When these kinds of questions have been answered, managers are ready to develop a department mission and philosophy statement that has real meaning for every staff member.

Once you have a mission statement, appoint a "quality service team" comprised of knowledgeable employees from each operational unit. Empower them to identify obstacles to the mission and make recommendations.

Len Berry, in an article for the *American Banker,* mentioned one of my clients, **Society Corporation** of Cleveland, Ohio, as an example of what quality service teams can do. At Society's customer service department, the principal vehicle for change is the Q-SEI team (quality Society employee involvement). There are 11 teams in customer service and allied departments, with 8 to 11 members per team. Membership is voluntary, with about 85 percent of the staff participating. Each Q-SEI team meets one hour per week on company time, comes up with its own service improvement ideas, and carries them through to completion. The teams have fun names like "Ninth Street Jammers" and "South Side Niners."

Dave Herron, senior vice president, and Dave Tillery, vice president of Society Corporation, are inspiring these people to deliver exceptional service through the power of teamwork. According to Len's article, the

Q-SEI teams accomplished 37 specific tasks in 1988. Some of their accomplishments included:

★ Revising an employee handbook titled "Quality Service Begins with You," which includes a statement of customer service objectives, the 10 commandments of good business, hints on telephone courtesy, and other material

★ Developing a regular customer service newsletter and distributing it to various parts of the company

★ Creating a service self-improvement exercise for all ninth-floor staff, in which employees scored themselves on how well they communicate and interact with coworkers and clients

★ Developing a "Special Touch" thank-you card for employees to show appreciation to other employees

★ Developing a booklet titled "A Guide to Quality Written Communication," which includes newly revised sample letters and hints on effective writing

**Ameritrust** of Cleveland, Ohio, has also put quality service on the "front burner," according to an article by Paula Slimak in the September 1988 *Bank Marketing*. Operations and marketing have teamed up to improve service quality throughout the institution with "Project Franchise," the creation of A. Jay Meyerson, senior vice president of retail banking. "Project Franchise" gives branch managers unlimited earnings potential as they assume new responsibilities for customer service. The criteria for this program includes attaining deposit and loan goals as well as improving administrative controls. What impressed me the most about "Project Franchise" is that a committee involving members from all management groups was created to weed errors out of the system and help Ameritrust lead a "quality revolution."

The key then is to make service awareness a strategic priority for every unit in your organization. If you are interested in how to incorporate the total organization into your plan, see Chapter 13.

### *"Everyone-Has-a-Customer" Campaign*

To heighten the awareness of internal service, develop an "Everyone-Has-a-Customer" campaign. If you hear someone say, "I don't serve customers or members," you know you have a problem with how your employees perceive internal services. A loan originator can only provide a mortgage to a home buyer with the help of a loan processor. Therefore, the loan processor should ideally view the loan originator as a customer.

For this kind of program to be effective, it must be given a high level of priority and visibility and involve all units. Support materials, such as forms asking staff members who their internal customers are and what service commitments they will pledge, are needed to spread the message. If you have a small organization, the CEO and the executive management team can demonstrate their support and commitment.

Senior management must be behind this kind of program for it to succeed. Every employee should be asking, What departments or individuals benefit and rely on my services? Therefore, who are my internal customers? How can I deliver better service? Each unit should conduct meetings and ask questions to determine the levels of service it is currently providing. What ideas do the units have for improving the teamwork, cooperation, and quality of work for their internal customers?

Implementing an "Everyone-Has-a-Customer" program can have a significant impact not only on the quality of service behind the scenes, but also on morale and the spirit of comradeship within your organization.

### *Methods of Measuring Internal Service*

To support the concept of "Everyone-Has-a-Customer," devise a way of measuring internal service. You will then discover the kind of service you are receiving on a day-to-day basis from your support staff. Such a measuring device will also let your employees know if you are satisfied or dissatisfied with their current level of service. What kind of measuring device should you use?

When you check out of a hotel, you often rate the service you received by filling out a comment card. You can also use these comment cards to improve your internal service. Develop a comment card that employees can use to rate the service they receive from fellow employees in other departments. Items to rate can include friendliness, courtesy, responsiveness, knowledge, telephone skills, professionalism, and follow-up. The comment cards can be scored with 5 or 10 being a perfect rating.

Distribute these cards among all of your employees, both frontline and support staff. Every time an employee deals with another employee, they can rate the service received on a comment card. Those getting perfect scores should receive special recognition, such as publishing their names in the employee newsletter, or a reward. One credit union has a selection of special gifts for those with perfect scores.

Comment cards can help you hold managers and staff accountable for internal service performance (see Chapter 8 for an in-depth discussion on accountability). By taking the average score of all the comment cards returned each month or quarter, you can determine the overall service rating for each employee and for each department. For example, suppose I am the manager of loan processing. During the past quarter, I received 50 comment cards from my internal customers and had an average score of 6.5. My performance appraisal states that I must maintain a 7.0 or higher. From the comment cards, I know that I must improve my service performance. Likewise, managers and supervisors can use the average scores to coach a particular individual who has been receiving unsatisfactory comment cards.

In *Service Quality*, Berry, Bennett, and Brown give the example of **First American National Bank** in Nashville that asks branch employees to grade the service performance of the Operations and Information Systems Division. Branch employees complete "report cards" using an A, B, C, D, and F grading systems. This is an excellent example of how we can rate internal service.

Once you begin using internal department comment cards, publish departments' scores in your newsletter. In that way, all departments can see how they are doing in relation to other departments in meeting the needs of their internal customers.

**Valley National Bank**, Phoenix, Arizona, has implemented a Department Rating Survey to rate their internal departments on the following nine attributes (*Measuring and Monitoring Service Quality*, Bank Marketing Association):

1. Friendliness
2. Professionalism
3. Knowledge
4. Helpfulness
5. Accuracy
6. Accessibility
7. Follow-up
8. Prompt return of telephone calls
9. Overall telephone service

Every Valley employee is asked to complete a questionnaire asking about the service he or she received from various staff areas during the past year. At the end of the questionnaire, employees are given the opportunity to make suggestions. Findings from Valley's survey indicated that a big concern was the level of phone service. For example, "The phone rang ten times, then once someone answered, they acted as if the call was an inconvenience."

Results of the surveys are distributed to Valley's executive management as well as to the department heads of these rated areas. Information is shared and discussed with each department's staff to encourage teamwork and improvement.

**National Bank of Long Beach** (NBLB), Long Beach, California, also uses interdepartmental evaluations (see Exhibit 2.1). Terri de la Vega, a marketing officer, explains NBLB's program:

> According to our initial employee survey, we were falling short in the area of servicing other departments within the bank. So we wanted to measure this aspect within the incentive plan. We began in July 1989 and our objectives were to encourage greater teamwork and obtain better service from other departments, i.e., responsiveness, attitude, etc.

24

## Exhibit 2.1

### National Bank of Long Beach
### Inter-Department Service Evaluation Form (Non-officer)

---

Department: (Overall)

Completed by: _____

| Service Area | Extra-Mile | Excellent | Good | Fair | Poor | N/A |
|---|---|---|---|---|---|---|
| Attitude | ____ | ____ | ____ | ____ | ____ | ____ |
| Responsiveness | ____ | ____ | ____ | ____ | ____ | ____ |
| Competence | ____ | ____ | ____ | ____ | ____ | ____ |

Comments: _____

---

Department: _____

Individual: _____

| Service Area | Extra-Mile | Poor |
|---|---|---|
| Attitude | ____ | ____ |
| Responsiveness | ____ | ____ |
| Competence | ____ | ____ |

Comments: _____

---

Department: _____

Individual: _____

| Service Area | Extra-Mile | Poor |
|---|---|---|
| Attitude | ____ | ____ |
| Responsiveness | ____ | ____ |
| Competence | ____ | ____ |

Comments: _____

We established service criteria based on attitude, responsiveness, and competence. On a quarterly basis, each department's staff members get together and rate other departments. If there are specific individuals who went the extra mile or who gave poor service, they are identified with a description of their action. I tally evaluations, and quarterly, outstanding 'contact' and 'noncontact' departments are recognized and rewarded. One sign of success is employees frequently comment on the improved service levels they receive from other departments.

Terri recommends providing an incentive for those departments who submit their evaluations on time. Costs for NBLB have been approximately $1,200 for annual department awards.

Another measuring device is a form for reporting poor telephone service. **First National Bank of Chicago** created a "telephone hot sheet" (see Exhibit 2.2) to improve its internal telephone service (*Measuring and Monitoring Service Quality*).

Whether you regularly use comment cards, conduct an annual or quarterly survey, or devise a "telephone hot sheet" to rate internal service, such measuring devices are a key part of building a strong support team to complement your efforts to increase the quality of your service.

## *Branch Marketing Meetings*

How often do we hear frontline managers and employees commenting, If only those marketing people would ask us how we feel. The most common complaint is, We are the last to know when a new promotion is scheduled. To correct this situation, Hazel Martin, manager of the Advertising and Promotion Department at **VanCity Savings Credit Union**, Vancouver, British Columbia, implemented branch marketing meetings.

Her rationale was to establish two-way communications on VanCity's marketing strategies, increase staff commitment and support, and increase the sense of teamwork. In addition, she hoped to get frontline input for corporate marketing strategies and upcoming advertising campaigns.

## Exhibit 2.2

### First National Bank of Chicago

---

TELEPHONE HOT SHEET

PROMPT, COURTEOUS TELEPHONE SERVICE IS IMPOR-
TANT TO ME, MY CUSTOMER AND THE BANK!!!

THEREFORE, I WOULD LIKE TO REPORT THAT THE FOLLOW-
ING TELEPHONE LINE DID NOT MEET OUR BANK
STANDARDS:

Phone Line: _____

Date and Time: _____

Contact Area: _____

PROBLEM:

_____ Rang More Than 5 Times

_____ Discourteous Treatment

_____ Phone Was Never Answered

_____ Placed on Hold Without Permission

_____ On Hold For More Than One Minute

_____ Other _____

_____

_____

Please give us your name and extension so that we can contact
you if we need to do so.

_____   _____

Name                              Extension

Return to Beth Shaw, Suite, 0339, IFNP-PL.

---

The first step in this program was to gain the support of the Branch Operations area in implementing the branch meeting schedule. According to Hazel, "Each quarter, representatives from the Advertising and Promotion, and Product Planning and Development departments visit the branch system. A schedule is established based on the convenience of the branches. Topics discussed generally cover a review of current campaigns and a 'brainstorming' session for ideas for future programs."

VanCity feels the branch marketing meetings are well received. Since beginning this program, there has been a marked improvement in coordinated, consistent branch promotions. A word of caution, however. Hazel told me that it is important to obtain branch operations support for the concept before proceeding with this program, as their participation requires valuable time.

## On-Site Visits to Support Departments

It's so easy for frontline employees to become frustrated with support and operational departments because they have no hands-on knowledge of the challenges these departments face daily. Likewise, support and operational employees often cannot understand why a branch employee begs, "I need it now! The member is waiting." To alleviate this situation and to encourage teamwork and empathy among employees, schedule regular visits to all support and operational departments and have your frontline staff rotate through these departments at some point in their first three to four months of employment if possible.

Support and operational employees can visit a branch, talk with employees, and attend a staff meeting. These on-site visits and exchanges of frontline and operational employees can do much to improve your internal service. **First Metropolitan "Metro 1" Credit Union** in Concord, California, encourages employees to visit other departments. Gail Palmer, vice president of human resources, said, "The employees are much more empathetic and understanding as a result of their visits."

Department heads and branch managers should make a point of speaking at internal department staff meetings. For example, your loan processing manager could speak at a branch sales meeting, and your branch manager could reciprocate at the next loan department meeting. This is an excellent way to build strong relations. Be sure to praise your department heads and branch managers for their support and cooperation.

## *Praising Certificates*

To make service fun for everyone, make it a positive experience. **Monterey Federal Credit Union** in California decided to develop service appreciation certificates (see Exhibit 2.3). Service standards were distributed to each employee along with 10 certificates. Employees were encouraged to give the certificates to other employees within a three-month period. The certificates simply said, "Here's my personal thank you for your excellent service." Space was provided to describe reasons for the thank-you. For example, "Thank you for helping me with Mr. Jones' complaint and researching his last loan payment." Certificates were tracked and awards were distributed for those employees who received the most at the end of the program.

**National Bank of Long Beach** has an extensive service program, "Service Is Our #1 Priority"—"If it's to be, it's up to me!" Terri de la Vega, marketing officer at NBLB, got an idea from Ken Blanchard's "Legendary Service." All bank employees have a pad of paper that says "I caught someone doing something right" (see Exhibit 2.4). Anytime they witness an employee demonstrating exceptional service, they write it on one of the special slips and submit it to Terri.

These slips equal extra points on the employee's master scorecard for a quarterly cash pay out. A copy of the comment is sent to the employee—this really makes their day! According to Terri, "These slips of paper are flying around the bank. People take the time to express their appreciation which tends to create a higher motivation level for providing quality service and internal teamwork."

29

## Exhibit 2.3

**Monterey Federal**
C R E D I T   U N I O N

# IN APPRECIATION

HERE'S MY PERSONAL THANK YOU
FOR YOUR EXCELLENT SERVICE

FOR

DATE

SIGNATURE

## Exhibit 2.4

### National Bank of Long Beach

# I caught someone doing something right!

I caught _____

_____

_____

_____

_____

_____

_____

_____

_____

_____

_____

_____

_____

_____

Signed _____

Please return to Resource Planning

Terri cautions, "Communicate to your people that they should reward the 'above and beyond', not just 'good' service. Good service is expected." The cost of this program is $200 for printing.

This simple gesture can go a long way to heightening awareness of internal service and creating an atmosphere where the emphasis is placed on catching someone doing something right.

## *Host Open Houses for Support Departments*

When I worked at **Crocker Bank** in San Francisco, a centralized consumer loan center had recently been developed. As you can imagine, in the beginning there was much conflict between the frontline employees and the loan processors and officers at the loan center. To remedy this situation, the loan center hosted an open house one evening. Those of us who sold the loans got to visit employees at the center and see exactly what challenges they faced. This event had a tremendous effect on improving the morale, cooperation, and team spirit between the branch employees and the loan processing center.

Another time, a branch manager and the platform officers held a thank-you reception for the tellers and the operations employees for doing such good jobs. I'll never forget the look on the faces of the staff members—they were beaming and genuinely appreciative of being acknowledged for their contributions.

If you want to stimulate cooperation among support departments, consider hosting open houses and inviting your frontline employees to come and thank the support and operations people.

Until everyone in your bank or credit union truly believes that he or she has a customer to serve and that his or her contribution is important, your service program will flounder. I hope that these ideas presented will help you build a high level of internal service.

# Chapter 3

## Empowering and Listening to Your Employees

Many CEOs and managers believe that decisions and answers belong well within their area of control. Unfortunately, since managers are the most removed from daily problems, they are least able to offer a solution within a quick time frame. Empowering our employees to feel free to do whatever it takes to satisfy a customer or member is without question a key challenge. Financial institutions are typically so policy and manual driven that our employees are reluctant to take risks for fear of negative repercussions.

In his book *Moments of Truth*, Jan Carlzon shares how he encouraged those on the front line to put their skills and knowledge into action by seizing every opportunity to provide excellent service. The following story, excerpted from Carlzon's article in *Success!* (May 1987) based on *Moments of Truth*, is an excellent example of the kind of behavior we need to encourage in our own organizations:

> One day an SAS flight across Sweden had fallen far behind schedule because of snow. Taking responsibility for the situation, the purser decided on her own to compensate the custom-

ers for their inconvenience by offering free coffee and biscuits. She knew from experience that, because she was offering them at no charge, she would need about 40 additional servings. So she went to catering and ordered the extra coffee and biscuits.

The SAS catering supervisor turned her down. It was against regulations to request more than the amount of food allotted to a particular flight, and the supervisor refused to budge. But the purser wasn't thwarted. She noticed a Finnair plane docked at the next gate. Finnair is an external customer of the SAS catering department, and as such is not subject to SAS internal regulations.

Thinking quickly, the SAS purser turned to her colleague in the Finnair plane and asked him to order 40 cups of coffee and 40 biscuits. He placed the order, which according to regulations, the catering supervisor was obligated to fulfill. The SAS purser bought the snack from Finnair with SAS petty cash and served the grateful passengers.

In this case, the purser dared to find a way to circumvent regulations in order to meet the customers' needs—something she surely never would have tried under the old system. This is exactly the behavior that Jan Carlzon desired. He has a saying, "Run through walls." "Your goal may seem impossible, but don't stop trying until someone really says no. After we reorganized SAS and unleashed our employees' energy, our people began to break through walls routinely," stated Carlzon.

I had the pleasure of being a speaker at a bank marketing conference along with Bill Marriott. He, too, emphasized the importance of empowering frontline employees to make decisions. He told an interesting story. An honored guest of Marriott was checking out of his hotel one morning. The gentleman noticed a restaurant charge on his bill for approximately $10 that he felt he had not incurred. Upon checking out, he mentioned the error to the front desk representative, and the employee said, "I'm sorry, I'll have to talk to my manager." The manager looked at the guest and said, "I'm sorry, this charge appears to be correct." The guest was furious. He left the hotel and for many months thereafter proceeded to write scathing letters to the Marriott Corporation trying to get satisfaction. Marriott commented that by the time this gentleman's complaint reached his office, it had probably cost his corporation $900 to handle it! Not to mention the 20 days that this guest stayed at a Marriott hotel each year. He shared the following with the audience, "Our front desk representative should have felt comfortable waiving the $10 charge without asking her manager." He was quick to point out that it was not the fault of the front desk representative, but a challenge for his management to continually empower the frontline employees to satisfy guests on the spot.

If we applied this same rationale in our organizations, I'm sure we'd agree there's room for significant improvement. How many times do we hear our own employees say, "I can't approve this check, I'll have to ask my manager," or "I'm sorry about the $10 fee for your overdraft, Mr. Jones, but it is our policy."

When was the last time you personally made a special request in a store or hotel and the employee responded, "I'm sorry, I can't do that. I have to ask my manager"? Often, this kind of statement is so aggravating that we will walk out and never return again. Are our employees willing to take risks to respond to a customer or member? Or are they afraid to bend the rules one iota for fear of negative repercussions from management? Service-oriented organizations recognize that each employee must feel free to act spontaneously and do whatever it takes to ensure that the customer or member leaves happy. Consider the following approach to encourage decision making in your organization.

## *Surveying Employees for Ideas*

Dick Mangone, CEO of **Digital Employees' Federal Credit Union** (DCU) in Maynard, Massachusetts, is a service champion. To encourage risk taking among his staff and to solicit their ideas on how to improve service, he did an extensive survey, in November 1988, asking them what responsibilities and authority they needed to better serve their members. As a result of this survey, many ideas were implemented throughout the credit union.

35

According to Liz Hartel, director of human resources at DCU, "We wanted to improve service to a point where members and employees noticed it constantly. We think providing excellent service gives us a competitive edge over other financial institutions."

In November 1988, DCU started asking employees for any ideas they had for improving service. They also were asked what obstacles prevented them from delivering excellent service and what decisions they felt were necessary to make DCU more responsive to members' needs. There was no limit on the number of ideas an employee could submit. Employees were also polled through departmental meetings to ensure maximum employee participation. Every employee, including part-time employees, submitted at least one idea by January 1989. Once duplicates were eliminated, DCU compiled a list of 165 ideas and prioritized them as follows:

1. Low/no cost—will be implemented early in 1989
2. Increased cost/staff investment—will be started or completed during 1989
3. Ideas not yet implemented—will be reviewed in the fall of 1989 to determine future status

DCU has implemented 77 of the 165 ideas. Here are some examples:

★ A petty cash fund at each branch site was created for "member appreciation" events.

★ Authority to reverse fees, up to $50 limit, was granted, with appropriate documentation guidelines, to branch managers and head customer-service representatives.

★ Decision-making authority regarding stop payments and other account problems was given to West Coast regional management to expedite complaint handling.

According to Dick Mangone, "We regularly update our staff on the service ideas implemented through our employee newsletter, which gives a feeling of accomplishment, as well as encouragement that we do take their ideas very seriously."

**North Island Federal Credit Union** in San Diego began its IDEA$ (Improvement Demands Employees Action Suggestion) program in June 1989. The rationale for the program was to encourage staff to contribute ideas that would enhance service, profitability, or employee satisfaction. Mike Maslak, CEO, and Janet Madden, human resource director, developed the program.

Employees are encouraged to submit their ideas in writing. The IDEA$ Midmanager Committee then reviews and selects key suggestions for the Executive Research and Development Committee. Next, the Executive Research and Development Committee approves the ideas for research or implementation. Finally, $100 to $1,000 is paid to the staff member who submitted the idea.

North Island pays out approximately $7,500 annually for their IDEA$ program. They feel it is well worth the cost, since the savings from this program far outweigh the cost.

At **Penn Savings Bank**, Wyomissing, Pennsylvania, if the bank has done something to upset a customer, any employee has the authority to spend up to $50 on the spot to recover with the customer. Joni S. Naugle, director of marketing, comments in a January 1990 article in *Bank Marketing*, "It can be very upsetting when a customer wants an immediate response, but the employee must first 'check with their manager.' Customers want their problems handled immediately. The recovery program allows the bank to be more responsive."

**Richmond Savings Credit Union** of Richmond, British Columbia, developed a creative program in April 1988, "Cowbusters—the contest to change the way we do business!" An outline of this contest is provided in Exhibit 3.1. The objective of the program was to provide more efficient and effective service to members. Don Tuline, president of Richmond Savings, has made considerable progress in building his sales and service culture.

The following is an overview of the program as submitted by Diane Touchet, assistant vice president of human resources at Richmond Savings:

In 1987, we converted to a state-of-the art PC-based computer system which had capabilities far beyond the system we had been using. Many of the methods and procedures we had been using were no longer necessary because of the expanded capabilities of the system. Also, like most companies, we did some things from habit because we'd always done them that way, but the original purpose had become lost or unclear. We recognized that to reach our objective of achieving excellence in providing quality financial and related services to our members, we had to examine the way we did things and determine if it was the most efficient or effective way of providing that level of service. To encourage our staff to look for ways of improving, we introduced a staff contest called "Cowbusters" in April 1988.

The unusual name was derived from one of our planning mottoes—"There are no sacred cows." In a three-month period, we received over 440 suggestions from our staff, some of which were implemented immediately, many which have been implemented over a period of time on a priority basis and some of which we will implement in the future. Prizes included steak dinners and restaurant certificates.

We measured the success of the program by the number and quality of the replies and the benefits derived by identifying areas where communication had to improve, manuals needed to be updated, and areas where better and more consistent training was required. The contest was held for a three month period, and after that we formed task forces which continue to meet on a regular basis to bring forth new ideas and help implement more of the ideas brought forth in the contest.

Pitfall to avoid—make sure your staff understands that not all good ideas may be implemented immediately, but on a priority basis over a period of time and that some may not be implemented at all if the benefit does not outweigh the cost of implementation. Ensure feedback is given regarding suggestions which are accepted with expected implementation dates, and for suggestions not accepted, the reason should be given.

## Exhibit 3.1

**Richmond Savings Credit Union**
Richmond, B.C., Canada

# COWBUSTERS

*The contest to change the way we do business!*

## Exhibit 3.1 (cont.)

C    O    W    B    U    S    T    E    R    S    !

**We're doing a good job -- but what can we do to make it better?** How can we make our work experiences more satisfying and productive, and make our members perception of the level of service we offer increase?

Can you see things we do at Richmond Savings that we don't need to do, or perhaps shouldn't do? Can you see things we're not doing but should? Would these changes, if enacted, save (a) time, (b) money, (c) effort, or (d) all of the above?

Now there is **COWBUSTERS**, the contest designed to reward you for slaying the sacred cows at Richmond Savings.

A "sacred cow" is a way of doing something, or something that we do, that has become a habit, and one where the original purpose has become indistinct and unclear, and perhaps even lost.

For example, we used to record every utility bill payment in a journal kept by the individual tellers, as well as posting the payments and filling out credit slips. Now we simply post the entry and microfilm the stubs at the branch, and miss the extra step, saving time and speeding member service. The journal was not serving a useful purpose, and simply slowed down the transaction. The utility bill journal was a sacred cow.

Increasing Richmond Savings' productivity by doing the right things, at the right time, and doing them right the first time will allow us to provide better service, and to return a greater profit to the membership through SharePlan, and to receive larger productivity bonuses as staff ourselves.

If you have an idea, simply complete one of the attached entry forms, and drop it into an envelope marked **"COWBUSTERS"** in the internal mail system. All entries are anonymous, and if you don't remove your name before the entry is judged, then the staff in Marketing will.

Please be sure to think your entry through and highlight some of the key benefits as the entry form suggests, and to consider who should be responsible for actually making the changes.

If your entry is selected by the committee as a winner, then you will find your suggestion number posted in the branch as a winner, and even if you are not chosen as the best idea of the week, your entry will still be entered in a random draw for other exciting prizes!

**Get MOOOOVING!!! Enter the fabulous contest of ideas now!!!**

## Exhibit 3.1 (cont.)

C　O　W　B　U　S　T　E　R　S　!

**THEME:**

*"There are no sacred cows"*

**OBJECTIVE:**

To reward staff for suggesting ideas on ways that operations in any area can be improved and/or streamlined.

**DEFINITIONS:**

　　"Improved" means finding ways to :

　　　　　-Increase quality of product or work

　　　　　-Increase member's perception of service

　　　　　-Make money

　　　　　-Save time

　　　　　-Save money

　　"Operations": means creating or changing current

　　　　　-Procedures

　　　　　-Policies

　　　　　-Practices

　　　　　-Customer/Member Service Experiences

---

**Exhibit 3.1 (cont.)**

---

C     O     W     B     U     S     T     E     R     S     !

**PRIZES:**

Every two weeks starting **April 21st, 1988** the following prizes will be awarded:

**For the winning entries, as selected by the evaluation committee:**

# *STEAK DINNER PINS*

## *plus*

# *$25 KEG RESTAURANT GIFT CERTIFICATES*

*Plus*

**For all non-winning entries selected in a random draw:**

# *To Be Announced*

## Exhibit 3.1 (cont.)

NAME

SUGGESTION NUMBER:  **4 9 4**

RETAIN THIS PORTION -- YOU WILL BE KNOWN ONLY BY THE NUMBER SHOWN ON THE TOP
AND BOTTOM OF THIS FORM, AND NOT BY NAME WHEN YOUR SUGGESTION IS REVIEWED BY
THE COMMITTEE

MY COWBUSTERS SUGGESTION IS:

IT WILL BENEFIT THE CREDIT UNION BY:

WE WILL HAVE TO CHANGE THESE *OTHER* THINGS TO MAKE IT WORK:

THIS DEPARTMENT WILL HAVE TO MAKE THE CHANGES:

WE SHOULD DO IT BECAUSE:

**American Savings Bank**, El Cerrito, California, developed a complete program to empower its staff. A handbook with instructions, a poster, and a special video were distributed to each manager to generate enthusiasm with the staff. Managers led a series of discussions with the staff on empowerment examples and any concerns they might have. The program encouraged staff members to take responsibility for responding to a customer's needs on the spot. Nancy Smith-Becker, senior marketing representative of American Savings Bank, submitted some program materials for us (see Exhibit 3.2).

Rather than trying to guess what your customers or members want, or what responsibilities your employees need to give responsive service, conduct an employee survey. Give your employees the chance to come up with ideas for improving service. They can do it!

## *Employee Focus Groups*

Your customer-contact and support employees know better than anyone what is preventing them from being more responsive to your customers and members. Several financial institutions have conducted on-site focus groups with both frontline and operational employees who were asked the following questions:

1.  If you were president for a day and could make any changes or modifications to existing rules and policies, what would you do to improve service?

2.  If you could have the responsibility to waive fees and make exceptions or decisions of any kind, what would you ask for to better serve your customers or members?

3.  What is the biggest obstacle preventing you from delivering excellent service or being responsive to customers and fellow employees?

4.  What products and services do you feel our customers and members would enjoy and which ones do you think are no longer necessary?

5.  What complaints or comments do you frequently hear from our customers or members that you feel we should act on?

6. What could the CEO and senior management do to be better role models for customer service?

Organize an employee focus group at your bank or credit union. After conducting the focus group, tabulate all the ideas and then implement the best of them throughout your bank or credit union. Again, the purpose of holding a focus group is primarily to improve the responsiveness of the frontline employees by empowering them to be comfortable making decisions and taking risks.

Ask your employees—they know the symptoms and they have the cure to your customers' and members' ills.

## Reward Risk Takers

If you are serious about pushing decision making down the ranks, then acknowledge your heros for their independent action. Why not create a special award, "Risk Taker of the Month." A simple trophy or certificate will do nicely. Present this award to employees who take it upon themselves to make a decision, without asking a manager, in an effort to better serve a customer or member. By utilizing these certificates, your employees get the message, "We want you to make decisions and break the rules if necessary."

In a December 1988 article in *Retail Banking Strategist*, David R. Bennett, chairman of the board of Omega Consultants in San Francisco, gives this example of breaking the rules, "One institution has a little program they call 'throw out the rule book' where the local branch manager can basically create service policies that may be unique to that particular branch. As long as they document what they're doing and why, that branch manager is able to do it, change branch hours or whatever."

You should let your rebels lead the way. Pick a maverick—someone who will challenge accepted practices, such as "It takes eight days to clear an out of town check," or "Telephone transfers are not permitted."

Richard Hartnack, senior vice president of the personal banking group at **First National Bank of Chicago**, shared the following example of

---

### Exhibit 3.2

---

**American Savings Bank**
El Cerrito, California

# Who Puts
# The *Pow*
# in
# Empowerment?
# *You Do!*

## April is **EmPOWerment** month.

This handbook is designed to help you implement the **EmPOWerment** program in your branch.

### *EmPOWerment is for everyone!*

- We are all empowered to be successful and provide outstanding customer service.
- We are committed to quality customer service.
- We put the POW in **EmPOWerment.!!!**

---
**Exhibit 3.2 (cont.)**

---

# EmPOWerment Program Materials

1. EmPOWerment poster for branch breakroom

2. Three EmPOWerment bricks to attach to breakroom poster with EmPOWerment examples

3. EmPOWerment video for morning meeting

# Policy and Procedure

1. You are EmPOWered!!!  Do the right  thing for the customer and American Savings Bank.

2. If the occasion calls for gratuities please disburse from GL 61200 on your cost center. $25.00 is a guideline.

---

## Exhibit 3.2 (cont.)

---

# EmPOWerment Morning Meetings

The following pages are designed to assist you with developing exciting and informative morning meetings.

### I  PROGRAM GOAL

We will define and introduce EmPOWerment through discussion of EmPOWerment examples at three morning staff meetings. We will enhance the new Key Customer program by recognizing and providing Key Service for these customers. We will provide unexpected service to all American Savings Bank customers at all times.

### Morning Meeting One

*Ask*:
1. Have you used your EmPOWerment?
2. How did you use it?
3. What were the results?

*Explain:*  We don't wait for our customers to be inconvenienced or to have a problem before we use our EmPOWerment. We use EmPOWerment everyday to respond to customer requests.

### II  Video

At this time show the EmPOWerment video. The video includes three examples of using EmPOWerment.

After the video discuss the use of EmPOWerment shown in the video:

1. Provide the unexpected customer service for the Key Customer.
2. Offer to solve customer's dilemma by taking a money order to payee.
3. Encode checks for customer when they ran out of printed checks.

*Ask:*
1. Is there only one right answer for EmPOWerment?
2. What would you do?
3. Why would you do that?

*Explain:*  EmPOWerment will set American Savings Bank apart from all the rest. Senior management has empowered us to make the right decisions and provide outstanding and unexpected service!

## Exhibit 3.2 (cont.)

### III  Branch Discussion

*Ask:*  1. How is EmPOWerment the #1 key to success in this branch?

*Discuss:*  2. Select the top three EmPOWerment examples that have occurred in the branch and vote for the best one.

*Action:*  3. Ask the person with the best use of EmPOWerment to write their example on one of the enclosed peel-off bricks and then attach the brick to the EmPOWerment poster.
(There are three bricks for three morning meetings)

### IV  Key Customer Section

*Discuss:*  Key Customer program activity in your branch and how EmPOWerment supports Key Customer.

*Ask:*  1. What are your concerns about using your EmPOWerment?

*Discuss:*  Management supports your decisions and trusts that you will handle the situation for the benefit of the customer and American Savings Bank.

### Morning Meeting Two

The next two meetings reinforce using EmPOWerment. Discuss examples from the previous week and select the top one to be placed on the poster. (Play video again)

*Ask:*  1. How does using your EmPOWerment bring more sales to the branch?

*Ask:*  2. What reaction do you see from your customers regarding your EmPOWerment?

*Ask:*  3. What are your concerns about using your EmPOWerment?

*Discuss:*  Management supports your decisions and trusts that you will handle the situation for the benefit of the customer and American Savings Bank.

### Morning Meeting Three

Again select the top three examples of EmPOWerment and vote for the best one to be attached to the breakroom poster as in Section III.

1. If you have to ask, are you EmPOWered?

*Action:*  When poster is completed at the end of April please interbranch to:

**Corporate Marketing**
El Cerrito Branch #39

*POW!!!*

**That's EMPOWERMENT!!!**

decision making in an interview in the April 1988 issue of *Product, Marketing, and Technology.* It seemed there was one recurring complaint in their home equity lending area: After customers signed their loan papers, it took several days for their checks to be printed. This meant that the customers could not immediately access the money available to them. Some customers were very unhappy.

Why, Hartnack wondered, could the checks not be printed in advance? He was told that some customers might not sign up for the loans. "How much would that cost the bank?" he asked. The answer was, about $3 a customer. This seemed like a small price to pay for customer satisfaction—especially since few applicants ever failed to take the loans. Hartnack acted. Today, First National's home equity customers get their checks immediately.

To have a service-driven organization that responds directly and quickly to customers' needs, we must eliminate cumbersome tiers of authority. In essence, we must delegate the real "managing" from the executive suite to the operational level where everyone is then a manager of his or her own situation. Ownership and participative approaches must become a key part of our culture. We must remove the chains that prevent our employees from acting responsively. We must encourage and empower them to "run through walls" for our customers and members without fear of reprisals.

# Chapter 4

# Defining Service and
# Retaining Your Customers or Members

Peter Drucker once said, "The purpose of a business is to get and keep a customer. We can get customers, but then we've got to keep them."

Sometimes financial institutions are more obsessed with attracting new customers and members than with retaining existing ones. What good is it to bring new customers in the front door but have former ones leaving through the back door. Focusing on customer retention is a key strategy for ensuring customer satisfaction. How can you make your services unique? How are you different from all the others? How do your customers and members view your present service? To define service, you've got to ask your customers what they expect and then give it to them!

Marriott Hotels is always trying to be better. They provide faster check in, newspapers at the door, and a guarantee of breakfast within 15 minutes. A Marriott executive commented, "We must constantly strive to provide the 'little things,' the personal touch that will set us apart." (Dow, June 1988.)

Even the U. S. Postal Service is attempting to improve its service by meeting customers' expectations. In an article in the *San Francisco Chronicle,* Anthony M. Frank, postmaster general, said, "The American people have given us a clear message. In surveys of more than 27,000 individual and business customers conducted over 14 months, Americans have told us that the mail quality they place the highest value on is consistency. Yes, they want their mail delivered speedily and yes, they want it at a reasonable cost. But first and foremost they want to know with a high degree of certainty how long it takes for a letter to reach its destination. We are going to try to match customers' expectations with our service standards."

This chapter offers many tips on understanding how your customers perceive you and, thus, helps you retain those customers or members.

## *Customer or Member Opinion Surveys*

Dale Eicher, general manager of **Sunshine Coast Credit Union** in Vancouver, British Columbia, feels strongly that an annual survey of his members is the absolute minimum he should do to determine their needs. To quote Dale, "Give them what they want and listen to them." The only way to be certain that you are giving your members or customers what they need is to survey them periodically, ideally two to four times a year. In a survey, you can ask questions about customers' or members' expectations and perceptions of your overall service, your products and services, your employees, your phone system, and your competition. You can also find out through a survey what their primary financial institution is and why you do not have their total financial relationship.

Len Berry, in an article in the March 10, 1988, *American Banker*, defines customer expectations as what the customers want the service to be; and perceptions as what customers perceive the service to be. It is important to measure both expectations and perceptions. Berry also recommends asking the "killer" question, Would they recommend your institution to their friends?

Mava J. Hurd, of Total Research Corp., Princeton, New Jersey, points out another element to keep in mind when developing a survey. "In surveying customers, we ask not just why you are satisfied," but also what factors are contributing to this satisfaction or dissatisfaction (Schoultz, October 27, 1988).

**Champaign National Bank** in Illinois, **First National Bank of Chaska** in Minnesota, and **Alliance Federal Credit Union** in San Jose, California, are a few of the many institutions interested in meeting the needs of their customers or members. See Exhibits 4.1, 4.2, and 4.3 for the surveys used by these financial institutions to determine their customers' or members' needs.

Surveys are conducted by mail and sent either to your total customer or member base or to a random sampling by segmented markets. Do a small test survey initially to make sure the questions are clear. Most banks and credit unions use outside consulting firms to do surveys for them. However, if you are on a low budget, consider developing the questionnaire yourself and then finding a computer whiz to tabulate the results for you. You might try the marketing department of a local college since advanced students are often eager to offer their services for free. Lastly, consider splitting the cost of a consultant with your friendly competitors and associates.

The results of your survey can be used to develop a "score card" listing the attributes that customers or members seek in your organization, as well as additional products they want (Albrecht and Bradford, 1990). With this information in hand, you are ready to develop standards, a subject covered in Chapter 5.

The biggest mistake you can make is to assume that you know how your customers feel, that you know what they want from you in the future, and that you know what their overall expectations are. By conducting an annual opinion survey, you can rally the troops to reach your service goal. For example, if you received a rating of 75 percent *extremely satisfied* and 25 percent *somewhat satisfied* in your last survey, aim for an 85 percent *extremely satisfied* rating in your next survey. Create a theme, such as "Service 85," to generate enthusiasm and commitment from your entire organization.

## Exhibit 4.1

## Champaign National Bank

September 1986

Dear Customer:

You are one of our 14,000 customers we are privileged to serve. Your name was selected along with 1,199 other customers on a random basis to represent all of our customers. We are asking this group of 1,200 customers to give us an evaluation of our services and people who serve you.

I hope you will take the time to complete this questionnaire and return it to us in the postage free envelope. If you would be good enough to do so within the next two or three weeks it would be very helpful and very much appreciated. You need not sign your name. We are interested only in your honest evaluation and wish to keep all information confidential as it applies to any individual respondent.

We have left some space at the bottom of the questionnaire for comments which you might wish to give us concerning any of our services and suggestions that you think would improve our service to you and others.

Sincerely,

*Sandy Lyon*

Sandy Lyon, Marketing Director

- - - - - - - - - - - - - - - - - - - - - - - - - - - - - - - - - - - - - - -

1. Listed below are a number of services available at the Champaign National Bank. Please check those that you are now using or have used in the past 12 months and then indicate your evaluation of the quality of the service offered.

| Services Available | Use or Have Used | Evaluation of Service | | | | | |
|---|---|---|---|---|---|---|---|
| | | Excel-lent | Very Good | Good | Fair | Poor | Very Poor |
| **a.** Personal checking acct. | | | | | | | |
| **b.** Business checking acct. | | | | | | | |
| **c.** Savings (Passbook, IMMA, CD's, etc. | | | | | | | |
| **d.** IRA, KEOGH | | | | | | | |
| **e.** Borrowing money. | | | | | | | |
| **f.** Investment advice | | | | | | | |
| **g.** Financial Planning | | | | | | | |
| **h.** Farm management. | | | | | | | |
| **i.** Crescendo Club | | | | | | | |
| **j.** The Club | | | | | | | |
| **k.** Drive-up windows | | | | | | | |
| **l.** Easy Answer Machines | | | | | | | |
| **m.** Trust Department | | | | | | | |
| **n.** Newcomer Program | | | | | | | |

2. Please indicate about how often you use the following bank facilities:

| Frequency of Use | Main Bank | Bank Park | Bank West | Easy Answer Machines |
|---|---|---|---|---|
| Daily | | | | |
| Two to six times a week | | | | |
| Once a week | | | | |
| Less than once a week | | | | |
| Seldom or never | | | | |

## Exhibit 4.1 (cont.)

3. In the table below, indicate how you would rate the people who have served you at CNB.

| Character of Personnel | Evaluation of Personnel | | | | | |
|---|---|---|---|---|---|---|
| | Excel-lent | Very Good | Good | Fair | Poor | Very Poor |
| a. Courteous | | | | | | |
| b. Glad to help | | | | | | |
| c. Efficient | | | | | | |
| d. Knowledgeable | | | | | | |

4. How would you rate CNB to your friends? _____ Excellent; b. _____ Very Good; c. _____ Good; d. _____ Fair; e. _____ Poor; f. _____ Very poor.

5. How many CNB senior officers (president, vice president, department heads, etc.) can you name? a. _____ none; b. _____ one; c. _____ two or more.

6. Is Champaign National the only bank or lending institution in which you have accounts? a. _____ yes; b. _____ no.

   A. If NO, how many others? a. _____ one; b. _____ two; c. _____ three or more.

7. Do our business hours fit your needs? a. _____ yes; b. _____ no.

   A. If NO, what would be better? _____

8. Have you noted any of our advertising during the past month or so? a. _____ yes; b. _____ no.

   A. If YES, please check where you have noted it:
   a. _____ Newspaper; b. _____ Radio; c. _____ TV; d. _____ Other.

9. Do you recall receiving any direct mail advertising literature from us? a. _____ yes; b. _____ no.

   A. If YES, what is your reaction to it?
   a. _____ Helpful.
   b. _____ Interesting but of little help.
   c. _____ Of no help.
   d. _____ Seldom read it.

8. Any comments concerning any aspect of our operation would be greatly appreciated. (What do you like most, what do you dislike most, what non-traditional banking services would you like us to provide, etc.)

## Exhibit 4.2

### First National Bank of Chaska

Customer Survey

Dear VALUED CUSTOMER:

At First National Bank, our goal is to provide you with the highest quality service possible. In order to find out how well we are serving you and if there is something we can do to improve our service, please take a moment to answer the questions below. Your opinions are always very important to us. Thank you for your cooperation.

Please place a (X) in each area of service. Please (X) "don't use" if a factor does not apply to you.

| | Excellent | Good | Fair | Poor | Don't Use |
|---|---|---|---|---|---|
| **Lobby Tellers** | | | | | |
| Speed of Service | | | | | |
| Accuracy | —— | —— | —— | —— | —— |
| Friendliness | —— | —— | —— | —— | —— |
| Knowledge | —— | —— | —— | —— | —— |
| Willingness to help or make suggestions | —— | —— | —— | —— | —— |
| **Drive-Up Tellers** | | | | | |
| Speed of Service | | | | | |
| Accuracy | —— | —— | —— | —— | —— |
| Friendliness | —— | —— | —— | —— | —— |
| Knowledge | —— | —— | —— | —— | —— |
| Willingness to help or make suggestions | —— | —— | —— | —— | —— |
| **Customer Accounting/Bookkeeping** | | | | | |
| Speed of Service | | | | | |
| Accuracy | —— | —— | —— | —— | —— |
| Friendliness | —— | —— | —— | —— | —— |
| Knowledge | —— | —— | —— | —— | —— |
| Willingness to help or make suggestions | —— | —— | —— | —— | —— |
| **Receptionists** | | | | | |
| Speed of Service | | | | | |
| Accuracy | —— | —— | —— | —— | —— |
| Friendliness | —— | —— | —— | —— | —— |
| Knowledge | —— | —— | —— | —— | —— |
| Willingness to help or make suggestions | —— | —— | —— | —— | —— |
| **Customer Service Representatives** | | | | | |
| Speed of Service | | | | | |
| Accuracy | —— | —— | —— | —— | —— |
| Friendliness | —— | —— | —— | —— | —— |
| Knowledge | —— | —— | —— | —— | —— |
| Willingness to help or make suggestions | —— | —— | —— | —— | —— |
| **Loan Officers** | | | | | |
| Speed of Service | | | | | |
| Accuracy | —— | —— | —— | —— | —— |
| Friendliness | —— | —— | —— | —— | —— |
| Knowledge | —— | —— | —— | —— | —— |
| Willingness to help or make suggestions | —— | —— | —— | —— | —— |

## Exhibit 4.2 (cont.)

|  | Excellent | Good | Fair | Poor | Don't Use |
|---|---|---|---|---|---|

How would you rate the Automatic
Teller Machine?

Easy to Use
Reliability/working order
Conveniently located
Safe/well lighted

Location Of Automatic Teller Machine:

My choice of an alternate location in Chaska would be _____

Comments, concerns or needs_____

_____

_____

_____

If you are currently dissatisfied with a service and would like a personal
response, please indicate your name and address or phone number.

_____

_____

_____

|||| ||||

NO POSTAGE
NECESSARY
IF MAILED
IN THE
UNITED STATES

**BUSINESS REPLY MAIL**
FIRST CLASS    PERMIT NO. 29    Chaska, Minn.

POSTAGE WILL BE PAID BY ADDRESSEE

**FIRST NATIONAL BANK OF CHASKA**
P.O. BOX 37
CHASKA, MINNESOTA 55318

Attn: Customer Service

## Exhibit 4.3

## Member Survey
## Alliance Federal Credit Union
## San Jose, CA

### YOU AND THE CREDIT UNION

1. How do you usually conduct business with the Credit Union?

   ☐ In person.　　☐ Tell-A-Phone.
   ☐ By mail.　　　☐ Through an ATM.
   ☐ By phone.　　☐ By automatic payroll deduction.

2. At which branch do you conduct most of your business?

   ☐ San Jose.　　　　☐ GE Plant Site (Wilmington).
   ☐ Sunnyvale.　　　☐ Wellington (Wilmington).
   ☐ O'Connor Hospital.

3. What best describes your membership status?

   ☐ GE employee.
   ☐ O'Connor Hospital employee.
   ☐ Other North Carolina member.
   ☐ Other Northern California member.
   ☐ Southern California member.
   ☐ Family member.
   ☐ Retiree.
   ☐ Other _____

4. What is your **primary** source for information about Credit Union developments and products?

   ☐ Flyers about specific products.
   ☐ Quarterly statements.
   ☐ *Prime Interest.*
   ☐ Credit Union staff.
   ☐ Articles in company newsletter.
   ☐ Other (please specify): _____

5. What is your reaction to *Prime Interest*, the quarterly Credit Union newsletter?

   ☐ Find interesting; usually read.
   ☐ Sometimes read, if content is of interest.
   ☐ Rarely take the time to read it.

6. Would you be interested in phone contact by the Credit Union to communicate information about the Credit Union or to determine interest in a proposed new service?

   ☐ Yes.　☐ No.　☐ Not sure.

### CURRENT FINANCIAL ACTIVITY

To help us determine if we are offering you the range of financial services you need, please complete the following:

1. What is your approximate balance at Alliance Federal Credit Union and at other financial institutions?

   A. Savings (includes regular Savings, Checking, Liquid Asset Account, Certificates):

   AFCU: $ _____　Other: $ _____

   B. Loans (not including first mortgages):

   AFCU: $ _____　Other: $ _____

2. Indicate which of the following services you use at Alliance *and* which you use elsewhere. Check **both** columns if you have an account at more than one institution. Also, indicate if you have no account activity.

|  | Use at Alliance | Use Elsewhere | No Activity |
|---|---|---|---|
| A. Savings: | ( ) | ( ) | ( ) |
| B. Checking: | ( ) | ( ) | ( ) |
| C. Direct Deposit of net paycheck: | ( ) | ( ) | ( ) |
| D. Automated teller machines: | ( ) | ( ) | ( ) |
| E. Certificates of Deposit: | ( ) | ( ) | ( ) |
| F. IRAs: | ( ) | ( ) | ( ) |
| G. Credit card: | ( ) | ( ) | ( ) |
| H. Auto loans: | ( ) | ( ) | ( ) |
| I. Signature loans: | ( ) | ( ) | ( ) |
| J. First mortgage: | ( ) | ( ) | ( ) |
| K. Second mortgages: | ( ) | ( ) | ( ) |
| L. Other loans: | ( ) | ( ) | ( ) |
| M. Other: _____ | ( ) | ( ) | ( ) |

3. In addition to Alliance, where else do you conduct financial business (Check **all** that apply):

   [ ] Another credit union.　　[ ] Finance Company.
   [ ] Small community bank.　[ ] Other (please specify):
   [ ] Large bank.
   [ ] Savings & Loan.　　　　_____

4. Which organization do you consider your Primary Financial Institution (e.g. where you conduct most of your business and/or you check first when considering a loan or an investment?)

   [ ] Alliance.
   ☐ Another credit union.
   ☐ Small community bank.
   [ ] Large bank.
   [ ] Savings & Loan.
   [ ] Finance Company.
   ☐ Other (please specify): _____

5. Why do you feel this way?

   ☐ The relationship has been established over a period of time, I see no reason to go elsewhere.
   [ ] The staff is friendly and service-oriented.
   [ ] Savings rates are very competitive.
   [ ] Locations are convenient for me.
   ☐ I have had a positive loan experience there (e.g. rates, approval procedure, payments, etc.).
   ☐ Offers a full-range of services.
   ☐ I support the Credit Union philosophy of doing business.
   [ ] Other (please specify): _____

## Exhibit 4.3 (cont.)

**LOAN ACTIVITY**

Now we'd like you to answer some questions about your loan experiences, at Alliance and elsewhere.

1. Which of the following applies to you? (Check ALL that apply):

   ☐ I currently have a Credit Union loan.
   ☐ I have had a Credit Union loan in the past.
   ☐ I have never had a Credit Union loan.
   ☐ I currently have a loan from another financial institution.
   ☐ I have had loans from other financial institutions in the past.

2. I plan to apply for a loan during the next 12 months at (Choose ONE):

   ☐ Alliance.
   ☐ Another credit union.
   ☐ Small community bank.
   ☐ Large bank.
   ☐ Savings & Loan.
   ☐ Finance Company.
   ☐ Other (please specify): _____

3. If you do plan to apply for a loan during the next 12 months, what are the likely reasons (Check ALL that apply):

   ☐ To purchase a new or used vehicle.
   ☐ To purchase a home.
   ☐ Home Equity Loan.
   ☐ Second Mortgage.
   ☐ Personal reasons (education, vacation, etc.)
   ☐ VISA Credit Card.
   ☐ Share/Certificate-Secured.
   ☐ Other (please specify): _____

4. Do you believe the Credit Union's interest rates are:

   ☐ Competitive
   ☐ Low
   ☐ High

5. Have you borrowed from a lending institution other than Alliance in the past two years?

   ☐ Yes
   ☐ No (Go to question 9)

6. If "Yes", **where** did you borrow?

   ☐ Another credit union.
   ☐ Small community bank.
   ☐ Large bank.
   ☐ Savings & Loan.
   ☐ Finance Company.
   ☐ Other (please specify): _____

7. If "Yes", what type of loan?

   ☐ Auto Loan
   ☐ Personal Loan
   ☐ VISA Credit Card
   ☐ Real Estate (First Mortgage)
   ☐ Real Estate (Second Mortgage)
   ☐ Share/Certificate-Secured
   ☐ Other (please specify): _____

8. Why did you borrow from another financial institution?

   ☐ Better rates.
   ☐ More convenient location.
   ☐ Used to doing business there.
   ☐ Staff is pleasant and responsive.
   ☐ Credit Union turned me down.
   ☐ Other (please specify) _____

9. Assuming interest rates are competitive, would the Credit Union be your **first** choice for a future loan?

   ☐ Yes ☐ No ☐ Not sure

   Why do you feel this way? _____
   _____
   _____

ANSWER QUESTION TEN ONLY IF YOU HAVE APPLIED FOR A CREDIT UNION LOAN IN THE PAST.

10. Please check all of the statements that were true for you when you applied for your most recent Credit Union loan:

    ☐ The loan officer was friendly.
    ☐ The loan application was easy to complete.
    ☐ The loan officer was knowledgeable.
    ☐ All of my questions were answered.
    ☐ The loan was processed promptly.
    ☐ I would apply to the Credit Union for another loan.
    ☐ I was turned down for the loan. _____

ANSWER QUESTION 11 ONLY IF YOU HAVE BEEN TURNED DOWN FOR A CREDIT UNION LOAN IN THE PAST.

11. Please check all the statements that were true for you when you were turned down for a Credit Union loan:

    ☐ I was told why I was turned down.
    ☐ I was told how I might qualify for a loan in the future.
    ☐ I would apply for a Credit Union loan in the future.
    ☐ I received a loan from:
       ☐ Another credit union
       ☐ Small community bank.
       ☐ Large bank.
       ☐ Savings & Loan.
       ☐ Finance Company.
       ☐ Other (please specify). _____

## Exhibit 4.3 (cont.)

### QUALITY OF SERVICE

. Compared with other financial institutions, how do you feel about the quality of Alliance's services? Please circle one number rating for each subject.

|  | Poor | Neutral | Excellent |
|---|---|---|---|
| 1 Staff knowledge: | 1 2 3 | 4 | 5 6 7 |
| 1 Staff courtesy: | 1 2 3 | 4 | 5 6 7 |
| 2 Convenient hours: | 1 2 3 | 4 | 5 6 7 |
| 3 Convenient locations: | 1 2 3 | 4 | 5 6 7 |
| 5 Branch environment: | 1 2 3 | 4 | 5 6 7 |
| 1 ATM locations: | 1 2 3 | 4 | 5 6 7 |
| 1 Telephone answering: | 1 2 3 | 4 | 5 6 7 |
| Interest rates on savings: | 1 2 3 | 4 | 5 6 7 |
| . Interest rates on loans: | 1 2 3 | 4 | 5 6 7 |
| 1 Clear (monthly/ quarterly) statements: | 1 2 3 | 4 | 5 6 7 |
| Variety of loans: | 1 2 3 | 4 | 5 6 7 |
| Variety of investments: | 1 2 3 | 4 | 5 6 7 |
| Educational information you receive (newsletter, brochures): | 1 2 3 | 4 | 5 6 7 |
| Other _____ : | 1 2 3 | 4 | 5 6 7 |

2. Compared with other financial institutions with which you do business, how would you rate the overall quality of service provided by the Credit Union? (Add any written comments on the last page).

☐ The best.
☐ Better than others.
☐ About the same.
☐ Not as good as others.
☐ The worst.

### BACKGROUND INFORMATION

Please answer all questions to help us analyze survey results. Your replies are confidential. **Do not sign your name.**

1. You are: ☐ Male ☐ Female

2. You are:

☐ Single (includes divorced, separated or widowed.)
☐ Married (spouse is employed).
☐ Married (spouse is not employed).

3. Your age is within the following range:

☐ 18-25      ☐ 46-55
☐ 26-35      ☐ 56-65
☐ 36-45      ☐ 65 or older

4. How long have you been a member of the Credit Union? _____ Years.

5. Including yourself, how many family members are in your household? # _____

6. How many of these are under age 14? # _____

7. Which of the following ranges is **closest** to your annual combined household income (before taxes)?

☐ Under $20,000      ☐ $50,001 to $60,000
☐ $20,001 to $30,000      ☐ $60,001 to $70,000
☐ $30,001 to $40,000      ☐ More than $70,000
☐ $40,001 to $50,000

8. Do you

☐ Own your home (or purchasing).
☐ Rent

9. If you own your home (or purchasing), how many years have you lived there?

_____ Years.

10. What is your zip code? _____

11. Do you use advertising (TV, Radio, Newspapers, etc.) to make choices for financial services?

☐ Yes.
☐ No.
☐ Sometimes (please specify) _____

NORTHERN CALIFORNIA MEMBERS ONLY:

12. If the Credit Union opens another branch in Northern California, where should it be?

[ ] Oakridge area
[ ] Blossom Valley/Almaden
[ ] North San Jose
[ ] Other _____

13. Which radio station do you listen to most often?

_____

**ALL MEMBERS:** Please add any comments regarding Credit Union experiences or suggestions for the future.

COMMENTS:

_____
_____
_____
_____
_____
_____

Thank you.

## *Customer or Member Focus Groups*

Holding customer or member focus groups is another effective way of determining what is important to your customers and members. The main reason to hold a focus group is to determine customers' or members' buying behavior and their feelings about your products and services. Focus groups are frequently used by large banks and credit unions and are underutilized by small ones. Whether you are $5 million in assets or $500 million, you should be able to gather a group of both customers and noncustomers to give an honest assessment of how they perceive your organization.

Some tips to consider in structuring your focus groups, as mentioned in *The Service Advantage* by Karl Albrecht and Lawrence Bradford, are:

★ Invite a minimum of 5, up to a maximum of 10, people to participate in each group.

★ Send a special invitation from the president to a cross section of your customers and members.

★ Be prepared to pay each of them an honorarium, from $25 to $75.

★ Conduct the meeting on your premises or in a local hotel, and offer refreshments.

★ Start with approximately five different focus groups.

★ Prepare some general questions, such as:

1. When you think of "Main Street Bank," what comes to mind?

2. What is it like to be a customer of our bank?

3. What is your perception of our overall quality of service?

4. What problems have you experienced as a customer? What would cause you to leave us?

5. What are our competitors doing to attract your business?

6. What products and services do you currently use or wish we had?

7. What does good service mean to you?

★ Arrange for a note taker, and audio or video tape the session.

I think you'll find the following comments taken from a June 1988 article in *Bank Marketing* by Roger J. Dow, vice president of sales and marketing at Marriott Corporation, about input from customers quite interesting.

> I think we grew as a company by really knowing our customer. That's so ingrained in our culture at Marriott. We research products tremendously. For example, we have a new division called Court-yard Hotels that has more than 100 branches. When we came up with this product, we wanted to make sure the room was right. So we rented a warehouse and we built a Holiday Inn room. We built all kinds of rooms in the warehouse, and we marched thousands of customers—people like you—through them. We asked them "What do you like, and what don't you like" and then did research and changed the designs. Then we built the hotel.

The next time you're about to develop or enhance a product, don't forget to ask your customers or members for feedback.

## *Customer Advisory Board*

Some banks and credit unions have begun establishing customer advisory boards. These boards are comprised of from four to eight customers or members, members of the business community, and representatives from the bank or credit union. They meet anywhere from once a year to four times a year. In choosing your board's participants, it is important that you do not select direct competitors. At the board meetings, the customers or members should feel free to critique your products, people, sales and marketing programs, and policies. This is an excellent opportunity to obtain valuable information about your competitors from your customers or members. As an incentive to serve on the advisory board, hold the meeting as part of a special luncheon or hold them at unique locations.

The following examples of customer advisory boards were taken from the January 1989 issue of *Community Bank Marketing Newsletter*.

**First National Bank and Trust Company of the Treasure Coast**, Stuart, Florida, has a 15-member board chosen to represent a cross section of the community, including retirees. The majority are business owners, and the bank strives to have an attorney, an accountant, and a medical professional on the board at all times.

At every advisory board meeting, a department of the bank is evaluated, following a presentation by senior executives. The remainder of the meeting is a private conference between the board and the bank's chairman and president to discuss sensitive matters. Charles R. Schad, senior vice president and chairman of First National's advisory board, says that their meetings have resulted in, among other things, the development of a queuing system in the teller area and changes in teller hiring practices.

At **North Houston Bank**, in Texas, both the composition and purpose of the advisory board are significantly different from the board at First National. All 14 board members at North Houston are bank customers, and all are under 40 years old. They are, says Russell F. Hughes, executive vice president, "the heirs apparent to businesses and are future leaders in the community."

Called the Business Development Board, North Houston's board was created in 1987 to help the $82-million institution increase in size. Accordingly, its primary goal is to encourage customers to make referrals. "We want them to represent us as salespeople in the community," explains Hughes. Thus far the program appears to have been a success with more than $500,000 in new loans and $200,000 in deposits attributable to the board in less than one year.

In addition to reviewing bank programs and products, advisory boards can also help banks keep lines of communication open with certain groups of customers. **Commonwealth Bank and Trust** in Pennsylvania formed three advisory boards comprised of senior citizens for just such a reason.

The advisory boards, located in three of the bank's markets in North Central Pennsylvania, make sure that its Golden Opportunity (GO) Club for mature customers is in tune with the wants of the club's members. Each advisory board has six to eight GO Club members and nonmembers, along with bank representatives from those offices in the region. The meetings are held monthly. The board members discuss what is happening within the GO Club, what is taking place within the bank, and what activities and trips club members are interested in.

## *New Member or Customer Contact Programs*

Shirley Grindeland, manager at **VanCity Credit Union** in Vancouver, British Columbia, began TeleService, a new member contact program in 1987. The following is Shirley's explanation of TeleService:

> Our research indicated we needed to find more effective ways to cross-sell services to new members. Service quality was initially a secondary objective.

> Our service objective was to identify and resolve any problems members might be experiencing. Our sales objective was to cross-sell products and services that might be of interest to our members.

> All new members are called by a TeleService representative after they have been with VanCity for approximately three months. We inquire about their satisfaction with VanCity and any problems and solutions are explored. Whenever possible, products and services are introduced (based on existing account holdings and age of the member) and printed material is mailed to the member if desired.

> Based on our feedback received to date, member response is very positive to this program. Our cross-selling success depends on efforts that were undertaken at a members branch when the account was opened. Approximately 40% of our members request additional information on other products and services.

Sounds like VanCity has a winning program. To make a program like this work requires consistency and a knowledgeable, sales-oriented staff.

## *Appeal Procedure for Turned Down Loans*

"Being turned down for a loan is one of the major causes for dissatisfaction with a financial institution," says Larry Wald, vice president of marketing and member service for VanCity Savings Credit Union. "We developed an 'appeal procedure' so our members feel that we have done everything reasonably possible to honestly and fairly consider their application.

"By documenting our review process, we allow dissatisfied members adequate appeal if their loan is turned down. As a result, complaints requiring senior management or board attention, have declined significantly."

VanCity's procedure is an effective and inexpensive way for retaining customers or members, even when you can't give them the service they want. Loan customers who know they've been treated fairly—even though their loan request was turned down—will probably turn to your organization again when their circumstances have changed.

## *Thank You Note Contests*

Many banks and credit unions send thank you notes to *new* customers or members. What about *existing* and loyal customers? When was the last time that large depositors and longtime customers received thank you notes? A branch manager at **Zion's National Bank** in Salt Lake City decided to do something about it.

He announced to his staff that he was holding a thank you note contest to thank existing customers. Every employee received a supply of personal thank you notes and was asked to send out at least three a day for one month. As there was no limit to the number of thank you notes employees could send out, the branch manager offered an incentive to the three employees who sent out the most thank you notes.

Employees were initially unsure as to what they would say in their notes. Many of them thanked customers for cookies, organized deposits, additional funds, and their loyalty. By the third day of the contest, the manager was thrilled with the many calls from customers thanking him and his staff for the thoughtful notes. This program was so popular that it was extended to many other branches.

Zion's program is an excellent example of not taking our loyal customers or members for granted. Let's start sending those thank you notes today.

## *Customer and Prospect Luncheons*

**Orange National Bank** of Orange, California, is a small, community bank with an excellent reputation. Some time ago, I attended a first-class luncheon that the bank was holding for its top customers and prospects. Each month, Orange National holds two customer and prospect luncheons. This lovely lunch is catered in the bank's private dining room and lasts approximately two hours. Officers and managers are asked to submit to the marketing director names of customers and of prospects they are pursuing.

At the luncheon, Wayne Miller, president of Orange National, and various officers mingled with the attendees prior to sitting down. The number of bank officers was limited, however, so the customers would not be overwhelmed. When the lunch began, each customer and prospect told the group a little bit about themselves and their business. This ice breaker worked wonders to create an open and friendly atmosphere.

At the end of the luncheon, a video was shown on the history of, and the benefits of doing business with, Orange National Bank. I was most impressed at the conclusion of the video when Wayne got up and said, "I thank you all for coming. Those of you who bank with us, we sincerely appreciate your business. Those of you who do not bank with us, we hope you choose us in the future. You will be hearing from us again." Now that's a CEO role model for sales and "asking for the business."

We understand from Orange National that a significant portion of their loan volume and deposits is directly attributable to these luncheons and the referrals they receive from their impressed customers and prospects. If you do not have a dining room, a simple catered affair in a conference room will do very nicely.

## *Customer or Member Appreciation Week*

It is important that your customers or members know that you appreciate their business. When I worked at **Crocker Bank** in San Fransisco, I remember a fabulous event that a branch manager held to acknowledge the customers. The customer appreciation week was announced to employees at least a month in advance to generate enthusiasm. During the entire week, senior management and employees from support and operational areas greeted customers at the door. Customers received flowers and their children got lollipops and other candy.

For ambiance, the branch manager arranged for a student to play the harp in the lobby during lunchtime. To reflect the bank's upscale market area, all of the employees dressed in black and white attire and the branch was decorated in black and white. Attractive balloons were also displayed. Tellers and platform employees made a special effort to thank the customers for their business.

Finally, the manager took advantage of the event by having customers fill out a special coupon for a savings bond drawing. The coupon was actually a prospect sheet, in that it asked many sales questions such as, what major purchases or remodeling will you be undertaking in the coming years? Not only did the manager succeed in thanking his customers, but he got the entire staff involved and generated some good referrals.

Customer appreciation weeks work very well. Consider making them part of your organization's customer relations program. Ask your managers to hold at least two a year.

## *Customer or Member Education Day*

In addition to saying thank you, we can also add value by providing educational information to our customers or members. **Honeywell Florida Federal Credit Union**, Clearwater, Florida, holds an annual event, "Savvy Saturday," for its members. This event is an information day that provides members an opportunity to meet with the various companies and groups that they interface with. T. Adrian Brown, president, commented enthusiastically, "We also have music, entertainment, and food along with a display of autos, vans, and boats. Financial planners and people from our mortgage company, insurance vendors, Better Business Bureau, title company, and others are available to provide our members with information and answer any questions they may have." Honeywell submitted a write-up on "Savvy Saturday" that appeared in its member newsletter (see Exhibit 4.4).

## Customers or Members of the Year

*Personal Selling Power* magazine had an interesting write-up on Federal Express in the January-February 1990 issue. During its annual black-tie, sales award banquet, Federal Express presented awards to six "customers of the year" selected from different industries. On the following day, these customers delivered seminars to Federal Express's salespeople on how their industries work. They also shared their views on Federal Express's performance.

When planning your quarterly or annual sales meetings, why not present your top customers or members with awards and have them comment on your service?

### Salespeople Advisory Committees

Your frontline personnel and sales force have an amazing amount of knowledge about the market and customers. Why not consider establishing an advisory committee made up of frontline personnel from many different areas of your organization? Meetings can be held at the head office or at a special location from one to four times a year. You can have the same salespeople attend all the meetings, or you can arrange for a totally new group at each meeting (Matega, October 1987).

To make the most of these advisory committee meetings, develop a formal agenda to keep everyone focused on the task. Another key to making this meeting a success is picking a good moderator. During the meeting, each employee critiques the sales and marketing programs of your company—from catalogs and brochures to compensa-

## Exhibit 4.4

Phone (813) 539-2222                                              October 1987

The Pride of Honeywell.

## Honeywell Florida Federal Credit Union

P.O. Box 4300, Clearwater, Fl 34618-4300

### Did You Know ...

That we can wire money for you - from your account here at the Credit Union - to yours or anyone else's account at another financial institution? Your money is credited to that account the same business day.

That we can send money for you via Western Union as a commercial money order and this reaches its destination in an hour!

That you can set up periodic payments from your account to your mortgage holder, car insurance, etc. at no charge? ($100 minimum check sent)

That we're going to be offering Visa cards this year?

And you thought we were just here to give you those cute little calendars!!!

JOIN YOUR CIRCLE OF CO-WORKERS

CREDIT UNION GROWTH

The Pride of Honeywell

**Purchase a home or refinance through**

CU MORTGAGE Corporation

MEMBERS BENEFIT

**Call: 578-4663**
**St. Petersburg/Clearwater**

HOT LINE 1-800-722-3121

### Savvy Saturday

October 17th, here in Plant 5 parking lot, you're going to see a big tent, and inside that tent you're going to find representatives from credit bureaus, Credit Union Mortgage Corp., Consumer Credit Counseling, title companies, Career Apparel, IRA Plan and many, many more.

There will be give-aways and refreshments, but best of all, an opportunity for one-stop consumer information shopping.

This day ends Credit Union Week, so please come and meet and mingle with staff and our manager. Get to know us and the services that are available to you as well as being able to ask those questions of the companies that we hear of and deal with, but really don't know a lot about.

Remember, circle October 17th on your calendar and join us for "Savvy Saturday" from 9 to 4:30. Let us show you in one more way how we value your membership.

Your savings federally insured to $100,000

# NCUA

National Credit Union Administration, a U.S. Government Agency

---

### CREDIT UNION OFFICE HOURS

#### CLEARWATER MAIN OFFICE

Monday through Friday 9:00 A.M.- 4:30 P.M.

#### TAMPA & GATEWAY BRANCH OFFICES

Monday, Tuesday, Thursday, and Friday
9:00 A.M.- 12:30 P.M. and 1:00 P.M.- 4:00 P.M.
Wednesday Closed
Please note: These are Eastern Times; you should allow for zone differences.

---

### STATISTICS 8/87

| | |
|---|---|
| SHARES & DEPOSITS | $31,063,162 |
| LOANS | $18,839,733 |
| RESERVES | $1,939,521 |
| ASSETS | $33,415,246 |
| MEMBERS | 9187 |

tion policies and training programs. An open discussion then takes place on any new products and programs, or any obstacles, that hinder them in their sales and service efforts.

## Customer or Member Seminars and Educational Programs

Commercial banks and mortgage companies frequently offer their customers educational seminars in such areas as arranging for financing, preparing taxes, and understanding basic accounting issues. Why not utilize this same strategy for your customers or members as well? I'm sure your customers or members would appreciate seminars that deal with issues such as tax and investment strategies, child psychology, decorating tips, and any other hot topic of the day. The seminars do not necessarily have to be on business topics. Any topic of interest to your customers or members, even travel videos, will do.

## Senior Management, Telephone Thank You Programs

Several years ago when I worked for **Bank of America**, they took the time to identify their top customers. To make sure that senior management was in touch with the customers, each senior manager was asked to talk to 10 to 20 customers a month by telephone and thank them for their business. This was also an excellent opportunity to get feedback from their customers.

Many financial institutions have their midlevel managers and employees call their customers to thank them. Few, however, have senior management committed to a high-touch telephone program.

## Selling Packaged Accounts

While selling packaged accounts is certainly an old idea, it is amazing how many banks and credit unions have not yet developed this type of account. A packaged account is a core account that is bundled with other services. For example, a checking account, a money market savings account, and a credit card. Of those organizations that do have an excellent package, their employees often receive no extra compensation for their cross-selling efforts.

The real key to selling packaged accounts is to offer incentives to your frontline employees—such as a special reward if they sell three or more products. **First Interstate Bank** of California, in the Los Angeles region, for example, called it a "Grand Slam" when an employee sold at least four products. The cash award was considerably higher when an employee sold a packaged account versus a single service. If we give our employees a reason to actively sell our services, they will deliver a higher level of personal service to our customers or members. Such service is a key for retaining customers or members.

## *Evaluating Form Letters*

How many of you have received a harsh letter from a business? If so, you might have said, "That's it, I'm closing my account and never doing business with them again." Perhaps we should evaluate our own written correspondence. Is it driving our customers or members away?

One way to do this is to set up a task force comprised of employees with good writing skills from all levels of your organization. Ask each department to submit to the task force a copy of each form letter they mail to your customers or members. The task force can then evaluate the tone and friendliness of each letter and make modifications as necessary.

Task force members should sit back, and as they read each letter, try to put themselves in the customers' shoes. They should ask themselves, Is the tone friendly? How would I feel if I got one of these letters? While our letters may be serious, our customers or members deserve fair and courteous treatment. Just because a customer is behind on a payment, doesn't mean he or she is out to cheat our bank or credit union.

When each letter has been evaluated, you are now ready to mobilize your task force. Ask each task force member to replace one letter by drafting a new one, using input from coworkers. Each new letter should then be submitted to the task force for final approval.

The task force could also develop entirely new categories of letters. How about customers who are making their last loan payment? Why not send them a warm letter thanking them for their business? Such letters help balance the impersonal form letters we mail asking our customers and members to send specific information to complete their loan files or transactions.

## Scheduling Appointments Flexibly

The name of the game is differentiating yourself from your competitors. Everyone seems to be extending their hours and bending over backwards to impress their clientele. Why shouldn't we be more flexible by scheduling early or late appointments for our top customers or members.

I definitely know there are financial organizations who are currently doing this. Unfortunately, they are in the minority. If promoted adequately to our customers, flexible scheduling of appointments could be quite a differentiator, particularly in a branch environment.

## Distinctive Touches

In the February 1990 *Customer Service Report*, Geraldine Sticknen of Dallas, Texas, shared the following story. "I checked into the Baton Rouge Holiday Inn, very tired after driving for over six hours. I was pleasantly surprised by having been chosen 'Guest of the Day.' The staff had placed my name on the outside marquis, and had decorated my room with balloons, ribbons, and a basket of fruit and cheese. All this was a very nice ending to a not-so-nice day." Why not consider a customer- or member-of-the-week program?

To differentiate yourself from your competitors, always be thinking (as the Holiday Inn did) of ways to add little distinctive touches to your existing service. The appreciation you will get from your shocked and pleased customers or members is well worth the effort. Here are a few examples of distinctive touches that some organizations use.

★ At **First American Bank** in McClean, Virginia, the Waterman Square office provides a calculator and scratch pads for customers to use on the lobby tables. The Apple Blossom branch has city maps, with popular sections highlighted, ready to give to customers when they ask directions.

★ **Dime Savings and Loan** in Lake Grove, New York, provides chairs for elderly people at its branches when there is a long line. Another bank provides a little table, chairs, and toys to occupy children while their parents are conducting their banking business.

★ **Bay Area Bank** in Redwood City, California, puts out cookies and coffee for their customers each day.

★ **University National Bank and Trust** in Palo Alto, California, offers free shoe shines.

★ One customer of **City Bank,** Richardson, Texas, commented, "After performing a transaction at the drive-thru window, I received my receipt along with an envelope addressed 'Dog.' Curious, I opened the envelope to find the teller had enclosed a doggie biscuit for my dog who was in the backseat of my car." (*Customer Service Report*, February 1990.)

★ At Ray's Amoco Service in Dubuque, Iowa, customers receive a free bag of popcorn with a fill up, regardless of whether they used full service or self-serve. Ray reports that many customers will stop at his small station rather than go to the big Amoco three blocks away just because they want the popcorn. He says the popcorn costs him six to seven cents per customer, which he easily makes up with more sales (*Customer Service Report*, February 1990).

Have a brainstorming session with your employees to see how many distinctive touches, such as selling stamps, setting up a courtesy phone, and having candy for children, you can come up with to set you apart from the competition in your area. Distinctive touches are fun and easy to do, and your customers or members will remember you for them.

Look at your strategic plan and your sales and service action plan. Is there an objective with specific implementation steps for a customer- or member-retention program? If so, congratulations! If not, get started with some of the fun and easy ideas in this chapter.

# Chapter 5

## Developing Quality Service Standards

Now that you have identified your customers' or members' expectations from your opinion surveys, focus groups, and other kinds of research, you are ready to develop quality service standards. Quality standards are measurable levels of performance for meeting customers' expectations. They give your employees direction on what is expected of them and provide your management with criteria for evaluating and monitoring performance.

Here are some specific examples of quality service standards. Domino's Pizza has a standard that their pizzas will be delivered in under 30 minutes; Federal Express is famous for its guarantee of "absolutely, positively overnight"; and the Deluxe Corporation has a standard of "48-hour turnaround, zero defects." Winning retailers like L. L. Bean and Lands' End also set clear standards: satisfaction guaranteed or they'll take the merchandise back—no questions asked. Federal Express's salespeople are expected to follow a detailed list of 29 well-defined performance standards. The first one reads, "Do it right, the first time, no matter how insignificant the task may seem." (Levine, March 1989.)

Standards are created for every key service given to both internal and external customers. They answer the questions *what* and *how*. Examples of quality standards include the following:

★ Answer all inquiries and complaints within 24 hours of receipt

★ Produce correspondence that is neat, professional, and error free

★ Deliver a commitment to the customer within 14 days of receiving the application

Generally speaking, your CEO should insist that, at a minimum, standards be developed in every department for the following:

★ Telephone etiquette
★ Complaint resolution
★ Time to settle complaints
★ Frequency of reviewing accounts
★ Internal service
★ Turnaround time
★ Status of customer applications
★ Communication of compliments
★ Lost business
★ Customer visits/phone calls
★ Error reduction
★ Courtesy
★ Written correspondence
★ Waiting time

## Conduct Research

The best way to determine what standards you want to establish is to contact national associations in our industry, such as the Bank Marketing Association, Credit Union Executives Society, and many others.

Another way to determine standards is to find out what others in a variety of industries are doing. Perhaps you have existing customers or members who presently work in well-respected corporations, such as Hewlett-Packard, IBM, or Xerox. Their human resources director or quality of service director might share information with you on how they created their service quality standards.

The business library is also a valuable source of information. There are many books available on service that address the issue of establishing standards.

## *Have Each Department Develop Standards*

Once you have determined your internal and external customers' expectations, take the information to each of your department and branch managers to get your employees involved in developing team and individual standards. Negotiating standards with team involvement creates a sense of ownership and accountability.

Begin by sharing your research about your users' expectations with your staff. Find out what the staff feels its primary responsibility is in the area of service quality. For example, you found out that your branch managers expect your Data Processing Department to deliver accurate reports with a quick turnaround time. After discussing this expectation with your staff, they agree to strive to deliver error-free reports to your branches by the fifth of each month. By finding out your internal customers' expectations and getting input from your team, you have paved the way for success.

Each employee also needs to know exactly what his or her individual standards are for a particular position. For example, do you want your secretary to answer the phone within three rings? Would you like all complaints solved within 48 hours? Be as specific as possible.

It is recommended that specific standards of telephone etiquette, especially concerning handling complaints, be set for your entire organization. The following is a list of items that you can measure regarding telephone service:

★ Number of rings it takes to answer

★ Number of calls coming in and going out

★ Types of calls coming in and going out

★ Length of incoming and outgoing calls

★ Quantity of hang ups

★ Number of calls handled per person

★ Volume of business per call

★ Number of incomplete calls

★ Number of return calls required

★ Number of calls per phone location

★ Number of requests for information

★ Time required to fix problems over the phone

★ Number of calls that have to be transferred to a second or third person

★ Number of complaints about how phones are answered

★ Volume of calls per time of day

★ Types of transactions handled over the phone

★ Amount of backlog of calls to return

★ Time spent on hold

★ Number of times customers use your phones to make calls

To help you develop your own service standards, I have included examples of service standards from four institutions. Exhibit 5.1 has branch standards from **First Pennsylvania Bank**, corporate standards from **Citytrust** are shown in Exhibit 5.2, and operational/support standards from **Society Bank** are in Exhibit 5.3. Larry Wald, vice president of marketing and member service at **VanCity Credit Union**, was generous enough to share standards for branch operations, the overall branch, the teller department, the member service department, and the loan department. For these standards, see Exhibits 5.4 through 5.8.

Now it's your turn to develop some service standards. To begin, ask each manager to conduct a meeting with his or her own staff and explain that they are to develop their own standards as a department, as a branch, and on an individual basis. The following are four simple guidelines to help your staff establish service standards:

## Exhibit 5.1

### First Pennsylvania Bank

*These are standards, or "commitments," which each employee in a customer contact position will be expected to meet. They reflect a conviction that for First Pennsylvania Bank, the customer comes first. These standards demonstrate to our customers that we value them, that we want their business, and that we deliver on our promise of personal, responsive, and efficient service.*

## All Employees

1. **Greeting:** to greet each customer with genuine friendliness, to make eye contact with the customer. Example: a friendly "good morning." "Next" is not considered a greeting.

2. **Promptness, Efficiency:** to immediately acknowledge customers and to minimize delays in providing service. Acknowledgment alone is insufficient; the customer must also be served quickly.

3. **Courtesy:** to treat customers with friendliness, respect, and consideration; to treat customers as you would wish to be treated.

4. **Personalization:** to treat each customer as an individual, with individual needs; to look for innovative solutions which are tailored to the individual's specific situation.

5. **Accuracy:** to provide up-to-date, accurate information which is clear, precise, and easy to understand. For example, this would entail paying attention to rate changes and communications from Branch Operations and Marketing.

6. **Professionalism:** to conduct oneself with dignity, displaying an attitude which projects knowledge, confidence, and ability.

7. **Conduct:** to refrain from gum-chewing, smoking, eating and drinking, and socializing in the presence of customers (either in person or on the phone).

8. **Grooming:** to wear appropriate clothing, (nothing loud, extreme, or provocative). To be clean and free of excessive jewelry and/or makeup.

9. **Listening:** to hear the customer out, without interrupting. Example: to listen carefully and attentively to learn the nature of a customer's problem with an account.

10. **Going the Extra Mile:** to do whatever is necessary to help the customer. To focus on the solution, going out of your way to solve a customer's problem.

11. **Close:** to end all customer interactions with a sincere closing greeting. A pleasant, "have a nice afternoon" would be an example of this.

## Platform Employees

12. **Probing:** to ask open-ended questions to determine customer needs and goals, to listen attentively to the response.

13. **Cross-selling:** to suggest appropriate products or services and relate them to customer needs.

14. **Product Knowledge:** to know, to thoroughly understand, and to be able to clearly answer detailed questions relating to First Pennsylvania and competitor products.

15. **Overcoming Objections:** to tactfully and pleasantly provide information which relates to customer objections.

16. **Organization:** to maintain a neat, clean workspace; to be able to locate all forms.

17. **Suggesting Specific Follow-up:** to suggest a concrete next step to interested customers.

# Exhibit 5.2

## Citytrust

---

### CITYTRUST CORPORATE SERVICE STANDARDS

#### TELEPHONE COURTESY STANDARDS

1. Citytrust employees will answer their phones by the 3rd ring.

2. Citytrust employees will return all phone calls (internal and external) within 24 hours.

3. Citytrust employees will answer their phones in the following manner:

   (Receive mostly internal customer calls):

   | | |
   |---|---|
   | Department: | "Customer Service" |
   | First and Last Name: | "Anne Sullivan" |
   | Offer Assistance: | "How may I help you?" |

   (Receive mostly external customer calls):

   | | |
   |---|---|
   | Bank Name: | "Citytrust" |
   | First and Last Name: | "Anne Sullivan" |
   | Offer Assistance: | "How may I help you?" |

4. Citytrust employees will not transfer customer calls. Requested information will be secured and personally phoned back to the customer by the original call recipient. On rare occasions, when the information requested is complex or specialized in nature, Citytrust employees will ensure that the caller wants to be transferred, explain why the call will be transferred, provide name and phone number of the person to whom the call is being transferred, remain on the line, and announce the caller and the nature of the inquiry.

#### ERROR RESOLUTION STANDARDS

Citytrust employees will resolve any problem or service request within five business days. If the resolution requires more time, Citytrust employees will continuously update the customer on its status.

#### WRITTEN COMMUNICATION STANDARDS

Citytrust employees will adhere to the corporate typing standards, will use professional verbage, and will represent Citytrust accurately and clearly in all written materials and communications.

---

## Exhibit 5.3

### Society Bank
### Cleveland, Ohio

# QUALITY  SERVICE  COMMITMENT

DATA I/O
DATA INPUT OPERATOR - VIPS - A.M.

| SERVICE PROVIDED | TIME FRAME |
|---|---|
| Provides quality, courteous, and timely support to both our external and internal customers on a consistent basis. | At All Times |
| Controls the security/access to the Regional Operations Center. | At All Times |
| Distributes interoffice correspondence to appropriate area within department. | Same Day |
| Balances the Goshen Cash Management run and reports totals to the Cleveland Cash Management Department. | Daily By 9:30 A.M. |
| Prepares company ACH payrolls for transmission to Cleveland; reports dollar totals to Cleveland ACH Department; prepares entries for both company payrolls and correspondents; returns processed tapes to customer after three business days. | Daily By 2:00 P.M. |
| Rotates back-up tapes received from Cleveland as well as from internal departments. | Same Day |
| Records Block/Run totals on the Item Processing System; inputs data; reconciles input; prepares adjustments; microfilms rejects; sorts rejects; records balanced COA totals; requests and balances Extract at specified times; verifies confirmations to Extract Transmission files. | By Current Deadlines |
| Purges Four Phase data according to procedures; enters data on system; transmits data to Cleveland; makes corrections to programs/formats; performs back-up procedures to system. | By Current Deadlines |
| Records/Balances/Batches Branch Recap totals. | Same Day |

## Exhibit 5.4

Vancouver City Credit Union
Vancouver, BC, Canada

Branch Operations
**Standard of Performance**

Defined as "results which will exist when a job is completed competently"

### 1. Services
All loans submitted for approval will receive same day turn-around. Any declines will be discussed with the Branch prior to returning the application. A member of Branch Operations will be available for assistance to Branches and members from 8:30 AM-5:30 PM Monday through Thursday; 8:30 AM-6:15 PM Friday; and by ASPEN on an hourly basis, to 3:00 PM on Saturday.

### 2. Telephone and Correspondence
Any telephone messages from staff will be responded to the same day. Correspondence and telephone calls from members or personal visits from members will be given priority and will be responded to upon receipt. Calls returned the same day; correspondence within 3 days.

### 3. Marketing
Branch Operations Vice President to meet with 2 or 3 Branch Managers (on a rotating basis) quarterly to encourage the informal exchange of ideas relating to marketing and business development.

### 4. Administrative
Branch Managers' meetings will take place every other month. District meetings will also take place every other month. Supervisor meetings will be held quarterly. Branch Operations are responsible to ensure that Branches adhere to the standards of performance.

## Exhibit 5.5

Vancouver City Credit Union

### Standards of Performance
### Overall Branch

1. **Housekeeping**
   - Janitorial contract must always be maintained
   - Cheque writing stands and brochure racks to be updated twice weekly
   - Exterior and interior of Branch to be checked daily to ensure garbage is cleaned up, pens are working, lights changed, etc.
   - All staff working items are kept neat and up-to-date.

2. **Promotions**
   - No more than *two* services promoted at any one time
   - Location of in-Branch material changed every *two* weeks
   - Brochure racks full stocked with items covering the three member functions (Teller, Member Service, Loans)
   - Branch must undertake at least *one* community event each quarter
   - Develop a quarterly market plan
   - Each branch will have a Realtor program in effect
   - Send Thank-yous to members and ask for referrals

3. **Accessibility to Senior Management**
   - No member complaints—that they were denied the opportunity to speak to the Branch management
   - Member complaints will be acknowledged the same day and dealt with by Branch management within three days, or forwarded to superior with acknowledgment of this procedure to member the same day

4. **Branch Climate**
   - Member will be addressed by name at some point during serving
   - Any wait time for member service or management will not exceed 5 minutes without an acknowledgement
   - All department standards are to be consistently adhered to
   - All sick employees must advise a supervisor at least 30 minutes before their starting time
   - A Branch staff meeting is held at least weekly and departmental meetings at least monthly
   - All incoming telephone calls will be answered no later than the third ring. Call forward will be used when a telephone is to be unattended

## Exhibit 5.6

Vancouver City Credit Union

### Standards of Performance
Teller Department

**1. Services**

Smile and acknowledge the member immediately. Use the member's name during the transaction and thank them for coming in. Under no circumstances will member complaints be acceptable for a teller not complying with the foregoing.

**2. Marketing:**

Cross sell and/or refer one new product per day and record the results on a daily basis.

**3. Administration Responsibilities**

- Tellers are to be set up and ready to work at their scheduled starting times.

- Scheduled duties must be completed within 15 minutes.

- Daily lunch and coffee breaks are to be taken as scheduled unless otherwise directed by the supervisor.

- Maintain 95% of the average Branch volume of work as determined by the branch Teller Transaction report.

- C.D.M. Tellers are to sight balance 4 days out of 5 within a maximum of fifteen minutes.

- Cash holding Tellers are to balance 4 days out of 5 within a maximum of thirty minutes without requested assistance. If assistance is required, the supervisor must be advised within 20 minutes.

- The cash drop for deposits must be cleared every hour with any exceptions reported to the supervisor.

- Daily work must be completed and bundled in an orderly fashion. The bundle is to be labelled for filing with the teller's name, date and operator number.

- Wickets are to be kept clean and fully supplied.

(continued)

## Exhibit 5.6 (cont.)

4. **Product Knowledge**
   To be able, by the end of the probationary period, to:
   a)  explain the features and benefits of the following products:

   | | |
   |---|---|
   | Chequing/Savings | Terms |
   | Convenience | U.S. Accounts |
   | Plan 24 | Exchange cards |
   | T-Bill | |

   b)  explain the Deposit Rate and Service Charge Bulletins.

All new services and products will be reviewed in detail to ensure a clear understanding and marketability within one week of advice of launch or change date. Self-development of product knowledge will be ongoing.

## Exhibit 5.7

Vancouver City Credit Union

### Standards of Performance
Member Service Department

### 1. Service

Each member will be greeted with a smile and called by their name whenever possible. Each member will be acknowledged no later than one minute after reaching the next in line. At the close of service, each member will be "thanked." Members unattended in other departments will be acknowledged no later than 5 minutes after entering the department.

### 2. Marketing

Each member will be solicited in product or service at every visit. In-Branch marketing campaigns will receive full support by participating in cross selling and involvement in campaigns from the set up of plans.

### 3. Administrative Responsibilities

All administrative functions to be completed daily and records neatly maintained. Any exceptions to be reported to supervisor, daily. All correspondence will be responded to within 3 days.

### 4. Product Knowledge

All new services and products will be reviewed in detail to ensure a clear understanding and marketability within one week of advice of launch or change date. Self-development of product knowledge will be ongoing.

## Exhibit 5.8

Vancouver City Credit Union

### Standards of Performance
Loans Department

**1. Service**

All loans and mortgages will receive same day decision based on sound lending judgement. Any declines will be discussed with the member on the same day. Telephone messages from members will be responded to as soon as possible and without exception the same day. Each member of the Loans Department will be available to assist members from 15 minutes prior to opening the doors and 30 minutes after closing the doors.

**2. Marketing**

All loans officers will be involved in a Realtor program. This program will include weekly contacts and keeping Realtors advised of interest rate and policy changes. Each loans officer will make a minimum of two follow up or new contacts per week. All loans staff will cross sell a minimum of two products per new mortgage/loan application and one new product on rewrites. In addition, the loans officer will be accountable for soliciting the transfer of all business at other institutions on all mortgage/loan applications. Each loans officer will meet the penetration percentage objective set by the Branch Manager and Branch Operations for loan and mortgage insurance.

**3. Administration Responsibilities**

Each loans staff member will record the reasons for the loss of a mortgage or loan after making every attempt to maintain that business. The clerk will keep these records to assist the department to reduce further loss of business. All administration and records are to be neatly prepared and kept up-to-date. These records should be easily accessible.

**4. Product Knowledge**

All new services and products will be reviewed in detail to ensure a clear understanding and marketability within one week of advance of the launch or change date. Self-development of product knowledge will be ongoing.

1.  Create a group discussion that will allow everyone to contribute their thoughts and feelings on service standards. Discuss the typical frustrations that come up when dealing with problems concerning both coworkers and customers.

2.  Ask each employee to draft a copy of what he or she considers to be reasonable standards to measure the quality of the work he or she delivers as part of a team and as an individual. Once you have all of the draft copies, review them, make comments, and then return them to your employees.

3.  Share these draft standards with other internal users in your organization to get their feedback. Modify and refine them as necessary, and distribute the final standards to your staff.

4.  Revise your performance appraisals to incorporate the new standards.

Now that you've gone through the challenging exercise of setting standards, you must incorporate them into everyone's performance appraisal, as just stated in the preceding guidelines. In this way, every manager and employee is accountable for meeting the quality service standards. Accountability is the subject of Chapter 8.

# Chapter 6

## Providing Creative Training

In *Thriving on Chaos*, Tom Peters argues:

> If we view our employees as our primary asset and a powerful
> weapon against our competition, then we must prepare them for
> the battle by continually upgrading their skills. . . .
>
> Federal Express and Disney have thrived with similar training
> rigor. Both treat everyone as a potential career employee. The
> training Federal Express gives its customer service people in
> Memphis and Disney's training of a 17-year-old would-be jungle
> boat driver, far surpasses the technical and product knowledge
> programs of most firms. These excellent firms include extensive
> training on the goals and vision of their organization.

Richard Hartnack at **First National Bank of Chicago** had this comment on training in the April 1988 issue of *Production, Marketing,
and Technology*: "We find that almost without exception, employees
want to do a good job. In many cases where they give poor service, it

is because they do not know what to do. The solution is likely to lie in supervision. We work constantly to improve the quality of our supervisors so they can teach their subordinates how to deal with customers effectively and give them the resources to do it. Thus, we place a great deal of emphasis on supervisor training."

Many training programs fail because midlevel management is not included or asked to implement follow-up action. Therefore, include senior and midlevel managers when you are developing your training program. They need to understand their role in making your organization's vision come alive, in encouraging teamwork, in holding people accountable for results, in developing standards, in measuring quality, and in understanding their customers' or members' expectations. What good does it do to train everyone in sales and product knowledge if they do not understand the strategic direction, the goals, and the values of your organization?

If you are committed to developing a first-class service team, then training is not an option but a requirement. Many larger banks and credit unions have put significant dollars into comprehensive classroom training. But training can also be done on a low budget with some creativity. This chapter presents many ideas for giving your managers and employees the skills and knowledge they need to deliver the kind of service you expect.

### Let's Make a Deal!

The following idea came to my attention from Debbie Liester, formerly with **Society Bank**. The objective of Society's program was to improve product knowledge, increase referrals, and increase cross sales of products. Every time a sale or referral was made, "bonus bucks" in a specific amount of play money was awarded over a two-month period. At the end of the two-month period, a live auction was held, similar to "Let's Make a Deal." Each employee could bid for specific gift items with the "bonus bucks" they had accumulated. For example, Susan, a teller, got 20 referrals over two months and $500 in play money. The night of the auction, Susan could bid for a Sony Walkman or a night on the town with dinner for two.

This exciting program generated enthusiasm and encouraged employees to actively make referrals and cross-sell. The event was spectacular, with everything from a Monty Hall look-alike as emcee, to a professional auctioneer; curtains 1, 2, and 3; food; and music. I was honored to be the guest speaker at this successful event.

## Product Knowledge Certification

How can we consistently deliver excellent service if our employees are unable to answer our customers' or members' questions? Lack of product knowledge among bank, savings and loan, and credit union employees is a major problem.

**Mid-America Federal Savings & Loan** of Columbus, Ohio, decided to get serious about product knowledge and have fun at the same time. In 1987, a Financial Service Associate Certification Program was developed by James E. Marcos, Jr., to address the organizational goal of improved customer satisfaction and increased product sales and referrals. More specifically, Mid-America Federal expected maximum participation in the program, with a goal of 90 percent of their contact employees and corporate officers becoming certified in all products and 75 percent of their noncontact employees becoming certified. To improve service, Mid-America Federal targeted higher product knowledge and overall satisfaction scores in their customer surveys.

Each employee received a pocket-sized guide for each product, with definitions, benefits, features, cues, and sales tips. The back of each booklet contained a quiz that employees could take to see how well they knew the product. When employees felt ready, they called a designated coordinator who asked them five questions over the telephone. If they got all five questions correct, they were certified in that product. If they got any questions wrong, they could try again another time.

Certified employees then were presented with an attractive wood and bronze plaque with slots for a dozen product inserts. For example, if you were certified in checking accounts, your manager or a senior executive would present you with a plaque and your first insert for "checking." On the plaque might be the following: In attainment of the recognition of specialized knowledge, this is presented to Mary Smith, Financial Service Associate. You, or Mary would, of course, strive to fill up the entire plaque with inserts for all of the products.

Mid-America indicated that this program had the following benefits:

★ It prompted customers to ask questions when they saw the plaques.

★ It improved the morale of the support and back-office employees who also felt comfortable bringing in referrals from friends and associates.

★ It improved the levels of service as it minimized phone calls being passed to several employees until one was found who could answer a customer's or member's question.

★ It generated many sales and referrals.

Tangible recognition in the form of the plaque provided the pressure needed to encourage involvement in the program. Only employees certified in a particular product could participate in incentive programs for that product's promotion. Officers were provided the opportunity to be certified first so they could then encourage their staff.

**IBM Endicott-Owego Employees Federal Credit Union**, Endicott, New York, has also developed a comprehensive product knowledge certification program. Managers and staff members complete a written course of study on their own time. The course's four sections cover: core services, loans, CDs, and other products and services. Participants must contact competitors and can use reference material to complete each section.

Each section is essay style and asks questions such as:

1. List five benefits of each product listed (e.g. share draft, VISA, Readi-Reserve) and five features.

2. Name a prospective member for the following products and give reasons why the member would use them.

3. What does our competition offer in each of these areas?

4. List typical member objections to each of the following products and the responses you would give.

5. What does each product or service cost?

When section is completed, it is sent to the director of marketing. Sections are graded and returned to the employee if corrections are necessary. Upon completing all sections, a comprehensive exam is given. A score of 80 or better is needed to receive the course certificate. At IBM Endicott-Owego Credit Union, certified employees receive $100, a certificate of achievement, and a nameplate that says "product certified." See Exhibits 6.1 and 6.2 for an overview of the program, and a sample certificate.

## *Training and Testing for Product Knowledge*

With the vast array of products and services you offer, conducting product knowledge training is an ongoing challenge. Two California banks decided to get serious about product knowledge by testing employees and asking them to achieve a specific score. When I worked at **Bank of America**, each branch manager received monthly a set of product knowledge tests with a guide. Managers conducted the training on the product and gave a test to every employee. The tests were mailed from the branch to a central area where they were graded and returned to the manager for review. All of the scores were averaged, and each branch was expected to achieve a certain score.

Let's imagine I am the manager of the Main Street branch and that my 10 employees just completed a test on our home equity line of credit. I'm disappointed because their average score was 65 percent. Furthermore, my performance appraisal indicates that my branch must achieve at least an 80 percent score for me to get an excellent review in this category.

The beauty of this training system is that you can hold your managers accountable for product knowledge and can put this expectation in their performance appraisals. If you're thinking, "But Barbara, that will only work in a large bank," you're wrong. **Orange National Bank**

# Exhibit 6.1

## IBM Endicott-Owego Employees Federal Credit Union
### Endicott, New York

PRODUCT CERTIFICATION PROGRAM INFORMATION

This packet contains the Credit Union's Product Certification Program. This correspondence course was initiated to insure that employees are knowledgeable about our core services and the different products/ services offered by the Credit Union and its competitors.

The course has four sections which may be completed separately or as a group. Section 1 is on our core services; Section 2, loans; Section 3, CD's; Section 4, CUSO Products and Services. You may use any reference material available to you to complete each section. Answer all items and contact competitors as necessary for information.

Submit completed sections to Jerry Wilber. Sections will be graded and returned to you if corrections are necessary. Upon successful completion of all sections, a comprehensive exam will be given to you. A score of 80 or better is needed to receive your course certificate.

COMPLETION DATES

Section 1 _____

Section 2 _____

Section 3 _____

Section 4 _____

## Exhibit 6.2

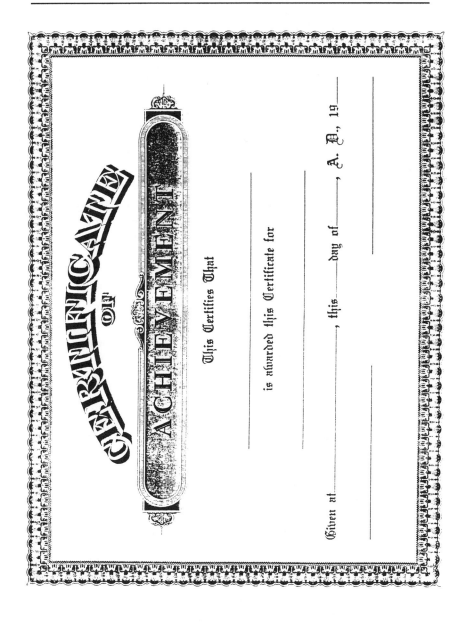

Certificate of Achievement

This Certifies That

is awarded this Certificate for

Given at _____, this ___ day of _____, A. D., 19

in Orange, California, is a highly successful community bank. Wayne Miller, president of Orange National, asks his employees from the top on down to take product knowledge tests, and he reviews the scores.

Show that you're serious about improving product knowledge. Start testing your employees so you can hold them accountable.

## Product Knowledge Games and Sales Tools

At Bank of America, we played an exciting product knowledge game called "Banking Bonanza," fashioned after a popular TV game show. Announce to your staff that you intend to have a product knowledge contest. Make it easy on yourself, and stimulate learning at the same time, by giving each employee at least 10 blank index cards and assigning them each a different product. Have your employees develop questions, with answers, about benefits, features, and sales cues, and open probing questions, as well.

After several weeks, the questions, with answers, should be returned to you. Review each question and answer for accuracy, and assign a point value to the question according to its difficulty. For example, 25 points for simple questions, 50 points for intermediate questions, and 100 points for difficult questions.

To play the game, you need two teams, a bell, a timer and a fun emcee. Here is an example of how the game is played. Each team picks a team captain. The emcee asks the first question, "What is the main benefit of a personal line of credit?" The team captain from the Tigers team jumps for the bell and gets the first question. The Tigers have 30 seconds to answer the question. The timer is on and is ticking away while they consult. They answer, "Cash available for any reason." Correct. They get 50 points and get to answer the next question. The Tigers continue answering questions until they get one wrong. When they get a question wrong, all the points they've accumulated go to the other team and then that team begins answering questions.

Set a time limit for the game. The team with the most points wins. This game can be played in each office or in an entire bank or credit union if it is small. If you have a large institution, you can pick the most knowledgeable employees from each office or department and hold a big event—an Olympics of product knowledge.

**First Security Bank** of Lexington, Kentucky, developed a game modeled after Trivial Pursuit. It is called Extra Special Product Review and Internal Training (ESPRIT). A game board and situation cards were developed by Leigh Reding, a graphic artist in the Communications Department. Between 8:00 and 8:30 in the morning, time is given for everyone to read, study, and answer the questions. Between 8:30 and 8:45, employees call a telephone number and give the correct answers. The first person to answer all the questions correctly wins extra hours off.

**Richmond Savings Credit Union** in Richmond, British Columbia, developed "Make Cents Trivia" in May 1989 (see Exhibit 6.3). Diane Touchet, assistant vice president of human resources, submitted the following overview:

> One of the suggestions which came from our employees in our "Cowbusters" ideas contest was for a game format for learning about our products and services. We felt the idea had tremendous potential for motivating staff to learn and have fun doing it, so we formed a task force to put the idea into reality.
>
> We started by asking our staff to help in making up the questions and encouraged participation by having random draws for prizes. The game is called "Make Cents Trivia Game." There are 10 categories such as Deposits, Loans, Mortgages, etc. with up to 10 cards in each category. A sample card is enclosed. Once someone has completed all the cards in a category, they must pass a written test before they can move on to another category. Cards are marked by a branch co-ordinator, while tests are marked by the Training Services Department. After successfully completing five categories, a specially designed medal with key chain is awarded. Upon successful completion of all categories, a gold pin and a check for $100 is awarded. Successful completion of all categories gives eligibility to play-offs held once a year. Teams of

# MAKE CENTS TRIVIA GAME

### The fun way to learn

**Read on to find out how
you can have fun ... and
win prizes, too!**

## Exhibit 6.3 (cont.)

MAKE CENTS TRIVIA

Knowing all about our products and services is an important part of our jobs - but learning all the details hasn't always been easy or exciting.

Now, thanks to Heather Coppen of our Broadmoor Branch and her Cowbuster's suggestion, we're about to change that and make it fun and easier to learn - and provide us with even better skills for serving our members.

But first we need your help - and you could win a prize!

Make Cents Trivia will consist of a series of cards, each with several questions about a specific product or service on one side plus some Trivia questions. On the other side is a scenario -

... here's a sample card:

---

MAKE CENTS TRIVIA

### TARGET 2000

1. Why is the account called "Target 2000"?
2. Can a child have a Target 2000 account if he/she is too young to sign?
3. Do these accounts have voting privileges if they want them?
4. At what age does a target 2000 account become a regular plan 24 and require $25 in the vote shares account?
5. How does the interest work on target 2000 account?
6. How is the account converted over (automatically or by member)?

### *Trivia Bonus*

a) What was RSIS originally called?
b) Who is the manager of Brighouse Branch?
c) Name three types of mutual funds available at RSCU.

---

MAKE CENTS TRIVIA

The correct answer to the following scenario will lead you to the next card.

### Scenario

A member has no need for cheques, but makes 5 - 6 withdrawals per month; makes deposits at irregular intervals and has a balance between $200 and $700.

What is the most suitable product/service we can offer to suit this person's needs?

---

---

## Exhibit 6.3 (cont.)

---

### Make Cents Trivia

The cards will be in sets and as each set is completed, a prize will be awarded—and a special prize when all the sets have been completed. There's even more—but we want to save that surprise for our launch.

Now this is where you come in—and have a chance to win prizes!

We need your help in making up the questions, and everyone who sends in an entry form will have their name entered in a draw for prizes.

—and if you get your entry in early, you have an additional chance to win!

To complete an entry form:
1.  Fill in your name and branch.
2.  Select a category.
3.  Choose a product or service in the category selected.
4.  List six questions related to the product or service.
5.  Give answers to all six questions.
6.  Write three trivia questions pertaining to RSCU.
7.  Give trivia answers.
8.  Write a brief scenario that will lead the player onto another card (product or service) in the same category.

### Contest Rules

1.  Entry forms must be complete with questions and answers.
2.  You may submit more than one entry.
3.  Entries received by March 9th will be eligible for the "Early Bird" prizes.
4.  All entries must be received by March 23rd to be eligible for the final draw.
5.  Entry forms—one form is included in this package. Additional forms are available in the lunchroom or the Training Department.
6.  Send completed forms to the Training Department, 5611 Cooney Road.
7.  Prizes will be awarded on a random draw basis as follow:
    Early Bird Draw:

    *   Entertainment '89 Books
    *   Pocket Calculators
    *   $25 Keg Restaurant Gift Certificates
    *   RSCU Pens

    Final Draw:

    *   Dinner for Two ($50 value)
    *   Entertainment '89 Books
    *   RSCU Jacket
    *   Theater Passes

## Exhibit 6.3 (cont.)

### "Make Cents Trivia" Staff Contest
### Entry Form

Date: _____

Name: _____

Branch: _____

*Please Print*

**Categories**

- ☐ Demand Accounts
- ☐ Loans
- ☐ Mortgages
- ☐ Registered Products/Life Services
- ☐ Foreign
- ☐ General Insurance
- ☐ CUDIC Ins/ SharePlan
- ☐ Miscellaneous (ie. SDB, ATM, travellers cheques, etc.)

---

MAKE  CENTS  TRIVIA

_____
NAME OF PRODUCT OR SERVICE

1.

2.

3.

4.

5.

6.

*Trivia Bonus*

a)
b)
c)

**RICHMOND SAVINGS**
CREDIT UNION
Much More Than Banking.

---

**Answers**

1. _____

2. _____

3. _____

4. _____

5. _____

6. _____

a) _____

b) _____

c) _____

Scenerio - To lead player onto another card (product or service) in the same category.

_____
_____
_____
_____

Answer: _____

three compete with each other for 1st, 2nd, and 3rd place. Gold, silver, and bronze medals (similar to Olympic medals) are awarded, along with prizes. Our first play-offs will be held in May or June and prizes have not yet been determined.

Our results to date are positive. Two hundred staff [members] are currently participating. Over 20 [of them] have completed all categories successfully. We are receiving letters from customers commenting on how knowledgeable and helpful our staff [members] are.

Some pitfalls and mistakes to avoid: We launched this program at the end of May 1989. It was far more successful than we initially anticipated, so the administration of the game was taking too much time. We overcame this problem by having set times for getting cards marked and receiving new ones, and for writing tests. It is important to emphasize the fact [that] this is a training program—but in a format that makes it more fun to learn about products and services. We have now built into the job, standards for each job—requirements for completing the categories pertinent to that position.

Product knowledge can be fun and stimulating. If your product knowledge training program needs some life, consider developing a game.

Product knowledge guides can be valuable sales tools. The best guides include not only the benefits and features of your products, but also tips on "how" to sell the product. Include ideas on identifying cues, handling objections, cross-selling opportunities, and, most important, probing questions to determine needs. **Society Bank of Cleveland** has the best format I've seen to date (see Exhibit 6.4).

## *Field Trips for Training*

To heighten the awareness of service and to stimulate creativity among your managers and employees, consider developing fun and informative field trips for training. For example, if you are asking your managers to package and merchandise their financial services in a

## Exhibit 6.4

### Consumer Savings Products
Money Market Savings Account

PRODUCT PROFILE

SUMMARY

Society's Money Market Savings (MMS) Account is a liquid investment account that enables the customer to earn variable money market rates of interest on funds. Ready access to funds on which there are no maturity restrictions assures the customer of having the flexibility to meet financial obligations without incurring any penalties for early withdrawal.

CUSTOMER NEEDS

- To take advantage of potential increases in interest rates with a variable money market rate of interest on savings.
- To have the peace of mind that funds are insured by the FDIC up to $100,000.
- To increase flexibility by having ready access to savings with no maturity restrictions.

FEATURES

- Interest on Society's Money Market Savings Account is
  - a money market rate
  - reviewed weekly
  - adjusted to reflect current market conditions
  - compounded monthly

- The customer may withdraw funds from a MMS Account in any amount at any time; there are no minimum withdrawal amounts or penalties for early withdrawal.

- The customer may access the MMS Account by:
  - over-the-counter transaction
  - automated teller machine (ATM)
  - direct deposit (ACH Credit)
  - automatic payment (ACH Debit)
    (NOTE: Federal Regulations limit ACH Debits to three per account cycle).

BENEFITS

- Increases return on investment, since funds earn competitive money market interest rates.

  Enables the customer to take advantage of potential interest rate increases, since the MMS Account is variable rate investment.

  Maximizes interest earnings, since monthly compounding increases the effective yield.

- Provides financial flexibility by giving the customer ready access to his/her funds to meet financial obligations.

  Preserves principal and interest when early withdrawal penalties are avoided.

  Increases convenience and preserves savings, since the customer can withdraw the exact amount of funds needed.

- Increases convenience, since the customer can choose the mode of access which best meets his/her personal preferences and time schedules.

ELIGIBLE CUSTOMERS/PROSPECTS

- Be an individual, sole proprietor, partnership, corporation, governmental agency or non-profit organization.
- Make a minimum $1,000 opening deposit.
- Provide a Social Security or Tax Identification Number.
- Clear Chex Systems.
- Be an existing customer or have two pieces of personal identification with photos.

# Exhibit 6.4 (cont.)

OPPORTUNITY CUES

- The customer has other accounts, loans or services with Society.
- The customer maintains a high average balance in his/her checking or savings account.
- The customer comments that he/she expects interest rates to change.
- The customer deposits checks into his/her other accounts that are payable through a money market fund or brokerage firm.

DISCUSSION LEAD-INS/PROBING QUESTIONS

- What kind of savings account do you currently have?
- What amount would you intend to deposit in a savings account?
- How do you currently invest your savings?
- How important is it to you that your funds are insured against loss?
- How convenient is it for your to access your invested funds?

RESOLVING OBJECTIONS

*Your rate is too low*

- Determine to what the customer is comparing our rate and in what direction he/she thinks rates will move in the future.

- Explain that our money market rate is reviewed periodically and adjusted to ensure that it is competitive with those rates offered by other financial institutions. Additionally, compounding interest monthly increases the effective yield that the customer will earn on his/her investment. Also, the MMS Account has no broker or management fees to reduce interest income.

PRICING -- See PHOENIX and the Fact Sheet.

DOCUMENTATION

- Have the customer sign the signature card.
- Give the customer the Rules and Regulations and Interest and Fees Brochure.

CROSS-SELL OPPORTUNITIES

- Automated Teller Machine (ATM) Card
- Certificate of Deposit
- Direct Deposit
- Money Market Checking Account
- Credit Card
- Credit Line
- Investor Services
- Individual Retirement Account

IN-BANK CONTACTS

- Joan Greitzer, Deposit Products (4-5193)
- Barb Brodnick, Deposit Products (4-3630)
- Marcy Ginsburg, Deposit Products (4-3653)
- Roseanne Colleran, Deposit Products (4-3652)

3/87/N/MMSA

more attractive way, send them to a retailer such as a book or department store. At your next managers' conference, have them share their experiences. What ideas did they pick up that they can use back in the office? After a field trip, one manager decided to display a beautiful kitchen in his lobby with a sign that said, "Let us finance your dream." This display generated many inquiries from customers and resulted in half a million dollars of consumer loan business. It also got some business for the contractor as well!

Keeping up with the competition is important if we are to serve our customers or members properly. Send your employees on field trips to shop your competitors' products and customer service. Have them get rates and brochures. At the next staff meeting, they should share their perceptions of the competition and describe how they were treated. From these field trips, you can compare your products with your competitors' products and, thus, determine your strengths and weaknesses.

Another type of field trip is to have your frontline employees visit a nice restaurant, hotel, or department store. Ask them to observe how quickly they are acknowledged and how they are treated. If you want to stimulate awareness of service in your employees, consider using some of these field trip tips.

### Managers as Trainers

One of the best ways to gain the attention and respect of your staff is to have your senior and midlevel managers do part of your training. This shows the staff that their managers are committed to the training program. It is also an affordable way to get your training done. Admittedly, it requires time and energy.

If you're on a low budget, identify the key service areas in which you need to develop training—for example, courtesy, handling telephone calls, handling irate people, presenting benefits, probing for needs, and improving your image. Assign a topic to each senior manager and have that person be available to present a short, interactive workshop to various departments and branches upon request.

## *Utilize Guest Speakers*

Our employees can get bored and tired of hearing us drone on and on about service. Get a free guest speaker to carry and articulate your message. That's right, I said *free!*

There are at least three sources of free speakers. First, when was the last time you had one of your own customers or members come in to talk to your staff about what service means to them? Can you imagine how your staff might react if they could hear firsthand from a real live customer exactly how service affects them—what their preferences are and how they like to be treated. Second, the next time you get excellent service at a hotel, restaurant, or department store by an exceptional employee, invite that employee back to your office to talk to your staff. Third, invite a top performer from another branch or department to share his or her secrets with your staff.

Senior management and branch manager meetings also can get stale. Scout out your existing customers or members. Perhaps you can find a sales and service leader from another industry or an entrepreneur to give a presentation at your next meeting. Ask your guest speaker to address these questions: How do they manage their sales and service culture? What standards do they use? How is performance measured?

Customer panels can be quite effective, and entertaining at the same time. **Zion's National Bank** in Salt Lake City, Utah, decided to have a customer panel at an annual senior management and officer meeting. I emceed this event. We invited a business customer, a consumer customer, a CPA referral source, a former customer, and an entrepreneur to speak on this panel. Prior to the event, each panel member was given the questions they would be asked. They were asked to respond informally and not prepare any notes. They had one minute to answer each of the following questions:

1. What does good service mean to you?
2. What would we have to do to lose your business?
3. If we didn't have your business and wanted to try to win a relationship with you, what is the best sales approach to get your attention?

4. What products and services do you feel we should eliminate or develop?

5. What is our competition doing to get your business?

It took about 20 to 25 minutes to get through the above questions. We then opened up a 30-minute, question-and-answer session to all of the managers and officers in the audience.

It was amazing how many officers and managers asked the customers how they felt about rates and price. The customers, however, emphatically responded that service was far more important to them than price. In fact, one customer felt it was more important that his officer know about his business so the officer could service his account effectively.

Whether it be a customer or member, or a service employee from another industry, take the time to bring in guest speakers to spice up your service message.

## *Cross Training*

Cross training your staff to be able to fill in for one another is essential for improving the delivery of your service. There is nothing more infuriating to a customer or member than when an employee says, "I can't help you. My manager is out to lunch and he knows about the loan products." Or, "Mary orders all our checks and she's out sick." Does delivery of service stop when one of your key employees is on vacation? If so, address the area of cross training in your organization. Your goal should be to see that every employee can fill in for another employee at a moment's notice. A cross-training program does require a significant amount of time and effort, but the rewards can be big.

Besides improving service, another benefit of cross training is that employees have both more empathy for their fellow workers and a renewed sense of teamwork. Through cross training, employees who feel they are stagnating can enjoy assuming additional responsibilities. Cross training also reduces the "protecting-one's-turf" mentality we sometimes find.

## *Service Leadership Training, Customer Service Training, and Internal Service Training*

Service doesn't just happen. It is led by committed managers. These managers need sales and service leadership training. Include training on everything from driving the service mission to the process of measuring, monitoring, coaching, and rewarding—all the intricacies of reaching service excellence.

Customer service training is recommended for all employees from the top on down. Cover complaint handling, general courtesy, telephone etiquette, accuracy, quality, turnaround time, and any other areas that go into delivering good service.

Let's not forget our internal support departments. These individuals need to realize that they, too, have customers—other employees or departments who rely on their support. Training in how telephone and general courtesy affects internal service is essential.

**Chase Lincoln First Bank,** Rochester, New York, has developed internally a comprehensive eight-consecutive-week training program called Personal Selling Program or PSP. PSP is designed to give participating personal bankers and assistant branch sales managers experiences with skills that will:

- ★ Ensure a sense of common purpose and organizational identification
- ★ Assure consistently high service quality in all Chase Lincoln branches by fostering the redesign of the branch service delivery system
- ★ Enhance current self-marketing and personal sales efforts and skills
- ★ Increase participants self-confidence
- ★ Provide new, challenging career opportunities for Chase Lincoln employees
- ★ Instill a high level of product knowledge
- ★ Improve problem-solving ability

PSP participants are trained in the skills necessary to accurately read customers' needs, problems, and perceptions; to spot opportunities in the marketplace; and to respond with personal value-added service. They also learn how to develop proposals for redesigning a branch service delivery system. Because of these experiences, Chase Lincoln fully expects PSP graduates to be agents of change throughout the organization.

Inauguration of PSP carries with it new job titles, one job grade change, and creation of a new exempt sales position. But most importantly, says Mark Haefele, manager of compensation and employment, "This results in better-defined career paths for branch personnel."

The challenging eight-week program brings together customer service representatives and assistant branch sales managers from across the state at the Corporate Human Resource Development Center in Rochester. For the duration of the program, participants are relieved of job responsibilities at their home branches. Out-of-town participants are provided with lodging.

To prepare for the program, participants read Albrecht and Zemke's *Service America,* which introduces key issues of service quality—the central focus of the program. The program includes an orientation to Chase Lincoln's business strategies and values. Participants learn where the bank is going and where they fit in.

Other PSP sessions support individual professional development, such as self-marketing, interactive listening, written communications, presentation skills, professional image, and motivation. A full week is devoted to specialized financial products such as mutual funds and tax shelters.

"The core of the program, however, focuses on service quality and services marketing," says Denise Selak, the senior management development specialist responsible for PSP. "Participants learn that service quality is the essence of success in a services marketing business."

Several graduates of the pilot program give extra kudos to the program's self-marketing segments. "The things I learned in those sessions have directly helped me with my sales," said Cindy Tate, assistant branch sales manager of the Ellicott Square office.

In a series of special exercises, participants, working in teams, learn to formulate specific sales and service strategies for their branches. They develop performance standards and communication plans to dissemi-nate these standards, and they reexamine their individual sales plans.

In field exercises, participants learn to take the customer's perspec-tive. They learn to develop and use service quality assessment skills and tools, taking into consideration such issues as physical environ-ment, operations, and the value added by service providers.

"They discover the value of 'going the extra mile' for a customer," said Cheryl Chester, senior sales training coordinator. Cindy Tate, re-called, "We shopped other banks, and how they treated us was not how we wanted to be treated. It was a real eye opener." Customers also are invited to hear and react to PSP presentations.

In advanced assignments, teams of participants audit branch service quality, measuring factors ranging from performance and policies to procedures and systems support. They compile reports on their audits and present them to branch and group managers. All participants design a model of a high-performance branch, including service quality statements and standards, and action plans for implementing changes. Their written reports are followed by oral presentations to a panel of PSP faculty. Their final assignment is a written comprehen-sive sales plan that has to be defended orally.

Finally, within three months of graduation, PSP graduates return to Rochester to report on implementation of their proposed changes within their home branches. Graduates of the PSP program report that along with increased self-marketing and sales skills, they have taken home increased confidence. "I feel confident about what I do. I feel confident about the ideas I present," said Anita Leitgeb, an assistant retail sales manager at the Syracuse Division's DeWitt office. "I believe that because of the training I received in PSP, my branch manager and others are more receptive to my ideas. . . . They know I have a good understanding of what we need to do. . . . I feel part of the cultural change in the bank."

David A. Jacobs, manager of Eastern Banking Group, said about PSP, "These people are expected to spread the word among their coworkers when they return." John Kikta, manager of human resources development, put it another way, "This program is designed to provide participants with an ability to redefine how we currently do our business. By coming at needed change from the top, the side, and the bottom, we can make it happen. This is perhaps one of the most significant lessons we have learned about organizational change. It must have involvement from all levels of the company."

Chase Lincoln has also launched an equally extensive, state-of-the-art training program, called "Winning the Future," for their branch sales managers. This program covers everything from leadership to conducting innovative sales meetings, managing service quality, penetrating your market, profitability, and much more.

**National Bank of Long Beach,** Long Beach, California, embarked on an extensive training effort in July 1989. According to Terri de la Vega, marketing officer, "In order to provide exceptional service, we needed to educate our employees on the standards we established. We also wanted them to be knowledgeable about NBLB's products and services." Through training, National Bank of Long Beach hoped to achieve a consistent service culture bankwide and to develop knowledgeable, competent employees in all areas of the bank.

Terri went on to explain more about the training program:

> According to our employee survey, we identified areas where our employees needed training, i.e. product and department training. We also identified critical service areas such as dealing with the irate customer and telephone techniques. Internal training modules for these topics were developed. We require all non-

officers who wish to be eligible for our incentive plan to complete the above mentioned service courses, as well as attend a 10-week Zig Ziglar additional course.

Our telephone skills [see Exhibit 6.5], product knowledge and service awareness have all improved according to our evaluations. The approximate costs are Ziglar course materials at $1,000 annually, and a $1,200 annual subscription to a video library.

## Exhibit 6.5

### National Bank of Long Beach
Long Beach, California

### Telephone Tips

**Forbidden Phrases Used in Telephone Techniques Training**
These annoy, frustrate, and irritate our customers.

| Eliminate | Recommended |
|---|---|
| 1. I don't know | I'll find out |
| 2. We can't do that | Here's what we can do |
| 3. You'll have to | You'll need to |
| 4. Just a second | This may take a few minutes |
| 5. No (at the start of a sentence) | Offer a positive alternative |
| 6. Can I (or May I) take a message? | If you'll give me your name and number, I'll see he gets your message |
| 7. Hold please | Are you able to hold? (Give length and reason for hold) |

★ ★ ★
★ ★

Training is an important part of the total picture of improving service. As you have seen in this chapter, however, training can be fun and, depending on which methods you use, relatively inexpensive.

# Chapter 7

# Monitoring Complaints and Measuring Service

A program for achieving quality service does not have a beginning or an end. It is a process needing continual refinement. The only way you can measure your success is by asking your customers or members for feedback every chance you get. With the current competitive environment, your annual opinion survey may be outdated by the time you tally the responses. Informal feedback, comment cards, employee focus groups, and mystery shoppers are all needed to give you regular reports on the quality of your service. All employees should see the results of these reports for your organization as a whole, their department, and their own personal level of service.

If you are preaching the service message in your bank or credit union, but measuring only expense control, staff reductions, and operating efficiency, your service program will flounder. By measuring service, providing feedback, and setting clear priorities, however, all of your staff will focus their efforts on quality service.

## *Create a Quality Service Position or Department*

We have CEOs to lead our organization, and CFOs to keep us financially sound. Who is the dedicated champion of the service crusade? Why don't we have a director of customer service or a chief service officer with the same power and influence as the CEO (Liswood, 1988)?

Organizations that are serious about service quality select a senior level manager as service champion to assist the CEO in improving the overall service of the organization. This sends out a strong signal to the entire organization that service is a priority. The service champion drives the service program and gets all units involved in setting standards, measuring service, monitoring complaints, and creating programs to improve member or customer perception.

Selecting a senior, well-respected, take-charge type of person and supporting him or her in his or her efforts is crucial. **North Island Federal Credit Union** has created such a position with Bev Kjer as the service officer. Kjer spends a great deal of time monitoring and measuring North Island's service and has the total commitment of executive management.

I am particularly impressed with **Society Bank's** commitment to service quality. Robert Maddox spearheads the service department and was generous enough to share an overview of his department.

Affecting cultural change and supporting the initiatives required to realize service quality superiority requires full-time staff support. The Sales and Service Department area has shown the need for such a unit as demonstrated by their support in moving our organization from an operational culture to a sales culture. To this point we made substantial progress in the implementation of sales initiatives. While service and sales are considered to go hand in hand, the service quality imperative requires the same resources, support and commitment. We must concentrate on supporting the sales efforts of the organization with superior service quality.

114

The Service Quality Development Department at Society is charged with this responsibility. We are responsible for addressing service quality issues by developing and implementing strategies for:

★ Measuring and Tracking Service

★ Communication and Awareness

★ Quality Improvement Processes

★ Training and Development

★ Recognition and Rewards

Our department reports to Mike Trigg, director of sales and service development, to insure that sales and service initiatives mesh and are aligned with internal and external customer expectations. The Service Quality Development Department interfaces with, and supports, the initiatives of the Service Excellence Council [see Chapter 1] as well as the objectives outlined by individual departments and areas [see Exhibit 7.1].

Our Service Quality Development Department's objectives are to:

1. Champion the service quality vision through interaction and support at all levels of the organization

2. Support the requirements and improvement efforts of the Service Excellence Council

3. Support the quality planning and improvement process by developing and implementing overarching measurement and recognition strategies

4. Provide management/departments with the resources, expertise, and tools they require to impact service quality excellence in their areas

5. Facilitate ongoing communication strategies to continue the expansion of a service quality, customer-focused culture

Our Service Quality Development Department's action plan covers the following six areas:

## Exhibit 7.1

**Society Corporation**, Cleveland, Ohio

### Service Quality Development Team

| | |
|---|---|
| **Manager, Service Quality Development** | • Promote and Communicate the Service Quality Imperative<br>• Develop Support Strategies and Processes in the Areas of Recognition, Measurement, Communication, and Training<br>• Coordination and Support of Service Quality Initiatives Statewide<br>• Administer the Efforts of the Service Excellence Council and Its Support Groups |

**Support Specialist**

• Provides Administrative Support
• Inputs and Compiles Data
• Prepares Reports and Presentations
• Coordinates Process Schedules

| **Recognition Manager** | **Research/ Measurement Analyst** | **Service Quality Consultant II** |
|---|---|---|
| • Coordinates/Administers All Statewide Recognition Programs<br>• Coordinates All Recognition Events<br>• Consults Where Needed on Recognition for Individual Areas<br>• Manages Recognition Database | • Measurement Research Planning and Design<br>• External/Internal Research (Surveys and Focus Groups)<br>• PC Analysis and Reporting<br>• Coordinate Statewide Customer Panels | • Consults with Middle Management on Quality Improvement Programs<br>• Supports the Initiatives of the Service Excellence Council<br>• Promotes Service Quality Awareness throughout the Organization |

116

1. Measurement
   - ★ Implement a service measurement process to determine customer expectations and quantify perceptions
   - ★ Further define service quality gaps with:
     - ☆ Focus groups
     - ☆ Customer panels
     - ☆ Shopping programs
   - ★ Track and analyze gap-closing efforts with:
     - ☆ Productivity/accuracy measures
     - ☆ Performance data
     - ☆ Complaint/suggestion tracking
   - ★ Coordinate measurements throughout the organization
   - ★ Standardize quality reporting formats

2. Service Quality Process (departmental)
   - ★ Provide managers with a customized service quality process structured for their area or needs (such as value analysis, creating value for the customer, etc.)
   - ★ Bring about change in individual areas by measuring customer expectations and implementing gap-closing solutions
   - ★ Support managers in an ongoing measurement process to track success of efforts

3. Training and Development Process
   - ★ Distribute quality and leadership periodicals, books, and audio and video tapes
   - ★ Develop modular, ongoing service quality video series
   - ★ Target service quality training and development programs for employees at all levels
   - ★ Provide speakers/consultants to share examples of service excellence and spread the service quality vision

4.  Communication

    ★ Develop and implement corporatewide service quality
      awareness and enhancement communications

    ★ Continue to utilize both internal and external speakers
      promoting the service quality imperative

    ★ Open communication channels across functions through
      quality improvement efforts

5.  Service Excellence Council [see Chapter 1]

    ★ Support the administration and mission of the council

    ★ Support the council with the required resources and
      service quality improvement tools

6.  Recognition

    ★ Monitor current programs and determine recognition
      voids

    ★ Develop corporatewide programs with consistent levels
      of criteria and rewards

    ★ Support sector/departmental recognition efforts

## *Customer or Member Comment Cards for Analyzing Complaints*

A credit union CEO approached me after my presentation on service
quality. "I enjoyed your program, Barbara, but I'm pretty happy with
our service." I asked him how he knew his service was satisfactory to
his members. "Well, I'm only getting a handful of complaint letters
each month," he responded. I then asked, "Do you mean that the only
way you know about your service is if a member is angry and motivated
enough to write you a letter? What about those members who don't
give you the chance to respond, and just take their business elsewhere?" He silently raised his eyebrows and nodded his head.

Only 4 to 6 percent of our customers or members will take the time to
register a complaint. Instead of letting us know they are unhappy, they
just leave and go to our competitors. Complaints are an opportunity

to save loyal customers or members. In addition to soliciting our customers' perceptions and expectations, we've got to make it easy for them to complain.

For example, at Stew Leonard's grocery store, there are signs everywhere inviting customers to comment on the service. Each comment card is reviewed daily by management. Randall's Food Markets in Houston, Texas, also is fanatical about utilizing comment cards (Berry, *American Banker,* November 1985). Marriott uses the Guest Satisfaction Index, a voluntary survey form, found in every room, that asks guests to rate the service. Results are posted in employee work areas, and meetings are held to discuss the scores and comments.

Whether you hand out comment cards at each financial transaction, mail them with your statement stuffers, display them in your branches, or hand them out quarterly, these can be valuable tools for spotting any negative trends or troublesome areas in your organization. Some banks have created slogans such as, "We want to know," or "Tell us please." **Valley National Bank** in Phoenix uses "The Buck Stops Here" as the slogan for its Value Report Card (see Exhibit 7.2).

Key areas to include on comment cards are:
- ★ Friendliness
- ★ Courteousness
- ★ Eye contact
- ★ Acknowledged by name
- ★ Responsiveness
- ★ Accuracy
- ★ Knowledge
- ★ Offered additional services
- ★ Thanked you for your business
- ★ Overall impression
- ★ Waiting time

119

## Exhibit 7.2

# The Buck Stops Here

When it comes to providing quality service, we don't pass the buck. Every Valley Banker is responsible for giving our customers the best service possible, because your satisfaction is very important to us. Please let us know how we're doing by completing the questions below on our VALUE REPORT CARD.

*Name:* (optional) _____

Address: _____

Telephone: _____

Today's Date _____ Time of Day in Branch _____

Branch Location _____

|  | YES | NO |
|---|---|---|
| **1.** Did we greet and help you in a friendly manner? | ☐ | ☐ |
| **2.** Did we efficiently handle your transaction? | ☐ | ☐ |
| **3.** Did we thank you for your business? | ☐ | ☐ |
| **4.** Was our office clean and neat? | ☐ | ☐ |
| **5.** Would you refer Valley National Bank to your friends, relatives and/or associates for their banking needs? | ☐ | ☐ |

**6.** How long did you wait for service? _____ minutes

**7.** VALUE REPORT CARD Final Grade on Today's Overall Service (A is superior, F is inferior).     A ☐  B ☐  C ☐  D ☐  F ☐

COMMENTS: _____

_____

_____

Please drop your completed card in the VALUE REPORT CARD COLLECTION BOX or any postal mailbox. Thank you for helping us serve you better.

*(VNB employees should not complete this survey.)*

## VALLEY NATIONAL BANK
*Member FDIC*

0-501-0154

Simply displaying comment cards in a rack will not ensure that they are used. I recommend having all frontline employees hand them out during the first week of each quarter for a random sampling.

The key to utilizing customer comment cards is to act on them and make sure every comment is responded to by someone in your organization. **A word of caution:** Sometimes financial institutions jump on the service bandwagon, print comment cards, distribute them to their staffs, and have no follow up. If you are going to take the time and effort to develop comment cards, give equal attention to analyzing the results, responding to your customers or members, and sharing the comments with your management team and employees.

I have included three examples here of organizations that follow up on comment cards—Mrs. Fields Cookies, Contra-Tel Federal Credit Union, and Bank of Marianna.

Mrs. Fields Cookies is a service-driven company. According to an article by Bill Kelley in the May 1988 issue of *Sales and Marketing Management*, one of the magazine's editors had stopped at a Mrs. Fields store in Manhattan. There was only one clerk available, making it a long wait, but that wasn't the problem. When the editor placed her order, the clerk questioned her by asking if she was sure she knew what she wanted. When she said yes, the clerk answered that she better be certain because once he started to fill the order he wasn't going to change it.

Surprised by the rudeness, the editor wrote a letter to the company, using the address on the cookie bag requesting comments or complaints. A few weeks later she received a letter from the president, Debra Fields, who wrote:

> Thank you for taking the time to let us know about your recent experience. We are sorry about the incident and appreciate your comments. Caring customers like you are invaluable. I will look into the matter immediately. Mrs. Fields stands for 100% quality and customer service. I am enclosing a complimentary card for cookies of your choice. . . . Please give us another chance.

**Contra-Tel Federal Credit Union** in Pleasanton, California, is also serious about service. Herb Hunter of Hunter-Thomas and Associates helped Contra-Tel develop a program to measure the quality of service that its employees delivers to members. The objectives for the Quality Member Service Program are:

★ To achieve a system of measuring member service that is viewed as fair and objective by all

★ To hold people accountable for less than acceptable service

★ To recognize service excellence

★ To provide management with regular reports measuring individuals, branches, and the overall organization on the level of service to members

Specific transactions are selected at random and members receive (within five days of the transaction) a four-question survey asking them how the employee handled the transaction in terms of friendliness, professionalism, responsiveness, and accuracy. Members check either excellent, good, fair, or poor. Surveys are assigned point values of one to four, and quarterly reports summarize the scores by individual branches. Managers and employees review the surveys and their ratings. The results are used in staff performance evaluations. Employees not meeting minimal standards are coached. Exceptional performance is recognized at a quarterly recognition breakfast.

To date, Contra-Tel continues to achieve overall scores above 3.7 (4.0 is perfect). If a branch or individual seems to be slipping, steps are taken to improve. A 3.5 score is minimally acceptable. In terms of advice, Susan Haines, President, commented, "Be consistent in sampling transactions, and monitor enough to know that the results are meaningful. Be very timely with any recognition." The approximate cost for this program is $100 per month, plus stationery and envelopes.

The following story is taken from the February 15, 1989, issue of *Community Bank President*. **Citizens Bank of Marianna** in Marianna, Florida, asks randomly selected customers to fill out short questionnaires after they've been helped by tellers, personal bankers, drive-up staff—even loan officers. "I spend about 30 minutes a week on this," says Rebecca Morris, marketing and training coordinator at Bank of Mariana. "A clerical person spends another 30 minutes, plus it costs about $5 a week in postage."

Once a week, Rebecca mails surveys to recent customers of the bank's loan officers and personal bankers. She sends four to five surveys for each personal banker, and one survey for each loan officer every week. Names are gleaned from weekly "new loan" and "new deposit" lists.

Twice a month, surveys are distributed to evaluate the bank's tellers and drive-up window personnel. An employee stands outside the bank and hands out surveys as customers leave. About 20 surveys are given out each time.

Rebecca has developed a slightly different questionnaire for each of the four job positions—teller, personal banker, drive-up staff, and loan officer. But all have just five or six questions, and they focus solely on the quality of service. The following is an example of the questions the bank asks loan customers. They are asked to rate each area or service on a scale of one to five (five being the best rating), as well as to make comments.

1. Was your loan officer friendly, professional, and courteous?
2. Was your loan handled in a timely manner?
3. Were you pleased with the service you received?
4. Was your loan officer knowledgeable about our product?
5. Were the terms and features of the loan described in a clear, easy to understand manner?
6. Are there additional services we could provide?

If the bank receives a negative comment about an employee, additional training assistance is provided. "The idea is to identify and correct a problem before it gets worse," Morris says. Once a month, she provides a copy of every survey to the bank's president. He reads the most favorable comments at an employee meeting.

By asking your customers and members to add up the total score for services, you can assign a point value to each survey and set targeted levels of service. For example, if your branch received 20 comment cards last month, averaging 6.0 on a 10-point scale, you clearly have some work to do to improve service. In Chapter 8, which deals with accountability, I will show you how to use these measuring devices in your performance appraisals.

Ask yourself the following questions. Is it easy for my members and customers to complain? Do we have an effective complaint handling system? If the answers are "no," utilize comment cards and read on for more ideas.

## *Error-Resolution Programs*

Federal Express executives believe that for every dollar they spend to prevent a problem from occurring, they would have to spend $10 more to correct the problem after it has occurred. If the problem goes unnoticed for a long period of time, they would probably spend 100 times more than what they would have spent to prevent it from happening at all (*Personal Selling Power*, January-February 1990).

The key is to prevent mistakes from happening and have a plan in place for dealing with them effectively when they do occur. For this reason, many banks and credit unions have developed error-resolution programs.

An error-resolution program establishes organizationwide procedures and standards for resolving problems or errors. In the November 1988 issue of *Bank Marketing*, Justin L. Moran outlined the following guidelines for a successful program.

1. Communicate your service mission and philosophy to all employees frequently, verbally, and in writing.
2. Develop specific standards for how problems are to be handled and in what time frame.
3. Evaluate your policies and provide for making exceptions when appropriate.

4. Develop a "service alert" or "error-resolution" form on bright colored paper. All employees need to feel a sense of urgency and ownership whenever one of these forms lands in their hands. (See Exhibits 7.3 and 7.4.)

5. Offer an incentive, reward or points, for each completed report. This is important to make sure you are getting all the correct data.

6. Have your service quality officer review and analyze all reports to identify problems that recur frequently. The sources of these problems should be addressed by senior management.

7. Have senior management demonstrate its commitment and support to the error-resolution program by recognizing top performers.

8. Emphasize in new employee orientation programs the importance of the error-resolution program and how it operates.

Quality service won't happen just because everyone is smiling and being friendly. A well-conceived and easily executable plan for consistently handling errors is critical to your long-term success.

## Customer Service Counter

Several years ago I went to use the outdoor ATM at my local **Bank of America** branch in Montclair, California. Unfortunately, the machine did not give me a receipt for my deposit. I was a bit frustrated because I knew I would have to go inside and thought I would have trouble getting someone to assist me. Much to my surprise, I walked in and noticed a large sign directly in front of me that said "Customer Service." I approached the counter and was greeted by a friendly woman who quickly took care of my needs.

On leaving, I asked the manager to tell me more about this customer service counter. The manager told me that they were experimenting with these special counters in several locations. Results to date had been positive—the customers loved the convenience they provided. Employees were rotated through the customer service counter. As

---

## Exhibit 7.3

---

# SERVICE ALERT!

Control #_____
(Obtain from Marketing)

Date: _____

---

**To:**    All Branch Managers

**From:** _____   _____
                 Name                             Department

**Subject:** _____

**Description:** _____
_____
_____
_____
_____
_____

**Potential Customer Impact:** _____
_____
_____
_____

**Units Impacted:** _____
_____
_____
_____
_____

**Resolution** (if applicable): _____
_____
_____
_____

**Contact:** _____   _____   _____
              Name            Department         Extension

**Citytrust**

## Exhibit 7.4

FIRST NATIONAL BANK OF CHASKA

```
┌─────────────────────────────────────────────────────────────────────────┐
│                        DISSATISFIED CUSTOMER FORM                         │
│                                                                           │
│  CUSTOMER NAME _____      ACCOUNT NUMBER _____      │
│  ADDRESS _____      PORT NUMBER    _____      │
│          _____      PHONE NUMBER  _____       │
│                                                                           │
│  NATURE OF COMPLAINT:   DDA ____   SAV ____   ATM ____   LOAN ____   OTHER ____ │
│  DESCRIPTION OF OTHER:  _____  │
│  DETAILS OF COMPLAINT:  _____  │
│                         _____  │
│                         _____  │
│                         _____  │
│                         _____  │
│                                                                           │
│  HOW RESOLVED:          _____  │
│                         _____  │
│                         _____  │
│                         _____  │
│                                                                           │
│  IF NOT RESOLVED, WHAT                                                     │
│  PROMISES WERE MADE:    _____  │
│                         _____  │
│                         _____  │
│                         _____  │
│                                                                           │
│  Employee Initials ____  Date of Complaint _____  Phone ___ Letter ___ In Person ____ │
│  Date of Follow Up _____  Phone Call ____  Letter ____  In Person ____   │
│                                                                           │
│                                                                           │
│  Triplicate copy:  Original + 1 copy to Marketing for follow Up.  Will be returned to │
│                    employee when completed.                               │
└─────────────────────────────────────────────────────────────────────────┘
```

customer service representatives, the employees received excellent training in solving problems and handling complaints, and best of all, had more time to focus on their sales efforts.

When you bring back a toaster or an item of clothing that doesn't fit, typically you go to a store's special customer service department. It makes perfect sense that we utilize this same idea in our own banking offices.

## Customer Service Hotlines

One of the more effective ways to improve customer satisfaction is to make it easy for complaints to be handled by telephone. What better way to do this than by advertising on all your statements and brochures that you have a special customer service hotline. Before you can do this, however, be sure you have an adequate telephone system to avoid long delays and other inefficiencies. Your customer service hotline should to be staffed by highly knowledgeable, friendly, and patient customer service employees who have on-line access to customer account information. You might want to check the sophisticated voice response systems that give detailed account information by phone. Many banks and credit unions are using them.

**Citytrust** in Bridgeport, Connecticut, established a centralized Customer Service Center when its managers learned that customers were annoyed at not being able to find the right person to answer questions or respond to requests. As a result of a survey, they expanded their center from 5 to 12 full-time representatives. In addition, the representatives were trained to handle a broad range of inquiries that were fielded previously by many different areas of the bank. Once the centralization was completed, Citytrust channeled all customer inquiries through an 800 number (*Measuring and Monitoring Service Quality*).

## Closed Account and New Account Surveys

Our employees are often approached by customers or members who say, "I want to close my account." Our employee responds, "Fine," and proceeds to close the account as requested. Instead, we should have our employees ask these customers why they are closing the account.

By not asking the customers for their reasons, we could be sending out a message that we don't care. By letting the customer explain, it is possible that the relationship could be saved.

Our employees need training in the procedure of closing accounts. They should keep a record of the reason for each closed account. This valuable information can then be used to generate a closed account report that can be distributed to the staff.

Demetra Takes Osterhoudt, vice president of **Harleysville National Bank**, in Harleysville, Pennsylvania, tells us in *Measuring and Monitoring Service Quality* that Harleysville National Bank finds closed account surveys useful for answering complaints, spotting trends, getting product ideas, and measuring and tracking performance. Every other month, a closed account survey is mailed to all closed checking account and savings account customers (see Exhibit 7.5). The bank receives a 40 to 45 percent response rate to these surveys. Following are some of the things that the bank does with the information:

1.  Every response is read, and all complaints are forwarded to the officer in charge of that account for an explanation. In many cases, follow-up letters or calls are done by the account officer.

2.  Compliments are identified by branch office and passed along to the staff that earned the praise. Fortunately, compliments far outnumber complaints.

3.  Each survey response is identified by branch office, by the reason for closing, by the average balance that had been maintained in the account, and by the length of time the account was open. This information is fed into a computer and sorted by reason-for-closing, then by reason-for-closing-by-branch to enable them to spot trends in specific markets.

The closed account survey allows Harleysville National Bank to determine what they are doing right, as well as wrong, and thus helps them fine-tune their service. Harleysville National also utilizes a new account survey (see Exhibit 7.6).

## Exhibit 7.5

HARLEYSVILLE NATIONAL BANK

The "closed account survey" is printed on continuous forms and prepared by the mainframe from information captured at the end of the month. The account number is printed on the reverse side so that we can track branch office designations and can locate names and addresses in case we want to correspond with the customer.

I closed my account for the following reason:

_____ I moved from the community.

_____ I had an immediate need for the funds.

_____ I transferred to a more conveniently located bank.

_____ Services I wanted were not available at HNB.

_____ I transferred the funds to another HNB account.

_____ Your service charges.

_____ Other _____

Comments_____

_____

Thank You.

The form is 2-part with an explanation attached (the reverse side of the explanation side is printed with the name and address so window envelopes can be used.) The Audit Department mails out and logs in the forms before forwarding to Marketing so that the survey is really a dual purpose one.

## Exhibit 7.6

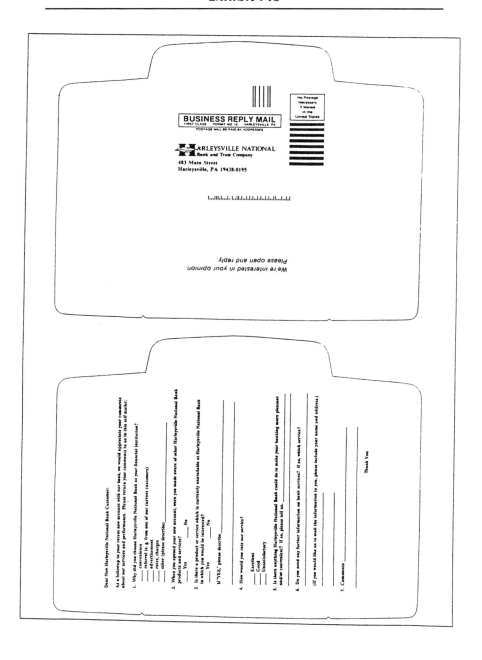

**North Island Federal Credit Union** in San Diego sends a survey to 10 percent of its new account and new loan transactions each week. A survey is also sent to 1-out-of-every-500 teller transactions. Bev Kjer administers this service program and tells me, "The member response is excellent with 20 percent returning the surveys." Members are asked to rate the service as either poor, satisfactory, good, or excellent. Managers receive copies of the summary reports and are held accountable for achieving a minimum percentage in the excellent and good categories. Each month, survey results are presented to the board of directors with suggestions for improvement. North Island also utilizes closed account surveys. See Exhibits 7.7 through 7.10 for North Island's teller transaction survey, new loan survey, new account survey, and closed account survey.

**Valley National Bank** periodically utilizes an extensive telephone survey for closed accounts to determine why customers left and where they took their business (see Exhibit 7.11). Several credit unions also do regular phone surveys each month on a random sampling of closed accounts to get a clear picture of why they lost the account. If you have a customer service hotline, your customer service reps, can make periodic telephone surveys of closed accounts.

Before we leave this section on account surveys, we should ask ourselves the following questions: Do we know how many customers or members we lose each month because of poor service or drawbacks in our product? Is our frontline staff filling out closed account surveys on the spot and trying to save business? Are our managers and employees familiar with new account and closed account surveys? And most importantly, is our senior management reviewing these surveys?

## Telephone Surveys

Many banks conduct monthly or quarterly telephone surveys to sample how their customers view their service. Typically, these are done by volunteers from the training department or by college students either for free or for minimal wages as part of their marketing program's curriculum. **Bank of America**, for example, uses students from time to time to call their customers. Rotating managers and

132

## Exhibit 7.7

```
TELLER TRANSACTION SURVEY

Our records indicate that you were in our Naval Supply Center
branch on JAN 26 1990.  Is our service meeting your expectations?
Please take a few moments to rate the service provided by our
Teller Service Representatives.

1)  Was the Teller Service Representative who helped you:

              Excellent      Good         Fair         Poor

Friendly      _____    _____    _____    _____
Knowledgeable _____    _____    _____    _____
Accurate      _____    _____    _____    _____
Helpful       _____    _____    _____    _____

2)  Was your transaction completed promptly?

              Yes _____        No _____

3)  Were any other services offered to you?

              Yes _____        No _____

4)  How would you rate our overall service?

              Excellent      Good         Fair         Poor
              _____    _____    _____    _____


5)  Comments:  _____

   _____

   _____

6)  Name:  _____    Phone #:  _____
    (optional)

    Account #:  _____

Thank you for your time.  Your comments are important to us.
```

## Exhibit 7.8

# New Loan Survey

Dear Member,

Would you please take a few minutes to rate the service you received on your new loan? Your comments are important to us in order to provide you with the best service possible.

Thank you for your time and response.

*Michael J Maslak*

**Mike Maslak**
President/CEO

1. Was the Loan Processor who helped you:

|  | Excellent | Good | Fair | Poor |
|---|---|---|---|---|
| Friendly | — | — | — | — |
| Knowledgeable | — | — | — | — |
| Accurate | — | — | — | — |
| Helpful | — | — | — | — |

2. How would you rate the loan processing time?
   Quicker than elsewere —
   The same as elsewhere —
   Slower than elsewhere —

3. Was it convenient to apply for your loan?
   ☐ Yes
   ☐ No

4. Would you recommend NIFCU's loan services to your family or friends?
   ☐ Yes
   ☐ No

5. Branch: _____

6. Comments _____
   _____
   _____
   _____

**Optional Information**

| Name | Phone (Day) | Phone (Evening) |
|---|---|---|
| Account Number | Date | |

NORTH ISLAND
FEDERAL CREDIT UNION

FOLD WITH RETURN ADDRESS PANEL SHOWING AND SEAL WITH TAPE

(5/84) OP070

## Exhibit 7.9

# New Account Survey

Dear Member,

Welcome to the benefits of NIFCU membership! We're here to help you meet all of your financial needs.

To assist us in serving you better, we would appreciate your completing and returning this survey regarding your initial contact with us when you opened your NIFCU account.

Thank you for your time and response.

*Mike Maslak*

Mike Maslak
President/CEO

1. Was it easy to find the branch office where you opened your NIFCU account?
   Yes    No

2. Was the branch office conveniently located to where you:
   Live    Work    Neither

3. Was parking adequate?
   Yes    No

4. Please rate the general appearance and cleanliness of the branch office.
   Interior:
   Excellent    Good    Fair    Poor
   Exterior:
   Excellent    Good    Fair    Poor

5. Was it easy to locate the Member Service area and everything you needed?
   Yes    No

6. Was the Member Service Representative who helped you:

|  | Excellent | Good | Fair | Poor |
|---|---|---|---|---|
| Friendly |  |  |  |  |
| Knowledgeable |  |  |  |  |
| Accurate |  |  |  |  |
| Helpful |  |  |  |  |

7. Was opening your account completed promptly?
   Yes    No

8. About which services would you like more information?

_____

_____

_____

_____

9. Comments _____

_____

_____

_____

_____

_____

_____

_____

10. Branch where your account was opened:

_____

**Optional Information**

Name

Phone-Day          Phone-Evening

Account Number     Date

NORTH ISLAND
FEDERAL CREDIT UNION

FOLD WITH RETURN ADDRESS PANEL SHOWING AND SEAL WITH TAPE

135

## Exhibit 7.10

# Closed Account Survey

1. I closed my account(s) because of the following:
   - I will be leaving the area
   - The branch is inconveniently located
   - I've had a problem with the service I received

   Please explain _____
   _____
   _____
   _____

   - Other _____
   _____

2. Please rate the following:

| | Excellent | Good | Fair | Poor |
|---|---|---|---|---|
| Service Quality | – | – | – | – |
| Services Offered | – | – | – | – |

3. How can we improve? _____
   _____
   _____
   _____
   _____
   _____
   _____
   _____
   _____

Dear Member,

Our records show you recently closed your account at North Island Federal Credit Union.

We value our members highly and regret losing your account. That is why we are asking you to provide us with information as to why you closed your account in order to help us serve our members better.

Thank you for your time and your response.

*Michael J Maslak*

**Mike Maslak**
President/CEO

4. Please share your comments _____
   _____
   _____
   _____
   _____
   _____
   _____

Optional Information

Name _____

Phone (Day) _____  Phone (Evening) _____

Closed Account Number _____  Date _____

NORTH ISLAND FEDERAL CREDIT UNION

FOLD WITH RETURN ADDRESS PANEL SHOWING AND SEAL WITH TAPE

## Exhibit 7.11

## Valley National Bank

VALLEY NATIONAL BANK

CLOSED ACCOUNT QUESTIONNAIRE

1. Which of the following reasons best describe why you closed your checking account at Valley National Bank (VNB). (Check all that apply.)

1 [] Moved (outside of Arizona) ⟶ PLEASE SKIP TO QUESTION 12
AND CONTINUE

2 [] Interest rates (on deposit accounts) not competitive    9 [] Discourteous/unfriendly personnel

3 [] Could not get errors corrected    A [] Slow service/long lines

4 [] Needed money to buy something    B [] Unable to get loan

5 [] To consolidate one or more accounts    C [] Unable to get VISA/MASTERCARD

6 [] This VNB Branch no longer convenient    D [] Made too many errors

7 [] Don't have free checking    E [] Due to a change in marital status

8 [] Fees/service charges too high    F [] Lost or stolen purse/wallet/ checkbook

   G [] Inconvenient banking hours

Other (specify) _____

## Exhibit 7.11 (cont.)

2. Which of these would you say was the <u>main</u> reason for closing your account? (Check only <u>one</u>)

1 [] Interest rates (on deposit accounts) not competitive

8 [] Discourteous/unfriendly personnel

2 [] Could not get errors corrected

9 [] Slow service/long lines

3 [] Needed money to buy something

A [] Unable to get loan

4 [] To consolidate one or more accounts

B [] Unable to get VISA/MASTERCARD

5 [] This VNB Branch no longer convenient

C [] Made too many errors

6 [] Don't have free checking

D [] Due to a change in marital status

7 [] Fees/service charges too high

E [] Lost or stolen purse/wallet/checkbook

F [] Inconvenient banking hours

Other (specify) _____

_____

3. How did Valley National personnel respond to your request to close your account? (Check only one)

   1 [] He/she asked why I was closing my account, but did nothing to retain my business.

   2 [] He/she asked why I was closing my account, then offered to attempt to resolve my problem and/or concern.

   3 [] He/she did not ask why I was closing my account.

   4 [] Other _____
           (please specify)

4. After you closed your checking account at VNB, did you open a new checking account at . . .

   1 [] Another financial institution   ⟶   CONTINUE TO QUESTION 5

   2 [] The same VNB Branch

   3 [] Another VNB Branch          PLEASE SKIP TO QUESTION 7 AND CONTINUE

   4 [] Didn't open a new checking account

## Exhibit 7.11 (cont.)

5.  Where did you open your new checking account?

    1 [] Arizona Bank              6 [] MeraBank

    2 [] Chase/Continental Bank    7 [] Pima Savings

    3 [] Citibank/Great Western    8 [] United Bank
         Bank

    4 [] First Interstate Bank     9 [] Western Savings

    5 [] Great American/Home
         Federal Savings           A [] Valley National Bank

                                   B [] A Credit Union

    Other (specify) _____

6.  Why did you choose that financial institution?

    1 [] Convenient hours          7 [] Overall reputation of
                                         the institution

    2 [] Convenient location       8 [] Directly solicited by
                                         one of its employees

    3 [] Recommended by a friend/  9 [] Attracted by a special
         family member or business     premium offer
         associate

    4 [] Already had other accounts A [] Lower fees/service
         there                           charges

    5 [] Attracted by the advertising B [] Interstate network

    6 [] Free Checking

Other (specify) _____

_____

7.  In the past 12 months, have you moved within Arizona; that is, have
you changed residences, but remained in the state?

              [] Yes              [] No (Skip to Question 12)

8.  Did you close your account at Valley Bank at the time of your move?

              [] Yes              [] No

9.  Did you open a new account after the move?

              [] Yes              [] No (Skip to Question 12)

## Exhibit 7.11 (cont.)

10. Where did you open your new account?

1 [] Arizona Bank

2 [] Chase/Continental Bank

3 [] Citibank/Great Western Bank

4 [] First Interstate Bank

5 [] Great American/Home Federal Savings

6 [] MeraBank

7 [] Pima Savings

8 [] United Bank

9 [] Western Savings

A [] Valley National Bank

B [] A Credit Union

Other (specify) _____

11. If you moved to an area where there was a Valley National Bank branch conveniently located, but did not open an account there, why not?

_____

_____

12. Compared to other financial institutions (banks, savings and loans, credit unions, brokerage firms, etc.) you may have used or know about, how would you rate VNB on: ("X" the appropriate box for each item).

| | 5<br>The<br>Best | 4<br>Better<br>Than Most | 3<br>The<br>Same | 2<br>Not Quite<br>as Good | 1<br>The<br>Worst |
|---|---|---|---|---|---|
| a. Providing quality service in the branch | [] | [] | [] | [] | [] |
| b. Innovative products and services to meet customers needs | [] | [] | [] | [] | [] |
| c. Convenience of locations | [] | [] | [] | [] | [] |
| d. Advertising message that applies to your needs | [] | [] | [] | [] | [] |
| e. Safe, strong, secure | [] | [] | [] | [] | [] |
| f. Arizona/community minded | [] | [] | [] | [] | [] |
| g. Delivering value to its customers | [] | [] | [] | [] | [] |

## Exhibit 7.11 (cont.)

---

13. Regarding other personal accounts you may also have had or have at Valley National Bank, please mark an "X" in the appropriate box.

| | 1<br>Closed When<br>Checking Closed | 2<br>Continue to<br>Have at VNB | 3<br>Never Had<br>at VNB |
|---|---|---|---|
| a. Regular Savings | [ ] | [ ] | [ ] |
| b. Certificate of Deposit | [ ] | [ ] | [ ] |
| c. Money Market Savings | [ ] | [ ] | [ ] |
| d. Credit Card | [ ] | [ ] | [ ] |
| e. Loan | [ ] | [ ] | [ ] |
| Other (specify) _____ | [ ] | [ ] | [ ] |

14. How long did you have your checking account at Valley National Bank?

    1 [ ] Less than 1 year     3 [ ] 3 to 5 years     5 [ ] Over 10 years

    2 [ ]  1 to 2 years        4 [ ] 6 to 10 years

The following information will be used to accurately group your answers for analysis purposes. Please "X" the appropriate boxes.

15. SEX

    [ ] Male

    [ ] Female

16. AGE

    [ ] Under 25

    [ ] 25 to 34

    [ ] 35 to 44

    [ ] 45 to 54

    [ ] 55 to 65

    [ ] 65 or older

employees to give them all a chance to call up customers is also an excellent idea. The key here is to call up customers or members who recently used your services and to have them rate their level of satisfaction by asking them identical questions.

Salespeople at the Longo Toyota dealership of El Monte, California, for example, are trained to call buyers within 48 hours of their purchase to find out if they were treated properly, got the car in peak condition, and had no problems or lingering dissatisfaction (Levine, March 1989). With more than $200 million in sales and near the top of *Auto Age's* ranking of the nation's largest dealerships, Longo Toyota reports that 60 percent of its volume comes from repeat and referral business.

Summit Health, Ltd., is another organization that uses telephone surveys to rate its level of service. Summit is a for-profit, investor-owned, health care system based in Los Angeles that has 15 hospitals and 24 nursing homes (Blume, September 1988). Sometime ago, senior management announced that it wanted to improve the quality of its health care systems and services—as perceived by the customer—by 100 percent. Summit hired an outside telephone research company to conduct a general survey of patient satisfaction with overall hospital service. The company calls on recently discharged patients and, in a 10-to-15-minute conversation, runs through the patient's experience. On a local basis, each hospital or nursing home asks patients who are being discharged to respond to questions on a written survey.

## *Mystery Shoppers*

A mystery shopper is an individual who acts like a customer or member and evaluates his or her experience in a report. Some banks ask their customers to be mystery shoppers. A branch manager I know has her friends shop her employees. Others hire professional shoppers who are trained in perception research.

In April 1986, **San Diego County Credit Union** in San Diego, California, developed a "Personal Touch Service Award," which is selected by an outside shopper service. Rene McKee, senior vice president of marketing and sales, gave me the following information:

We wanted to develop service standards and implement an outside shopping service as a measurement and accountability tool. It was important to introduce the program in a very positive, constructive fashion with employee recognition and rewards as a focal point.

Our objectives and expectations were to:

1. Improve the quality of service delivered by branch personnel and support staff.
2. Have specific standards met consistently that could be measured.
3. Provide a way to identify weak areas for further training.
4. Recognize staff who exemplify the high-quality service provider we wanted.

The program was kicked off at an all-staff service seminar. Employees were told this was how we could "catch them doing something right." We were up-front about the details:

1. They would receive additional training to meet specific standards when serving a member over the phone or in person.
2. We would have professional shoppers report on their service.
3. Once per quarter the shoppers would select the person they shopped who provided the finest service.

The Personal Touch Service Award recipient receives $100, a plaque, and their picture in our membership newsletter.

This program has improved our service significantly. In one year we averaged 7 to 8 "perfect reports" per month, compared to 1 to 2 when it began. After a point, some staff even started asking when they could get shopped and some employees set goals of "receiving a perfect report every time." [See Exhibit 7.12, 7.13, and 7.14 for shopper reports.]

## Exhibit 7.12

### First National Bank of Chaska, Chaska, Minnesota

### Mystery Shopper Rating Sheet

Date _____ Mystery Shopper's Name _____

Name of Employee Observed _____ Employee's Position _____

Name of Bank _____

| Did the Employee Perform the Following | Yes | No |
|---|---|---|
| **S** mile | _____ | _____ |
| **E** agerly & warmly greet you | _____ | _____ |
| **C** all you by name | _____ | _____ |
| **R** apid, accurate transactions | _____ | _____ |
| **E** ye contact | _____ | _____ |
| **T** hank you and ask you to return | _____ | _____ |

Was the employee courteous?                                   _____   _____

Were you kept waiting more than 2
minutes before the transaction began?                _____   _____

Was the employee willing to listen to you?         _____   _____

Did the employee offer suggestions
about other bank services?                                      _____   _____

<u>About the Bank</u>

Did you feel there was an excessive amount of
employee-to-employee conversation?                   _____   _____

Were you given answers to your questions . . .

• at the reception desk                                            _____   _____

• at the teller line                                                    _____   _____

• at the new accounts desk                                     _____   _____

• at the loan department                                         _____   _____

Did the employees you encountered seem to be
knowledgeable about the bank's products?          _____   _____

If not, who were they? _____

Other comments _____

_____

---

## Exhibit 7.13

---

### San Diego County Credit Union

### Shopper Evaluation Report

Branch___VISTA_____ Date___12/15/89___ Day___FRIDAY_____ Time_1:35____

Identity (name or description, teller #)        Position:__NEW ACCOUNTS_____

_____KATHY CAMMACK_____        Traffic Level:__MODERATE_____

|  | YES | NO | COMMENTS |
|---|---|---|---|
| Greet you? | X | | |
| Smile? | X | | |
| Use your name? | X | | |
| New Accts/Loans (shake hands)? | X | | |
| Use eye contact? | X | | |
| Efficient? | X | | |
| Respond to questions? | X | | |
| Excuse any interruptions? | | N/A | |
| Attempt to cross sell? | X | | |
| Thank you? | X | | |
| Personal Appearance | X | | |
| Hair groomed? | X | | |
| Appropriate attire? | X | | |
| Work area neat? | X | | |

General Information

  Upon entering the bank I had about a minute wait. Kathy greeted me warmly and directed me to have a seat at her desk. She said, "I'll be right there."

  She responded to my inquiry regarding opening a checking account. Her product knowledge was very good. She was professional and friendly throughout the presentation.

  Kathy did some cross-selling by mentioning the various services available.

  During the presentation she used a flip chart, maintained good eye contact and took out an application and pen very nonchalantly and placed them by my right hand.

  In closing Kathy thanked me by name and said, "Have a good weekend," and extended her hand to me for a handshake.

145

Make sure the reports are filed in personnel files and are considered when managers have position openings or are doing reviews. We had difficulty in this area initially. In terms of cost, we pay approximately $26 per report and $12,000 a year for this program.

The following case study is from "Rating Service is No Mystery" by Lynn Parker in the October 1988 issue of *Pacific Banker*. San Francisco-based **California First Bank,** which has more than $6 billion in assets, made a commitment to quality service several years ago. Since implementing a service and sales measurement program called "mystery shopper," they've seen a 22 percent improvement in overall service quality. People posing as customers ask for information on products and then rate the service they receive at a branch. Ruth Fall, vice president and sales development manager, hired Market Trends of Bellevue, Washington, to shop the bank's branches.

Shoppers from Market Trends visit each of the branches at different times and on different days to rate the service and sales abilities of the employees. No leading questions are asked; no notes are taken. The shoppers look and act like everyday bank customers. The results are then compared against industry norms developed by Market Trends.

According to Ruth Fall, mystery shopping works on many levels. First, employees aware that they are being rated improve their performance immediately, without any other training or reward system. At California First, the next steps are for regional sales managers to review the results of the mystery shopping, set service and sales goals based on the results, and then develop action plans consisting of training, reinforcement, and branch reward systems.

According to Ruth, "We reward good service by branches and make all mystery shopper results anonymous so that everyone learns from mistakes made. We remind our staff of the criteria for good performance and reward consistently high-performing branches with plaques." California First now mystery shops its branches every six months to monitor improvements and to catch slippage quickly.

Personally, I feel mystery shopping is an excellent way to monitor your employees' skills and service attitudes. It is not, however, an accurate indicator of how your customers and members perceive your service.

**Valley National Bank** has a successful Branch Manager Shopper Program to give branch managers an opportunity to measure service quality in other branches. Managers are given specific training and guidelines on how to conduct the shop, and the results are reported back to a central area. Service awareness hits close to home when you are rating another branch and wondering how your own branch is performing (*Measuring and Monitoring Service Quality*).

**Friendly Bank** of Oklahoma City pays select customers $50 a month to deal with the bank twice a week and report how they are treated (Rosenstein, October 13, 1988). What is unique about this program is that husbands or wives of community leaders are deliberately chosen as some of the mystery shoppers. "Word does get back to their organizations about the things that are going on at the bank," says Friendly Bank president, James R. Daniel. Loan officers, new accounts representatives, telephone problem solvers, and all customer contact employees are shopped to see if they are turning basic customer inquiries into sales opportunities. "When you call in to say, 'I'd like to have the Blue Book value on a 1986 Ford van,' if the officer doesn't find out who's calling and why, then he or she is scored down," he said.

**National Bank of Long Beach** conducts 50 telephone shops bankwide and 2 in-person visits per branch on a quarterly basis. Service criteria were established for both telephone and in-person behavior. They pay $550 per quarter for the mystery shopper fee. (See Exhibits 7.14, 7.15, and 7.16 for both telephone and personal-visit shopper evaluations.)

## *Annual Surveys*

Once you start utilizing annual opinion surveys (see Chapter 4), you can gauge the overall satisfaction rate of your customers or members. For example, if your first survey shows that 75 percent are extremely satisfied, 20 percent are moderately satisfied, and the remainder are dissatisfied, you can set a revised goal for service performance.

## Exhibit 7.14

### National Bank of Long Beach, CA

### Personal Visit Shopper Evaluation

Branch: _____

Employee Contacted: _____

Date: _____Time: _____

Type of Transaction _____

| Did the employee who served you: | YES | NO |
|---|---|---|
| 1. Acknowledge you immediately? (Within 30 seconds) | ____ | ____ |
| 2. Make eye contact? | ____ | ____ |
| 3. Smile and greet you in a friendly manner? | ____ | ____ |
| 4. Give their name and offer assistance? | ____ | ____ |
| 5. Use your name at least once? | ____ | ____ |
| 6. Respond politely to questions? | ____ | ____ |
| 7. Use terms you could understand? | ____ | ____ |
| 8. Thank you in a personal way? | ____ | ____ |

Answer ONLY if applicable. Was the employee able to:

| | YES | NO |
|---|---|---|
| 1. Ask for the business? | ____ | ____ |
| 2. Give basic information on core products and services, if requested? | ____ | ____ |
| 3. Skillfully refer you to new accounts, if applicable? | ____ | ____ |
| 4. Handle your transaction efficiently? (Did not leave workstation unnecessarily, or require unwarranted assistance) | ____ | ____ |

Answer for ALL employees. Did the employee appear to be:

| | YES | NO |
|---|---|---|
| 1. Wearing appropriate business attire? | ____ | ____ |
| 2. Neat and well groomed? | ____ | ____ |
| 3. Was workstation neat and uncluttered? | ____ | ____ |
| 4. Was workstation adequately supplied? | ____ | ____ |

Overall Rating: (5 being highest) __1 _____ 2 _____ 3 _____ 4 _____ 5 _____
     poor     fair     good     excel.  extra-mile

Employee could improve on:

Appearance _____Enthusiasm _____Eye Contact ____Efficiency _____

Knowledge ____Attitude ____Courtesy _____Friendliness _____

Additional Comments: _____

_____

_____

## Exhibit 7.15

### National Bank of Long Beach, CA

### Mystery Shopper
### Telephone Shopping Evaluation

Branch/Department Name: _____

Employee Contacted: _____

Date:_____Time: _____

**Switchboard:**

1. Were you able to get through to the switchboard operator on the first try?
   Yes____No____
2. How many time did the phone ring before the switchboard answered?
   _____(Actual Count)

| **Always answer. Did the employee contacted:** | **YES** | **NO** |
|---|---|---|
| 1. Answer by the third ring? | ____ | ____ |
| 2. Identify the department and himself or herself? | ____ | ____ |
| 3. Offer assistance? | ____ | ____ |
| 4. Ask your name and use it at least once? | ____ | ____ |
| 5. Respond politely to your questions? | ____ | ____ |
| 6. Use terms you could understand? | ____ | ____ |
| 7. Give accurate information? | ____ | ____ |
| 8. Thank you in a personal way? | ____ | ____ |
| **Answer ONLY if applicable. Did the employee:** | | |
| 9. Offer additional information? | ____ | ____ |
| 10. Cross sell other products or services? | ____ | ____ |
| 11. Ask for the business? | ____ | ____ |
| 12. Ask permission to place call on hold? | ____ | ____ |
| 13. Return to call on hold within one minute? | ____ | ____ |
| 14. Walk you through a transfer call? | ____ | ____ |
| 15. Transfer you to the correct department? | ____ | ____ |
| 16. Identify by name whom you would speak to? | ____ | ____ |

**Always complete. Was the employee's voice tone:**

1. Friendly/courteous _____

_____

2. Short/rushed/not receptive _____

_____

**Overall Service Rating: (5 being the highest)**

    1. _____2. _____3. _____4. _____5. _____

      poor      fair     good    excellent   extra-mile

Additional Comments: _____

# Five-Star Service Solutions

---

## Exhibit 7.16

---

### San Diego County Credit Union

### Branch Telephone Shopper Evaluation Report

Date:___12/18/89____    Employee Name:_____Donna_____
Day:___Monday_____    Branch:_____Encinitas_____
Time:___2:10_____
Number of Rings:___2___    Length of time waiting:___None_____

A check mark indicated that the call was answered with the following:

- ❑ "Country Credit Union
- ❑ Branch or Department
- ❑ Employee Name
- ❑ "May I help you?"

|  | YES | NO | COMMENTS |
|---|---|---|---|
| Use member's name | X | ___ | _____ |
| Respond to question thoroughly | X | ___ | _____ |
| Thorough product knowledge | X | ___ | _____ |
| Cross sell other services | X | ___ | _____ |
| Ask for the business (i.e. make appointment, get name, address or telephone number) | X | ___ | _____ |
| Ask if you need anything else | X | ___ | _____ |
| Thank you | X | ___ | _____ |

Inquiry:__I would like some information about membership___
services._____

Response: Donna greeted me with a friendly greeting and complete
identification of herself, the organization and of the branch.
Her attitude was helpful and pleasant. In response to my
inquiry, Donna was quite knowledgeable. Although she seemed
unsure as to what services she should mention, she did a
better than average job in selling the accounts. I was first
asked how I qualified to be a member before she went on to
explain about the $50.00 minimum in a savings account. I was
also told about the Star System access with the ATM card and
about the service-charge-free checking account. Donna offered
to send me the application in the mail. After she had my name
and address, she continued to use my name in the conversation.
        Donna closed with a friendly "Thank you," once again
using my name.

150

Announce to your entire organization that this year you are striving to reach an 85 percent rating of extremely satisfied. Each year thereafter, increase the expectations. Post a chart in every department and get everyone focused on reaching your goal.

## Service Guarantees

Other industries have been using money-back guarantees and customer bill of rights for years. These promises tell customers that they can expect to get superior service and be treated in a manner they cannot find elsewhere. In an effort to improve service and reduce errors, more financial institutions are using service guarantees and paying their customers or members for mistakes made by the institution.

**Peoples Heritage Bank** of Portland, Maine, decided to develop a quality service program that included a service guarantee. The objective of the program was to find a competitive edge that did not involve rate and price. Management hoped to retain and attract customers, track and monitor complaints, and improve internal relations between departments.

Susan Altshuler, who is in charge of this program, was very adamant in stating to me that this program must be driven from the top. Peoples Heritage Bank's CEO is very committed to the program and is the driving force behind it. Prior to introducing the program, Peoples Heritage Bank surveyed employees to get their thoughts on quality service and how they felt the bank was doing. The program basically guarantees that if customers are not happy with the service received, they tell the bank about it and are paid $5. Customer Research Forms are filled out and tracked by marketing to spot trends and problems that might be developing. Each problem is dealt with by a specific individual and referred internally to the appropriate person.

The results to date have been wonderful and the feedback from customers is complimentary. The tellers and customer service representatives consistently score higher on mystery shops than they did before this program was implemented. The branch people also feel that the relationships between departments are better than ever. In

151

terms of costs, other than printing brochures, the approximate yearly tab for paying customers for complaints is about $3,000 to $4,000.

The following case study is excerpted from an article by D. Dale Browning in the September 1989 issue of *Bank Marketing*.

> Several banks around the country have created service guarantees, often for the accuracy of their transactions. We have expanded this concept in a direction which we believe is more meaningful to our customers. And if we do not live up to our promise, we "put our money where our mouth is" and give our customers a "note from the President" in the form of a $5 bill.
>
> Specifically, our guarantees state that our customers will not wait more than three minutes to be served in our teller lines or more than five minutes in Personal Banking, Personal Loans, or Customer Assistance. We also guarantee a friendly greeting by name, a thank-you, no more than next-day turnaround on inquiries and on personal loan applications, and accuracy in all transactions.
>
> Before we put our guarantee into effect, we thoroughly evaluated our ability to deliver. We believe that a promise made must be kept. Logs were maintained by various departments and teller lines were timed for four months to determine how to structure our guarantee.
>
> We have consistently met our wait time guarantees in all areas, with minimal payouts for this simple promise. In instances where we have paid out for our accuracy guarantee, we have set up a problem reporting system to keep better track of when and why these problems are occurring. The success of our Service Guarantees is certified through the minimal amount of money paid out to customers, with only $885 in three months with more than 256,000 transactions.

**Marquette Bank** in Minneapolis also has a program that pays $5 to a customer if a mistake is made (Schoultz, March 24, 1988). The program pays on errors occurring from a teller transaction, such as a receipt, cash, or passbook error; or from an account transaction, such as a statement problem, encoding error, or incorrect service charge. The bank also pays for errors in account-opening or maintenance activities, such as name misspelling. "These kinds of errors cover most of the mistakes that occur on a consumer account," Marcia Hanson, group vice president of consumer services, commented. She said the guarantee program demonstrates to customers that the bank is serious about service.

**First Interstate Bank's** Los Angeles Division has a special service guarantee newsletter, highlighting success stories, for employees. A copy of this newsletter is shown in Exhibit 7.17.

Service measurement is an important key in keeping your service crusade alive. Getting an accurate picture requires many different forms of measurement, such as complaint monitoring, customer surveys, mystery shoppers, and closed account surveys. Communicating the results to your staff is as important as gathering the information. Clearly the service journey requires hard work and the tireless pursuit of excellence.

## Exhibit 7.17

*Service Guarantee*

Vol 2, No 1   Jan. 2, 1990

### *WHAT THEY'RE SAYING . . .*

**Bay Area:** "What goes around, comes around," says Customer Service Manager, **Wendy Leung.** "It's a popular phrase that has lost its punch somewhat from overuse, but perfectly captures the spirit of a recent $5.00 'goof' story at our San Leandro Industrial branch."

On a recent Friday, a longtime Customer visited our branch to make his weekly deposit. At the time, he was not aware of our new Service Guarantee which would pay him $5.00 for the inconvenience of waiting longer than five minutes in the teller line.

As he waited in line, the gentleman in front of him said, "Oh yeah, I'm going to get my five bucks!" Our Customer then asked teller **Troy Larson,** "Do I really get $5.00 if I wait more than five minutes?" Troy answered, "Certainly," and handed him a five dollar bill, apologized for the wait, and thanked him for his patience.

The following Friday, the Customer returned to the branch and told teller **Nancy Bold** that it was against his principles to keep the $5.00 because he felt he did not wait longer than five minutes the previous week. He further explained that he had inquired about the $5.00 only because the gentleman in front of him had mentioned the Guarantee. He said that our tellers are both efficient and friendly and insisted that he did not wait in line for five minutes. Our genuine and enthusiastic support of the Guarantee impressed him. Understanding our dedication and resolve, he realized that our commitment was genuine. He also realized he could not take advantage of our generosity and generously reimbursed our $5.00. So, good spirits encourage good spirits.

At the Danville branch, Financial Services Manager, **Jacqueline Laster,** received a desperate phone call from two Customers leaving in a few days for a trip to Europe. They expressed a need to obtain a Preferred VISA card because the card they had did not offer free car rental insurance in Europe. Jacqueline immediately called the Bancard Insurance Department. After quickly researching the information,

Bancard informed her that our Preferred card indeed carried the necessary coverage required in European countries. The Customers completed the appropriate application form to initiate the process.

Says Jacqueline, "I called **Don Stilling** in Credit and he picked up the ball and ran with it. The Bancard Company was wonderful and was behind us, not only in meeting our 24-hour Service Guarantee, but also by "going the extra mile Don was able to provide me with an account number that afternoon, and also gave me his personal phone number so the Customers' travel agent could call him and verify approval of the card and issue the Customers' airline tickets that same day. Because of Don's efforts, the VISA cards were sent Federal Express, arriving just in time for the Customers to enjoy their European vacation." Added Jacqueline, "It's this type of cooperation between different areas of First Interstate that help make the Service Guarantee a success."

**L.A. Metro: Rita Maus,** Customer Assistance Representative writes about the following incident that occurred at the Brentwood branch: A Customer approached teller **Linda Zardes** and said, "Is it true that you give $5.00 if I wait for more than five minutes?" Linda answered, "Yes, it's true." The Customer replied, "Well I've been here since 10:30 and it's now 10:35." Linda said, "Then we'll give you the $5.00. It's our Service Guarantee." The Customer responded, "I don't understand why you're not getting mad." "Well," said Linda, "There's no reason to get mad, because you are entitled to it. We're very sorry for the inconvenience."

Still finding it difficult to believe, the Customer questioned, "Aren't you going to call me a liar?" Somewhat amused, Linda smiled and said, "No, of course not, I'm going to give you the $5.00." Said the Customer, "I don't understand why you're not getting upset and fussing about it." Linda replied, "We just want you to have the $5.00. Have a nice day." The Customer left the branch both surprised and happy!

*(continued)*

## Exhibit 7.17 (cont.)

*What They're Saying (continued)*

**San Diego:** A Customer from First Interstate Bank of Oregon was having difficulty accessing the ATM at the San Diego Main branch. He approached teller **Greg Bloomfield** and explained what had happened. Greg told him he could complete his transaction in the branch and handed the Customer $5.00 for his inconvenience, apologizing for the problem with the ATM.

The Customer was unaware of the Bank's Service Guarantee and thought at first that Greg was joking. Greg explained the Guarantee to him, and the Customer literally became speechless. He stood in shock at the teller window for so long that the Bank security guard came over and politely asked him to move on. The Customer responded, "I never would have believed a bank would put its money where its mouth is. I'm very grateful they made good on their promise." He also added jokingly, "I think I'll come back again next week."

## *CUSTOMERS . . .*

. . . Are the most important people who will ever be in this office.

. . . Are those special VIPs who call on the phone.

. . . Are not interruptions of our work. . . they are the reason for it.

. . . Are individuals with names and feelings.

. . . Are not people I argue with.

. . . Are the reasons I have a job.

. . . Are not *always* right, but they are *always* . . .

THE CUSTOMER

*Pryor Resources, Inc.*

## *PROCEDURE UPDATE*

*Service Guarantee Customer Receipt*

The top portion of the 3-part Service Guarantee GL form is a *non-negotiable* receipt that is given to the Customer at the time a Service Guarantee is credited to their account. Some Customers have been attempting to deposit these receipts into their accounts either at the teller window or via the ATM.

At the time of honoring the Service Guarantee, it is important to inform the Customer that this is a receipt *only*, and that their account has been credited accordingly. The receipt cannot be deposited into his or her account.

Please do *not* encode these receipts. Tellers are encouraged to review their work carefully to ensure that the receipts have not been accidently included with the deposits *or* sent for processing. If there are any questions, please speak with your branch's Customer Service Manager.

*Bancard Fax Alert*

Help us to provide *your Customer* with quality service!

The quality of faxed applications is often poor. Please ensure that applications are legible and use a dark color pen when possible. Review applications for *zip codes, city, signature,* and *income*.

Also, please remember to include a branch contact name and telephone number.

We are receiving many duplicate applications. Please fax an application only *once*. If you have any questions, please call the Bancard Credit Department, 1-800-552-5050, ext. 5505.

---

### *SEND US YOUR STORIES*

Do you have a Service Guarantee story you wish to submit? Please contact the following:

**Branches:** Division Customer Service Manager

**OSG:** Vanessa Mooneyham (213) 239-5249 or 8+521+5249, mailsort S1-10.

**All other areas:** Carole Leonhardt, (213) 614-5138 or 8+522+5138, mailsort W27-S.

# Chapter 8

## Holding People Accountable for Service

> The entire measurement plan is made a primary goal of the corporation through compensation. For years, executives were paid in part based on how well we met our service goals. Beginning this year, all managers will have a portion of their salary based on corporate performance, including service goals.

In this quote, Bruce F. Grabell of Southern New England Telephone, in an April 1988 article in *Bank Marketing,* is telling us that service performance has got to be tied to compensation. I couldn't agree more.

The previous chapters have emphasized the importance of developing standards and a system to measure delivery of service. The most well-written standards and most sophisticated measurement system, however, will not guarantee a successful service program. Now that you've announced your expectations to your staff, how will you measure their performance at review time? If you are championing service, but measuring employees on assets, return on equity, and operational duties, you are sending out signals that you are not serious about service quality.

I'm sure you all expect excellent service from your staff members. The problem is that, in many banks and credit unions, whether an employee delivers exceptional, average, or poor service makes little difference at raise time. Often, the standards for service are subjective or not even included in the appraisal. In fact, I had a difficult time finding case studies and examples to include in this chapter. Many managers in financial institutions admitted there was little accountability in place for service quality.

Your service program's success depends on getting results from your people. People provide personal service, not computers and reports. Therefore, your staff must be willing to contribute and be held accountable for service performance. To my knowledge there is only one sure way to hold people accountable—in their performance appraisal. This chapter focuses on utilizing the performance appraisal process to improve service throughout your organization.

## *Include Individual Service Goals in the Performance Appraisal*

Earlier I discussed the following ways to measure individual service performance:

- ★ Comment cards with a point value, completed by customers or members
- ★ Internal comment cards with a point value, completed by employees
- ★ Mystery shopper reports scored with a point value
- ★ New account surveys scored with a point value
- ★ Teller transactions scored with a point value

By tabulating returned comment cards, new account surveys, and mystery shopper reports, it is possible to average the overall service scores and incorporate them into the appraisal form.

For example, Mary, a customer service representative, was shopped six times in the first quarter of the year and received an average score of

8 (10 being a perfect score). In addition, approximately 12 comment cards were filled out by customers commenting on Mary's performance. These averaged 7.5. By giving a high priority to the performance appraisal, we can help Mary raise her scores as follows:

Objective:   Customer Service Skills
Job Weighting:   35 percent

Obtain a satisfactory service score from mystery shoppings, customer or member comment cards, and new account surveys as follows:

| | |
|---|---|
| 9.0–10 | Superior |
| 8.0–8.9 | Excellent |
| 7.0–7.9 | Good |
| 6.0–6.9 | Fair |
| Less than 6.0 | Unsatisfactory |

Note that 35 percent of Mary's performance appraisal depends on her achieving an acceptable service score of 7.0. Job weighting is the process of ranking key job responsibilities in order of priority. This approach sends out a strong signal about the importance an organization places on service excellence. At TRW, for example, part of employees' compensation comes from the level of customer satisfaction. Likewise, sales, cross-selling, and referral goals can also be included in this manner. The performance appraisals in Exhibits 8.1 and 8.2 demonstrate how customer service, sales, and referrals can be weighted and included in the review form. You will note that service is 32 percent of the teller's job, and sales and service is 45 percent of the sales and service consultant's job.

## *Holding Managers Accountable for the Team Average*

By measuring your individual employee's service scores, you can ask your managers of both frontline and support areas to achieve a specific service score. Let's suppose a manager with 10 employees whose service scores range between 5.0 and 9.0 receives an overall score of 7.5. Now you can incorporate service goals in your manager's performance appraisal.

## Exhibit 8.1

## PERFORMANCE STANDARDS AND REVIEW FORM

| NAME | DEPARTMENT | DATE OF HIRE | CURRENT RATING PERIOD | Merit _____ 6 mo. Review _____ Promotional _____ Other |
|------|------------|--------------|----------------------|---------|

| TITLE/GRADE | SALARY RANGE | DATE/AMT/TYPE/LAST INC. | PRESENT SALARY | RECEIVED BY/DATE |
|-------------|--------------|-------------------------|----------------|------------------|
| TELLER | | | | |

INSTRUCTIONS: The Supervisor identifies key job areas and corresponding performance standards which are statements of what is expected during the rating period. At the end of the rating period, the performance is reviewed with the employee and a full explanation of the rating is recorded in the results section

**JOB AREA** CUSTOMER SERVICE

32%

**RESULTS**

Performance is Satisfactory When:
1. There are at least 24 teller referrals within the normal 12 month review period.

Rating/Scoring System
for review period:

| | |
|---|---|
| 36 or more | - 10 |
| 30 - 35 | - 8 |
| 24 - 29 | - 6 |
| 13 - 23 | - 4 |
| 12 or less | - 0 |

SCORE

**JOB AREA**

Performance is Satisfactory When:
2. The average score for all shops conducted within the normal 12 month review period should equal 4 points. (Each shop has a possible total of 5 points).

Rating/Scoring System
for review period

| | |
|---|---|
| 4.75 - 5.00 | - 14.0 |
| 4.50 - 4.74 | - 11.2 |
| 4.00 - 4.49 | - 8.4 |
| 3.99 - 3.00 | - 5.6 |
| 2.99 or less | - 0 |

SCORE

## Exhibit 8.1 (cont.)

| | RESULTS |
|---|---|
| **JOB AREA SALES AND CUSTOMER SERVICE** (continued) | |
| Performance is Satisfactory when: | |
| 3. There is no more than one justifiable complaint during the normal 12 month review period. | |
| Rating/Scoring System for review period: | |
| 0 complaints - 4 | |
| 1 complaint - 3 | |
| 2 complaints - 2 | |
| 3 complaints - 1 | |
| 4 or more - 0 | |
| Note: Four valid complaints during the normal 12 month review period could result in the Teller's termination. | |
| | SCORE |
| **JOB AREA** | |
| Performance in Satisfactory when: | |
| 4. There are no more than four occurrences of inappropriate or unacceptable customer service behavior as observed by a member of management during the normal 12 month review period | |
| Rating/Scoring System for review period: | |
| 0 occurrences - 4 | |
| 1 - 2 occurrences - 3 | |
| 3 - 4 occurrences - 2 | |
| 5 - 6 occurrences - 1 | |
| 7 or more - 0 | |
| | SCORE |

## Exhibit 8.2

## PERFORMANCE STANDARDS AND REVIEW FORM

| NAME | DEPARTMENT | DATE OF HIRE | CURRENT RATING PERIOD | Merit |
| --- | --- | --- | --- | --- |
| | | | | Promotional |
| | | | | 6 mo. Review |
| | | | | Other |

| TITLE/GRADE | SALARY RANGE | DATE/AMT/TYPE/LAST INC. | PRESENT SALARY | RECEIVED BY/DATE |
| --- | --- | --- | --- | --- |
| Sales & Service Consultant VII | | | | |

**INSTRUCTIONS:** The Supervisor identifies key job areas and corresponding performance standards which are statements of what is expected during the rating period. At the end of the rating period, the performance is reviewed with the employee and a full explanation of the rating is recorded in the results section

| JOB AREA    CUSTOMER SERVICE | 45% | RESULTS |
| --- | --- | --- |

**Performance is Satisfactory When:**

1. The total number of new services sold should average 20 percent. This would include cross-sells, new accounts, and referrals to other departments.

Rating/Scoring System
for review period:

26.0 or more - 18.0
23.0 - 25.9 - 14.4
20.0 - 22.9 - 10.8
18.0 - 19.9 -  7.2
17.9 or less -  0.0

SCORE

## JOB AREA

**Performance is Satisfactory When:**

2. The average score for all shops encountered within the normal 12 month review period should equal 4 points. (Each shop has a possible total of 5 points).

Rating/Scoring System
for review period

4.75 - 5.00 - 12.0
4.50 - 4.74 -  9.6
4.00 - 4.49 -  7.2
3.99 - 3.00 -  4.8
2.99 or less -   0

SCORE

162

## Exhibit 8.2 (cont.)

| | RESULTS |
|---|---|
| **JOB AREA SALES AND CUSTOMER SERVICE (continued)**<br><br>**Performance is Satisfactory when:**<br>3. The average score on all new account letters received should equal at least 92% excellent and/or good responses. (To calculate, take total number of excellent and/or good responses and divide by total number of possible responses). Each letter has 4 possible responses.<br><br>Rating/Scoring System     98.5 or more - 6.0<br>for review period:            96.0 - 98.4 - 4.8<br>                          92.0 - 95.9 - 3.6<br>                          91.9 or less - 0.0 | SCORE |
| **JOB AREA**<br><br>**Performance in Satisfactory when:**<br>4. There are no more than four occurrences of inappropriate or unacceptable customer service behavior as observed by a member of management during the normal 12 month review period.<br><br>Rating/Scoring System     0         - 6.0<br>for review period:            1-2      - 4.8<br>                          3         - 3.6<br>                          4         - 2.4<br>                          5 or more -  0 | SCORE |
| **JOB AREA**<br><br>**Performance is Satisfactory When:**<br>5. There are no more than 1 justifiable complaint registered during the normal 12 month period.<br><br>Rating/Scoring System     0         - 3.0<br>for Review period        1-2      - 1.8<br>                          3         - 1.2<br>                          4 or more -  0<br><br>*Note: Any excessive deviation which causes an unsatisfactory rating in any of the above performance standards could result in the entire area being rated "Unsatisfactory". | SCORE |

163

The following is a sample service performance standard in a branch managers performance appraisal:

Objective: Maintain high level of customer satisfaction and employee service performance.
Job weighting: 30 percent

Maintain average scores on customer comment cards, opinion survey, and mystery shopping as follows:

| | |
|---|---|
| 9.0–10 | Superior |
| 8.0–8.9 | Excellent |
| 7.0–7.9 | Good |
| 6.0–6.9 | Fair |
| Less than 6.0 | Unsatisfactory |

A back-office or operational department manager would be measured by the internal service ratings given by other departments and from quality-control spot checks. Use both internal and external customer service scores in all management performance appraisals whenever possible.

The following is a performance standard for internal service accountability for a data processing or member service department:

Objective: Provide a high level of service to all frontline employees and internal customers.
Job Weighting: 30 percent

Achieve internal service scores from comment cards and employee surveys as follows:

| | |
|---|---|
| 9.0–10 | Superior |
| 8.0–8.9 | Excellent |
| 7.0–7.9 | Good |
| 6.0–6.9 | Fair |
| Less than 6.0 | Unsatisfactory |

By incorporating service scores in your managers' performance appraisals and providing incentives and recognition, you will have a much higher probability of keeping your service mission alive. A partial appraisal for a banking center manager, incorporating team goals for mystery shops and variable sales index, is given in Exhibit 8.3.

Tom Frawley, vice president and manager of **Society Corporation's** Customer Service Department, has done an excellent job of setting specific standards for his staff and incorporating them into the review process. His department handles a large volume of telephone and written inquiries from Society's customers. Therefore, Society's performance appraisals outline expectations that deal with numbers of calls, speed, response time, and pieces of correspondence handled. See Exhibits 8.4 through 8.7 for Society's performance objectives.

**Irwin Union Bank and Trust Company**, Columbus, Indiana, believes that there should be a direct link between an individual's performance results and compensation. The bank's philosophy is that standards should be attainable, but should require some "stretch" to achieve. Mediocrity is discouraged. If standards are set too high, they provide no challenge because they are perceived as impossible to reach. If set too low, they are reached too easily, provide no motivation, and simply become an administrative exercise. Irwin Union recommends that the number of standards per employee range from 3 to no more than 10 for each appraisal period. Weights are assigned to each standard indicating the importance of each standard relative to the others.

Irwin Union utilizes a general performance criteria checklist and a specific goals' sheet with weighting by percentages. Judith Gaffney, vice president of consumer services, submitted the following samples:

1. Diagram of Performance Evaluation Process (Exhibit 8.8)
2. Salary Administration overview (Exhibit 8.9)
3. Establishment of Goals for Banking Center Officer (Exhibit 8.10)
4. Establishment of Goals for Teller III (Exhibit 8.11)

165

## Exhibit 8.3

# PERFORMANCE STANDARDS AND REVIEW FORM

| | | | Merit _____ 6 mo. Review |
| --- | --- | --- | --- |
| | | | _____ Promotional _____ Other |

| NAME | DEPARTMENT | DATE OF HIRE | CURRENT RATING PERIOD |
| --- | --- | --- | --- |

| TITLE/GRADE | SALARY RANGE | DATE/AMT/TYPE/LAST INC. | PRESENT SALARY | RECEIVED BY/DATE |
| --- | --- | --- | --- | --- |

BANKING CENTER MANAGER

**INSTRUCTIONS:** The Supervisor identifies key job areas and corresponding performance standards which are statements of what is expected during the rating period. At the end of the rating period, the performance is reviewed with the employee and a full explanation of the rating is recorded in the results section

| JOB AREA   BUSINESS DEVELOPMENT | 33% | RESULTS |
| --- | --- | --- |

Performance is Satisfactory When:
1. A total of 66 Business Development calls are completed per Banking
   Center for the annual review period.

    13.0 - 96 or more
    10.4 - 84 to 95
    7.8 - 66 to 83
    5.2 - 36 to 65
    0 - 35 or less

**NOTE:** Minimum of 48 calls annually should be made by the manager.

| JOB AREA | | SCORE |
| --- | --- | --- |

Performance is Satisfactory When:
2. Acquire a YTD Total of no less than 25 new services per Banking
   Center through Business Development calls.

    5 - 46 or more
    4 - 36 to 45
    3 - 25 to 35
    2 - 15 to 24
    0 - 14 or less

SCORE

## Exhibit 8.3 (cont.)

| RESULTS | |
|---|---|
| **JOB AREA - BUSINESS DEVELOPMENT (continued)** | |
| **Performance is Satisfactory when:** | |
| 3. The Average score for Banking Centers shops during 1988 should be no less than 75% when averaging the five major factors. | |
| Over 90% - 5 | |
| 85.01% to 90% - 4 | |
| 75.01% to 85% - 3 | |
| 60.01% to 75% - 2 | |
| 50.01% to 60% - 1 | |
| 50% and under - 0 | |
| *Only Shops beginning 1988 will be included. | SCORE |
| **JOB AREA** | |
| **Performance in Satisfactory when:** | |
| 4. Banking Center Variable Sales index should average 1.25% for the review period. | |
| 5 - 1.40% or more | |
| 4 - 1.31% to 1.39% | |
| 3 - 1.25% to 1.30% | |
| 2 - 1.20% to 1.24% | |
| 0 - 1.19% or less | SCORE |
| **JOB AREA** | |
| **Performance is Satisfactory When:** | |
| 5. The Banking Center's total combined new money deposits should increase 10% over the 1987 actual figure. This information should be obtained from the Comparative Financial Report. | |
| 5 - 25% or more | |
| 4 - 15.0 to 24.99% | 1987 Actual New Money |
| 3 - 10.0 to 14.99% | Deposits $_____ |
| 2 - 5.0 to 9.99% | |
| 0 - 4.9 or less | SCORE |

167

## Exhibit 8.4

### Society Corporation, Cleveland, Ohio
### Objective Planning Sheet

Objectives For: __Sample Objectives:  Vice President, Customer Service Dept.__

Use the spaces in the left column to list the most important objectives for the upcoming year. Inside specific business objectives and, as appropriate, one or two personal development objectives. After the objectives are determined, the employee and supervisor should sign and retain a copy of the form. The right column will be used to summarize the employee's performance to-date at mid-year.

| OBJECTIVES | MID-YEAR RESULT/STATUS |
|---|---|
| 1. Maintain and/or improve overall quality of service by<br> • Pursuing the implementation of music on hold for 800 Superior. | |
| 2. Effectively integrate Customer Service functions of Affiliate Banks without degradation of afore-mentioned service objective by:<br> • Identifying all issues relative to systematic or procedural changes and charting action plans needed for effective integration.<br> • Develop service level agreements to measure service quality.<br> • Monitor FTE totals and costs of integration to insure they are in line with projections. | |
| 3. Improve employee' salesmanship by having all employees attend the relationship selling workshop during 1989 and by:<br> • Developing an effective sales tracking system.<br> • Creating an effective sales reward system.<br> • Developing and implementing credit card retention programs. | |
| 4. Insure weekly meetings are held with the department's management and staff. | |
| 5. Maintain non-interest expenses for December, 1988 to December of 1989 at a variance of five percent or less of the approved budget by:<br> • Turning in a report of the contribution analysis by 15th of each month.<br> • Insuring effective controls and monitoring systems are in place.<br> • Implementing corrective actions as needed to bring overbudget categories into line. | |
| 6. Improve overall communications with internal bank customers and departments by:<br> • Meeting with regional counterparts and other regional management at least once per quarter.<br> • Attending at least one branch administrative managers' meeting each quarter.<br> • Meet as necessary with Retail division counterparts to ensure Customer Service is providing expected support.<br> • Insuring regional Service Level Agreements are completed and distributed by the 10th of each month. | |
| 7. Improve personnel qualities by:<br> • Have the management staff become active members of the Q-SEI program.<br> • Insure the performance reviews are completed expediently and fairly. | |

## Exhibit 8.4 (cont.)

### Objective Planning Sheet - page 2

| OBJECTIVES | MID-YEAR RESULT/STATUS |
|---|---|

|  |  |
|---|---|
| • Conduct training sessions periodically.<br>• Develop program of cross training between functional areas to meet peak periods and enhance sucession management opportunities. |  |
| 8. Maintain a thorough understanding of various systems:<br>• Investigate and recommend the purchase of new equipment that would enhance the sales/service levels.<br>• Insure the effective implementation of the voice response system.<br>• Insure the effective implementation of any other equipment purchased during 1989.<br>• Maintain the effective functions of the telephone system.<br>• Develop support system to assess technical failures and take required action.<br>• Coordinate the installation of the commercial loan system in Customer Service during 4th quarter of 1989. |  |
| 9. Accuracy and control<br>• Insure general ledger tickets are accurately completed and within corporate policy.<br>• Complete month-end statistical reports by the 19th of each month.<br>• Complete and implement procedures for the chargeback area.<br>• Reduce accounts receivable bank losses for 1989 from year-end 1988 figure. |  |
| 10. Interact with internal audit, federal bank examiners and external audit.<br>• Review previous audit finding, insure corrections are made and procedures are followed.<br>• Insure federal, state and local regulations are adhered to.<br>• Insure emergency recovery manual is completed by October 31, 1989, for all sections of Customer Service. |  |
| 11. Management staff development<br>• Develop plans for succession management.<br>• Afford managers the opportunity to attend seminars that would be appropriate for them and enhance their development.<br>• Hold individual meetings a minimum of once per quarter to discuss career development and job performance.<br>• Have overall structure reviewed by HRIS to insure a working environment is in place to facilitate sucession management.<br>• Hold monthly manager team meetings to discuss cross cutting issues and operational results. |  |

These objectives have been reviewed with and agreed to by my immediate supervisor. (Where matrix relationships exist, both supervisors should provide approval signatures).

Supervisor(s) Signature _____ Date _____

Employee Signature _____ Date _____

## Exhibit 8.5

### Society Corporation, Cleveland, Ohio
### Performance Appraisal

Principal Responsibilities & Duties for Cardholder Chargeback Representative

| Responsibilities and Duties:<br>List up to fie (5) Responsibilities/Duties<br>in decreasing order of importance. | Commendable | Competent | Conditional | Comments:<br>Should be job-related and acknowledging performance above or below Competent |
|---|---|---|---|---|
| 1. Prepare and process all cardholder to merchant chargeback requests. Insure all cardholder disputes are complete within Mastercard, Visa and Federal limits and regulations. Insure files are properly documented and follow-up is performed on each open file monthly. | | | | |
| 2. Maintain complete documentation in all chargeback files, notating all action taken to resolve case. Review all open items monthly for progress on chargeback or to resolve case. Review all open items monthly for progress on chargeback, or to follow action items. Follow departmental policies and procedures. | | | | |
| 3. Maintain organized filing system consistent with rest of chargeback area. Perform routine filing daily. Ensure all preliminary work is completed prior to progressing to chargeback, returning file as necessary to correspondence rep. | | | | |
| 4. Prepare monthly reports accurately and by date due. Perform monthly follow-up on charge off items or items submitted on a collection basis-Process sales ticket for cardholder verification within 3 days or receipt from processor Ensure proper documentation is completed prior to review of file. | | | | |
| 5. Insure all correspondence is neat, accurate and grammatically correct. Advise customers of the resolutions or reason for recharging their account. Assume additional duties as requested. | | | | |

We acknowledge that the above Responsibilities and Duties and Expected Performance Factors have been reviewed, discussed and mutually agreed upon.

Supervisor's Initials _____ Date _____ Employee's Initials _____ Date _____

## Exhibit 8.6

### Society Corporation, Cleveland, Ohio
### Performance Appraisal
Principal Responsibilities & Duties for Telephone Representative

| Responsibilities and Duties: List up to fie (5) Responsibilities/Duties in decreasing order of importance. | Commendable | Competent | Conditional | Comments: Should be job-related and acknowledging performance above or below Competent |
|---|---|---|---|---|
| 1. To promptly answer & service incoming calls pertaining to deposit products, credit card, & installment loan (Branch or Department) in a professional & Courteous manner. Measures and requires spec. IFIC performance and standards be met. | | | | |
| 2. Maintains a basic working knowledge of related products, policies & procedures. Effectively communicates the information to the customer over the phone. Correctly generates any forms needed to rectify problems, (name & address change, pymt. adj., serv. chgs., quote accurate pay-off figures, close status.) When reversing finance fees, late fees, overline fees, service chgs., NSF fees Always attach supporting documentation. | | | | |
| 3. Maintains a basic working knowledge of our bank card portfolio, the content of the cardholder's agreement, mc/visa rules & regulation & requirements of Reg. Z items which relate to the area. (Require. and Procedures for charge backs.) | | | | |
| 4. Effectively relates information to other areas, as well as, out own area. Transfers calls & correspondence to correct person/ area. Maintains a neat work area. Keep memo and training material filed in notebooks for quick reference. | | | | |
| 5. Work along with and assist Retail Loan & Support and other bank personnel. Assumes additional duties as requested. | | | | |

We acknowledge that the above Responsibilities and Duties and Expected Performance Factors have been reviewed, discussed and mutually agreed upon.

Supervisor's Initials _____ Date _____ Employee's Initials _____ Date _____

## Exhibit 8.7

### Society Corporation, Cleveland, Ohio
### Performance Appraisal
Principal Responsibilities & Duties for Correspondence Representative

| Responsibilities and Duties: List up to fie (5) Responsibilities/Duties in decreasing order of importance. | Commendable | Competent | Conditional | Comments: Should be job-related and acknowledging performance above or below Competent |
|---|---|---|---|---|
| 1. To respond to any incoming written correspondence within 5 days pertaining to general Bankcard & Installment Loan inquiries, credit balance refund requests, ratings & Closes. Quick Credit authorizations to be completed no later than 12:30 p.m. on date received. Bankcard balance transfers to be completed within 2 days upon receipt of request; Maintains currently established departmental average of 20 pieces per day for regular written inquires. | | | | |
| 2. Utilizes grammatical accuracy & good written communication skills when responding to written inquiries. Maintains well-documented files and complies with departmental adjustment formats. Insures appropriate research is complete prior to adjusting a customers account. | | | | |
| 3. Maintain a current working knowledge of Credit Card rules and regulations on Installment Loan policies and procedures. Follow up with related departments and/or necessary research in order to ensure accurate response to customers. Ensure general ledger items are cleared within corporate policy. | | | | |
| 4. Compile statistics on daily productivity and submit to supervisor by end of day. Submit month-end statistics by first business day of following month. | | | | |
| 5. Make supervision aware of potential problems in any of the above areas. Assist walk-in customers as necessary. Promote professional image of corporation in all communication or interaction with customers, internal or external. Assume additional duties as requested in all aspects of Customer Service. | | | | |

We acknowledge that the above Responsibilities and Duties and Expected Performance Factors have been reviewed, discussed and mutually agreed upon.

Supervisor's Initials _____ Date _____ Employee's Initials _____ Date _____

## Exhibit 8.8

### Irwin Union Bank and Trust Company

### Diagram of PerformanceEvaluation Process
Beginning of Evaluation Period for
New or Current Employee

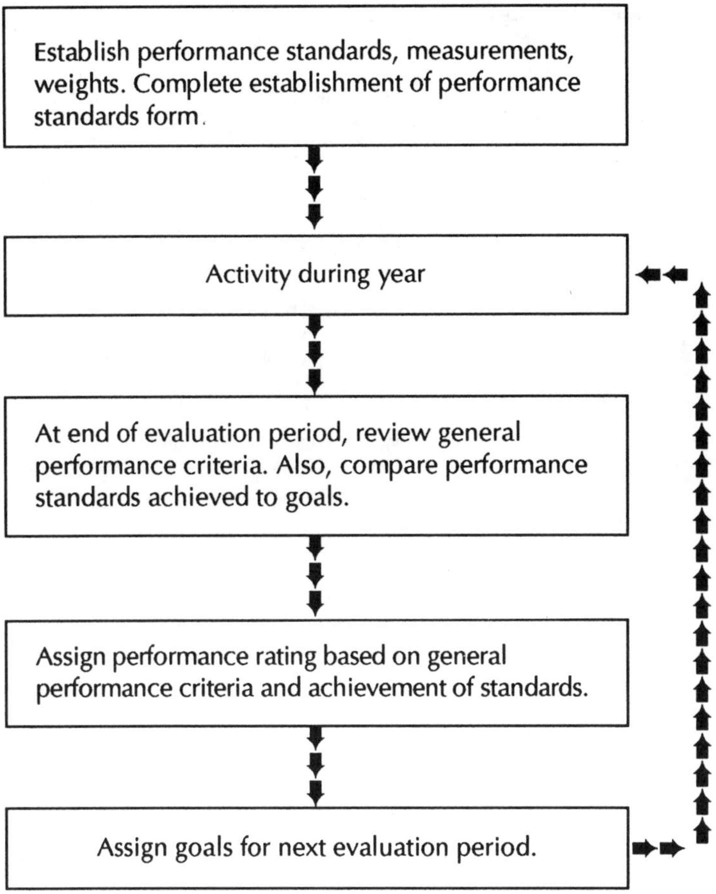

```
┌─────────────────────────────────────────────┐
│ Establish performance standards, measurements,│
│ weights. Complete establishment of performance│
│ standards form.                               │
└─────────────────────────────────────────────┘
                      ↓
┌─────────────────────────────────────────────┐
│ Activity during year                          │  ←←
└─────────────────────────────────────────────┘
                      ↓
┌─────────────────────────────────────────────┐
│ At end of evaluation period, review general   │
│ performance criteria. Also, compare performance│
│ standards achieved to goals.                  │
└─────────────────────────────────────────────┘
                      ↓
┌─────────────────────────────────────────────┐
│ Assign performance rating based on general    │
│ performance criteria and achievement of standards.│
└─────────────────────────────────────────────┘
                      ↓
┌─────────────────────────────────────────────┐
│ Assign goals for next evaluation period.      │  →→
└─────────────────────────────────────────────┘
```

## Exhibit 8.9

### Irwin Union Bank and Trust Company
### Salary Administration

Irwin Union's philosophy of compensation can be summarized as follow:

- There should be a direct link between the individual's performance results and compensation. (eg., average pay for average performance, above average pay for superior performance).

- Market pay levels, as determined by annual salary surveys, define average or above average pay.

- Individual performance ratings are determined by comparing individual results to performance standards at the end of the appraisal period.

The Human Resources Director is responsible for completing salary surveys annually to determine market pay rates. That information will then be used to establish pay ranges for various positions, and market pay rates for individuals. The information will be provided to the supervisor on a Market Analysis Form and should in turn be reviewed with the employee.

Generally new or inexperienced employees are hired in at the lower end of their pay range. As they gain experience and perform acceptably, employees are eligible for merit increases to get their base pay to their "target base pay levels". The target level, which is expressed as a percent to the outside market pay rate, is determined by the individual employees performance level. The target pay levels are as follows:

| If performance rating is | Target base pay level is: |
| --- | --- |
| Unacceptable | 80–85% of market pay rate |
| Level I | 90–95% of market pay rate |
| Level II | 100–105% of market pay rate |
| Level III | 110–115% of market pay rate |

If an individual's base pay is below their target level, the employee is eligible for annual merit increases to gradually bring their pay up to the target level. Merit increase guidelines are as follows:

| If performance rating is: | Suggested merit pay increase is: |
| --- | --- |
| Unacceptable | 0% |
| Level I | 3–8% |
| Level II | 5–10% |
| Level III | 8–15% |

Our objective is to bring an employee to the appropriate target pay levels by the time the employee has three years experience on the job, assuming acceptable job performance.

An employee who receives an unacceptable performance rating is ineligible for merit pay increases. A supervisor who gives an employee an unacceptable rating must also include in the review specifics about what performance is below expectations, what must be done to improve and by when. If performance does not improve after counseling and coaching by the supervisor, the supervisor should refer to our Personal Review Procedure to document serious performance deficiencies. Two unacceptable performance evaluations will generally initiate a work program which an employees must satisfactorily complete to remain employed.

Irwin Union is willing to pay superior salaries for superior performance, but is not willing to indefinitely pay a salary level above the corresponding performance level. In the event an individual's pay level is higher than the performance level would call for, the following will generally apply:

## Exhibit 8.9 (cont.)

- no action on base pay for one year
- if after one year performance rating is still below pay level, base pay will be adjusted downward to the target pay level which cor;responds to the employees performance rating.

This action may also apply if an employee transfers into a position at a pay rate that is higher than market for the new position. In this situation, the Human Resources Director will counsel the supervisor on a case-by-case basis.

<u>Salary Range</u>

Salary ranges are used to maintain a certain amount of internal equity among positions requiring similar skills, knowledge or ability. Positions with very different responsibilities may be slotted into the same salary range because they have similar market pay rates.

After a market analysis comparison is completed, a position is slotted into the pay grade whose midpoint most closely matches the market pay rates. If a position is graded appropriately, the market pay rate and the grade midpoint should be relatively close to each other.

For salary administration purposes, a supervisor may usually use the range midpoint as a "proxy" for the market pay rate. This can be helpful to the supervisor wh has several positions whose market pay rates are closely clustered together around the midpoint. This allows one market pay rate to be used for several comparable positions.

The only time this should not be done is when a position is slotted into a salary range higher than the market data calls for. In these infrequent cases, the Human Resources Director will "flag" the position to the supervisor and advise on appropriate strategy. Usually the individual will remain at the higher pay rate and salary grade for one year. After performance is evaluation, the pay rate may be adjusted accordingly. The person's position may also be regraded after one year to be matched into the appropriate salary range, if it has not already been regraded. As noted above, such situations will be evaluation by the Human Resources Director and Supervisor on a case-by-case basis.

<u>Discretionary Bonuses</u>

Individual employees may earn additional compensation from Irwin Union in a variety of ways. The primary one is achieving a merit increase based upon performance. Others include participation in the bankwide incentive plan, sales and referral programs, suggestion awards, or accomplishment of AIB certificate or diploma.

Occasionally a supervisor may wish to reward an individual for an accomplishment which fits none of the above categories. In that case, a discretionary bonus may be appropriate. A discretionary bonus is a one-time payment and is not an adjustment to base pay.

A discretionary bonus may be appropriate if the following apply:

- significant contribution or accomplishment above and beyond normal expectations
- generally one-time or non-recurring circumstances
- other types of recognition are inappropriate or insufficient

The amount of the bonus may vary, depending on the event. A $100 bonus may be appropriate for one event; a $3000 bonus for another. The Human Resources Director can provide guidance on appropriate amount.

A discretionary bonus should be initiated by the supervisor and approved by the division head, Human Resources Director and President. It is documented by use of a Supplemental Pay Authorization Form.

175

## Exhibit 8.10

---

### Irwin Union Bank and Trust Company
### Establishment of Goals for Upcoming Appraisal Period

Name _____ Dept. _____

Title _____ Banking Center Officer _____ Hire Date _____

Evaluation Period From _____ To _____

Time on Present Job_____

| Standard | Current Measurement | Current Weight |
|----------|---------------------|----------------|
| Office Sales | Stretch180 Referrals/Yr 65% Sold<br>195 Cross sales<br>Minimum140 Referrals/Yr 55% Sold<br>150 Cross sales | 20 |
| Own Sales Performance | Stretch18 calls/Qtr.<br>60 Referrals      65% Sold<br>1.75 Cross Sales<br>1.25 D/L Cross Sales<br>Minimum15 calls/Qtr.<br>40 Referrals      65% Sold<br>1.5 Cross Sales<br>1.20 D/L Cross Sales | 20 |
| Deposit Growth | Stretch$180M DDA<br>$1500M SAV<br>Minimum$90M DDA<br>$1200M SAV | 15 |
| Loan Volume | Stretch$300H      MF 70% Life<br>Minimum$150M      50% AH | 5 |
| Budget | StretchMeet 1990 Budget<br>MinimumMeet w/i 5% | 15 |
| Service Quality | Maintain highest standards<br>for service quality | 10 |
| Personnel | Weekly staff meetings<br>quarterly events, immediate<br>response to personnel issues | 15 |

## Exhibit 8.11

### Irwin Union Bank and Trust Company
### Establishment of Goals for Upcoming Appraisal Period

Name_____ Dept. _____

Title _____ Teller III _____ Hire Date _____

Evaluation Period From _____ To _____

Time on Present Job_____

| Standard | Current Measurement | Current Weight |
|---|---|---|
| Balancing | 85% Balancing Average | 10% |
| | No greater than 1.00 per day | 5% |
| | 6 proof corrections per month | 5% |
| Customer Service | Stretch: Zero compliants & | |
| | 8 positive comments | 20% |
| | Minimum: Zero complaints | |
| Referrals | Stretch: 32 per year | 20% |
| | Minimum: 24 per year | |
| Product Knowledge | Stretch: Score 100% on test | 20% |
| | Minimum: Score of 85% on test | |
| Attendance | Stretch: Perfect attendance | 10% |
| | Minimum: No more than 6 per year | |
| Versatility & Misc. | Supervisor observations cooperative spirit & enthusiasm for IUBT & its products | 10% |
| | Minimum Goal 25%   Current Weight | 100% |

## *Holding Managers Accountable for Product Knowledge Scores*

Earlier I talked about ways to improve product knowledge through certification and testing programs. Once you have begun these kinds of programs, take the average scores for product knowledge and ask your managers and staff to achieve a specific product knowledge score. For example:

Job category:   Branch Manager
Objective:   Improve product knowledge
Job Weighting:   10 percent

Achieve an average product knowledge score for your branch team from the testing program as follows:

| | |
|---|---|
| 90–100% | Superior |
| 80–89% | Excellent |
| 70–79% | Good |
| 60–69% | Fair |
| Less than 60% | Unacceptable |

Organizations that are serious about service recognize the benefit of holding managers and employees accountable for product knowledge results. I recommend that support and operational employees also have product knowledge goals in their reviews.

I work with many banks and credit unions who are seriously seeking to build a strong service culture. After some customer service, sales training, and incentive programs, however, things seem to slip a bit. Why? Because there is no accountability for service or sales in the employees' or the managers' performance appraisals. Everyone is asked to deliver service and to sell, yet no one is penalized if it doesn't happen. I believe the performance appraisal combined with proper coaching, leadership, and recognition and rewards will boost your sales and service program considerably.

178

# Chapter 9

# Rewarding and Recognizing Service Performance

An article by Robert L. Desatnik in the October 1987 issue of *Management Review* had some eye-opening statistics:

> In a national poll of thousands of workers, the question was asked, "If you were to improve service quality and productivity, do you believe you would be rewarded accordingly?" Only 22 percent said yes. As a consequence, 75 percent of the workers reported they deliberately withhold extra effort on the job. Imagine the potential impact on customer service!

Are your managers and employees holding back because they see no correlation between their extra efforts and personal rewards? Are you demanding *service* performance, but rewarding primarily for *sales* and *operational* performance? Admittedly, it is difficult to tie service rewards to every position, but that is a weak excuse for avoiding recognition of extra efforts.

If we truly believe that service is a key strategy and competitive weapon, then we must identify our service heros and give them the recognition they deserve. The rest of this chapter describes tried-and-true ideas for recognizing service excellence.

## *Cash Incentive Plans*

Cash incentives can be a powerful motivator, particularly for those employees who don't earn large salaries. **N. W. Gasco Federal Credit Union,** Portland, Oregon, with a total of 13 full-time employees, created a highly successful cash incentive program. Gail James, vice president, shares an overview of the program with us here:

> We wanted to involve staff more in the achievement of credit union goals assigned by the board of directors, and reward them for their individual and departmental efforts and achievements. The objective was to achieve all assigned credit union goals for the upcoming year.
>
> Our board established the goals at their planning session, and we placed a monetary reward on goals that each department would try to achieve. These departmental goals tied into the credit union's goals. Since bonuses and incentives are still a new venture, we have had to punt and learn by trial and error. For example, we had an asset goal to achieve. We assigned the Share Department a goal to increase certificates by 50 percent thus awarding them a specific dollar amount. If they achieved 60 percent, the incentive increased. The end result was an increase of 101 percent! Another goal was to increase loans by more than $1 million. The end result increased loans by $2.5 million.
>
> The program has been very successful and the credit goes to our president, Pat M. Porter. She has been very supportive of rewarding staff for their hard work. Total rewards for the past two years is approximately $8,000 divided among 10 employees. We have achieved most of our goals as a team project. The couple of goals that have not been achieved were due to economic setbacks beyond our control.

180

We originally took the stand that if we didn't achieve all goals there would be no reward and immediately saw that to be unfair since the staff devoted a great deal of time and effort in achieving what they had. So we left a loop-hole, if you will, in the program to allow management to at least reward the staff with a decent thank-you for their work, if not all goals were achieved.

Mike Maslak, president and CEO of **North Island Federal Credit Union** in San Diego, with his board of directors and executive staff developed an incentive plan to motivate all staff members to achieve the corporate goals. Jill Bechard, vice president of marketing, submitted the following overview for us:

The Excellence in Service Program (ESP) was introduced at North Island in March of 1988. We developed the program to gain the commitment of our staff in achieving our goals. Some of our expectations and objectives were:

1. To tie our staff to our 10 overall corporate financial goals

2. To meet above-average CAMEL ratios and be in the top of our peer group

3. To motivate staff with cash incentives if exceptional performance levels were achieved

4. To have our staff be aware of the board of directors commitment to performance excellence

At the beginning of the year, Mike shares the corporate goals with our mid-managers at our strategic planning session. Our board approves a cash payout with a specific budget. At the end of the year, if we exceed all of our 10 goals, all managers and employees receive their checks at our annual ceremony.

To date, our results have been excellent. We have met all of our financial objectives and the staff payout for 1989 was 5 1/2 percent of annual gross to general staff and 8 percent of annual gross to mid-managers. We had a total payout of $287,000 for 1989!

Jill also commented on some possible pitfalls. "You must communicate progress monthly and let the staff know what they need to do to achieve results on a monthly basis."

Both of the above credit unions recognize the power that being an employee-focused organization and paying for performance brings.

## *Mugging Program*

**North Island Federal Credit Union** also makes a big fuss over anyone going the extra mile. Chris Lamb, senior vice president of operations, and Beverly Kjer, assistant vice president of service, shared their unique "mugging" program with me. They began this program in January 1989 to encourage staff and members to write down compliments for excellent service and thus provide tangible proof for recognition.

When an employee provides exceptional service for a member or fellow employee, they are "mugged." Getting mugged means that they are given a lovely crystal mug with the credit union's logo on it, filled with chocolate candies. The mug is presented by the AVP of service, accompanied by the employee of the month who is introduced to the staff in the process. All of this is done in front of staff members for visible recognition. In addition, the employee is written up in the ESP service newsletter.

Anyone getting a letter from a member or fellow employee in praise of exceptional service qualifies to be "mugged." What is exceptional service? One employee at North Island drove to the airport to give a member the ID he or she had left behind. A mailroom courier, observing the long lines at the drive-up window one afternoon, pitched in and handed the members vouchers and pens to get their transactions ready. The staff nominated him to be mugged.

Employees can get mugged more than once. Beverly estimates that to date approximately 455 mugs have been distributed. Approximately 35 to 40 letters are received a month and about 35 mugs are distributed monthly. The cost is $7 for each mug, plus the candies, or approximately $3,500 annually.

The North Island staff raves about this program. Beverly mentioned, however, that some very good support people may not get recognized unless managers are encouraged to write a letter. What is fun about this simple, inexpensive, and unique idea is the surprise element: someone can be mugged at any time throughout the day.

To set the stage for the mugging program and to provide on-the-spot recognition, North Island developed a quarter-long program called "I've Got the Service Spirit." Attractive enamel pins, with that motto on them, were created and awarded instantly to anyone caught exemplifying excellent service. Through immediate recognition, both "I've Got the Service Spirit" and the mugging program reinforce the idea that service is a high priority.

## *Involving Customers or Members in Employee Recognition*

Years ago, an airline sent me a package of coupons and asked me to give them to any of its employees whom I felt gave exceptional service. The airline employees turned these coupons in and received special recognition.

Robb Evans, former president and CEO of **American Asian Bank** (now part of Security Pacific Bank), Los Angeles, California, in 1987 sent a lovely letter and three coupons, in both English and Chinese, to each bank customer. The letter asked the customers to assist in identifying eligible employees for the "Excellent Service Club." For months, customers mailed the coupons directly to the director of marketing, acknowledging a particular employee for service excellence. When a certain number of coupons had accumulated, the employee was given a cash award and invited to attend a special function.

The program was tiered to allow for different levels of performance. Ten coupons might equal a special gift; 15 coupons, a half-day off; and 25 coupons, a $100 award. This encouraged employees to be more aware of how they treated their customers. What I like best about this program is that it gets your customers or members involved in motivating and praising your staff. (See Exhibits 9.1, 9.2, and 9.3 for a copy of the letter and coupons.)

183

# Exhibit 9.1

 **AMERICAN ASIAN BANK**

May 15, 1987

Dear Customer:

In an effort to serve you better and make American Asian Bank the premier bank in the community, we have designed the *"Excellent Service Club"* to recognize those bank employees who provide excellent customer service.

I am writing to personally enlist your assistance in identifying the eligible employees to join the *"Excellent Service Club"*. It is very simple to participate. Just fill out one of the enclosed nomination coupons every time you come across an American Asian Bank employee who has gone that extra mile to serve you, be it in-person or on the telephone. For more information, please refer to the enclosed easy instructions.

This is an ongoing program and your continual participation and feedback are most important for its successful implementation. There is no limit to the number of employees you can sponsor or the number of times you can sponsor a particular employee.

Thank you in advance for your participation. We shall strive to provide the kind of excellent service which deserves your continued support.

Very truly yours,

Robb Evans
President & Chief Executive Officer

500 MONTGOMERY STREET • SAN FRANCISCO, CALIFORNIA 94111
TELEPHONE (415) 788-4700

## Exhibit 9.2

### Excellent Service Club

*Sponsor an "Excellent Banker"*

We have designed the Excellent Service Club
to recognize and reward those outstanding
American Asian Bank employees who
go the *"Extra Mile"* for you.

We ask your help in identifying these employees.

*(Please see reverse
for additional details)*

Attached you will find three Excellent Service coupons. These coupons
are also displayed in the lobby of each branch. Every time you come across
an AAB employee who, be it on the phone or in-person, has provided you with
excellent service, simply fill out a coupon and either drop it in the designated
box in the lobby or mail it back to us in the enclosed postage paid envelope.
This will give the employee bankwide recognition, a chance to enter the Club
and win awards and incentives.

In appreciation for your sponsorship, every time an employee you have
sponsored enters the Club you will be given a gift.

There is no limit to the number of employees you can sponsor or the
number of times an employee can be sponsored.

We thank you for your continued cooperation and patronage. We hope
that through your active participation in this Excellent Banker Program we
will continue to provide you with superior banking services.

## Exhibit 9.3

**AMERICAN ASIAN BANK**
WE MAKE IT HAPPEN

Date_____

AAB Employee_____

Office/Dept._____

Sponsored by:

Name_____

Address_____

_____

Telephone #(____) _____

Sponsor's Signature_____

**Excellent
Service Club**

I am sponsoring this
American Asian Bank
employee who has gone
the *"Extra Mile"* for me.

The following example, taken from Albrecht and Bradford's *The Service Advantage*, illustrates the use of coupons by customers:

> Steamboat Ski Corporation, located in Steamboat, Colorado, attracts skiers from throughout the United States and is well known for its friendly, family-centered environment. The resort has a very successful program called "Mountain Magic" that provides instant recognition of employees who go out of their way to provide extraordinary service to the ski resort's customers. Customers are selected at random when they purchase their lift tickets and are given an envelope. Inside the envelope is a certificate that can be redeemed for $10. The customer is invited to give the certificate to any employee in the resort who provides superior service. Hans Geier, president of the resort, says, "The Mountain Magic program has been the best way we've discovered to reward and recognize our employees."

Employees often enjoy getting praise from someone besides their direct boss or management. One bank decided to ask their customers to assist them in recognizing its staff for excellent service. Buttons that said "Super Service" were produced and displayed in baskets in each branch and department. The program was also outlined in the customer newsletter. On each basket a sign said, "If one of our employees gives you excellent service, please pin this button on them."

Imagine the beaming face of your teller or customer service representative as a customer or member pins a button on them. This fun and inexpensive program did much to improve the customers' perceptions that this bank was serious about service. In addition, employees felt appreciated for their hard efforts.

Every month at **Penn Savings Bank,** Wyomissing, Pennsylvania, two customers from each branch are randomly chosen to receive a $5 bill (Naugle, January 1990). A letter asks that the next time they visit an office, they should bring the $5 bill with them. If they receive good service, they are asked to give the $5 to the person who served them. If they receive an unacceptable level of service, they should keep the $5 and have lunch on the bank. Two weeks after the first letters went out, nine branch employees were $5 richer because of the service they provided.

## Special Awards Rallies

In Europe and Japan, managers know the value of hosting motivational rallies to reward their staff. In the United States, it appears to be making a comeback. Many top service organizations with loyal employees, such as Marriott Corporation, Xerox, and Hewlett-Packard make these exciting events a regular part of their culture.

To make your awards banquet a success try some of the following:

- ★ Use a special off-site location
- ★ Have a customer panel
- ★ Pick an employee with a TV personality as emcee
- ★ Have senior management and hosts dress in tuxedos
- ★ Have upbeat music playing as people arrive, break, and leave

★ Reward support and operational employees, as well as frontline staff for service excellence

★ Reward midlevel managers for their teams' results for sales and service

★ Communicate past successes and the future direction of the organization

★ Dramatically read, from the envelopes, the names of the runners up and then the winner—Academy Awards style

★ Have special music playing as the winner runs up on stage to accept his or her award

★ Encourage lots of applause

★ Give everyone noisemakers and favors to keep as a reminder of the banquet

Praise and recognition in front of one's peers is a powerful motivator. In some companies, this is the only opportunity for employees who may be isolated in a remote location, or routine function, to feel important.

## Recognizing Employees in Newsletters

Most banks and credit unions have a customer newsletter. A smaller number have an employee newsletter. Most of the ones I've seen contain recipes, anniversary dates, and community news. It is surprising how many of these newsletters contain little, if any, recognition of employees' sales or service achievements.

Don't underestimate the power of the written word. Use your customer or member newsletter to print success stories about your staff. Many people get excited about seeing their name in print. Even if you have only one location and 25 employees, there is no reason why a simple one-page flyer could not be developed.

**First Pennsylvania Bank** utilizes "Applause," a special column in their weekly employee newsletter, to publish excerpts from letters praising the actions of their employees (*Measuring and Monitoring Service Quality*).

Letters come not only from customers, but also from coworkers. In addition, each month in the "Doer's Profile" column, the newsletter spotlights a specific employee, who demonstrates a commitment to service quality. Exhibits 9.4 and 9.5 are examples of these recognition columns.

**North Island Federal Credit Union** recognizes its service hero's in its ESP (Excellence in Service Program) newsletter. This special newsletter was designed to communicate progress on ESP's goals. Do the employees read it? You bet. In fact, at North Island the staff calls to find out when the next issue is coming out; and if it's late, the Marketing Department hears about it! An example of the ESP newsletter is shown in Exhibit 9.6.

**St. Paul Federal Bank for Savings,** in the Chicago area, has one of the best sales and service newsletters I've seen. *The Sales Exchange* has a column from the president; sales, service, and product knowledge tips; recognition of employees; and most of all a comprehensive sales score card. I've included two pages from St. Paul's extensive newsletter in Exhibit 9.7.

The following is a list of reasons for recognizing employees in newsletters:

★ Receiving a perfect mystery shopping score

★ Receiving a perfect comment card score for internal or external service

★ Going the extra mile for a customer, member, or fellow employee

★ Saving a customer or member by being responsive in handling a complaint

★ Taking a risk and making a decision that differed from the organization's policy to better serve a customer

★ Receiving a letter of praise from a customer

★ Receiving special awards based on incentives

★ Achieving excellent scores for product knowledge

★ Passing certification programs

★ Achieving outstanding sales results

## Exhibit 9.4

### First Pennsylvania Bank

# FRIDAY'S WORD

*First Pennsylvania Bank* ..                                      November 13, 1987

# *APPLAUSE!*

Among the letters submitted to Applause, we occasionally receive one that stands out as an exceptional example of a First Pennsylvania employee taking "The Extra Step." Below you will find such a letter, reprinted in its entirety, which exemplifies "The Extra Step" philosophy.

Dear Mr. Butler:

On Thursday night a tragic fire struck a Bridgeport senior citizen complex, killing two residents and leaving some 70 more homeless.

On Friday October 30, after hearing news reports of the fire, Arlene Schecter, Branch Manger of the King of Prussia office, became concerned because some of her customers lived there.

Well, let me tell you, today too few business people demonstrate concern the way Arlene Schecter does.

After contacting the temporary shelter, Arlene contacted me to come to the aid of the homeless residents. Within 90 minutes of her phone call we had secured temporary shelter and mobilized the entire King of Prussia business network to provide amenities and comfort to those that were afflicted. Arlene personally intervened to see to it that families were contacted and personal belongings secured. She helped me in moving the people and seeing to it that they were cared for.

At First Pennsylvania, your slogan is "We hear you." Arlene Schecter is living proof of that commitment.

At your earliest convenience, I would like you to be present when Arlene Schecter will be honored by the Chamber of Commerce of King of Prussia for outstanding humanitarian services.

In the meantime, please see to it that she gets a well deserved pat-on-the-back. I am proud to have her on our team, I am sure you are too.

Most sincerely yours,

Albert F. Paschall
Chairman of the Board of Directors
King of Prussia Chamber of Commerce

## Exhibit 9.5

### First Pennsylvania Bank

## Exhibit 9.6

## ESP Update

by Beverly Kjer
AVP Service Management

June, 1989

### MEMBER SERVICE PLEDGE CLOSE TO GOAL

The **Member Service Department** had a 95% success rate, for the first month, on their service pledge:

"**If we can't solve your problem while on the line, we'll call you back within five minutes time.**"

This performance level was accomplished with a 50% staff reduction during two weeks of the month. With staff back up to full complement, they are going for their goal of 100%!

### 28 MUGGED IN MAY

The mail box was bulging with complimentary letters again this month. One special letter was received on **Frances Story** of **Member Accounting**. It reads:

"I wish to thank you again for all your help. It is not often that we come across people in this world who keep not only their cool but are pleasant, friendly and who also take what ever time is needed to help. It can become a very depressing job to do day in and day out. Sometimes people get tired or irritated and it comes across in their voices.

Again, thank you not only for taking care of this but because of your friendly and helpful manner. I also work with the public and know how hard it is to keep that quiet, friendly and helpful attitude when others lose theirs. I wish there were more like you."

**Donna Valdez** from the **University** branch impressed one member with the "long distance" help he received:

"She has provided excellent advice that was directly responsive to my needs and has expedited every transaction. And, most importantly, she has provided these services from the other side of the country with a courteous, personal and professional manner that I rarely encounter, even in face to face dealings with officers of local banks."

It was a pleasure to award mugs for excellent service to the following employees:

| | |
|---|---|
| Martha Arellano - Information Center | Phyllis Kennedy - Auditing |
| Cathy Bechtel - Information Center | Pam McGoldrick - Real Estate |
| Maria Behning - Central Lending | Diane Mefford - University |
| Cheryl Broome - HRD | Don Munson - Collections |
| Momi Cain - Imperial Beach | Randy Oliva - Administrative Services |
| Natalie Crowe - Information Center | Susan Payne - Item Processing |
| Laurel Cruz - Central Lending | Margie Pena - Item Processing |
| Bettye Davis - Information Center | Mary Simon - El Cajon |
| Kim Hartwick - North Island | Frances Story - Member Accounting |
| Colleen Henderson - Imperial Beach | Liz Taitague - Otay Lakes |
| Cheri Hill - North Island | Kelly Tieber - Item Processing |
| Marlene Holter - Naval Supply Center | Donna Valdez - University |
| Paula Jenkins - Real Estate | Mary White - Imperial Beach |
| Angela Jordan - Collections | Steve Wollert - Item Processing |

## Exhibit 9.6 (cont.)

### ESP FINANCIAL GOALS

| 1989 Goal | | 05/89 Actual |
|---|---|---|
| 14% | Share Growth | 9.9% |
| 12% | Loan Growth | 13.0% |
| 80.2% | Loan/Share Ratio | 81.7% |
| 8.26% | Reserves/Assets | 7.90% |
| 32.8% | Operating Expenses | 34.0% |
| 12% | Net Income | 9.02% |
| .6 | Del/Total Loans | .42 |
| .5 | Net Charge Offs | .49 |
| $3,300 | Average Share Balance | $3,183 |
| $5,540 | Average Loan Balance | $5,550 |
| 446 | Members/Employee | 435 |

### HAS THE CASH BALANCING PLAQUE FOUND A PERMANENT HOME?

The **Naval Supply Center** branch has decided they want to keep the cash balancing plaque permanently. To prove they are serious, they balanced perfectly for the second month in a row and are on their way to a three month sweep. **Doris McFadden** and her crew are doing a great job, but let's start giving them more competition. It would be fantastic to see a plaque in every branch.

There were 45 employees with perfect records in May. There are still fifteen employees (*) with perfect records for the year. Seven (**) of these are full-time tellers.

North Island

Pandora Brockman
Sue Brooks
Carol Burrell
Espie Helpling*
Michelle Marquis*
Rita Navarra*
Cindy Pace
Barbara Schock
Angelita Simmons**
Kim Zamora

El Cajon

Darleen Craig
Fran Marano
Kim Smith
David Stearns
Laura Steed*
Mary Templin**

Otay Lakes

Suzanne Antonio**
Brenda Thompson*
Kim Wenger

University

Michelle Belfiore
Crystal Davis
Gerly DelaVega
Diane Mefford
Tricia Montez

Bonita

Pat Rafferty
Leslie Souza
Tracey Walters
Monica Wilson

Mira Mesa

Lydia Barrett
Jim Huber
Ederlina Salvador

Cabrillo

Gloria Acosta
Maureen Maguire**
Lisa Massey
Betty Perkel*
Anita Tongco
Patsy Torres**
Angie Walsh*

Imperial Beach

Colleen Henderson
Mary White*

Naval Supply Center

J. Marie Bennett
Ellen Brown
Charlotte Burch**
Erlinda Ocampo**
Raquel Osuna

# Exhibit 9.6 (cont.)

## MBI SALES INCREASE

Four branches reached their MBI goals of 20% in May. Thanks to the outstanding work of **Marlene Holter,** the **Naval Supply Center** branch leads the pack with 44%. **Donna Valley's** sales meetings helped the **University** branch achieve 38%. The **Information Center** and **North Island** had 28% and 21%, respectively. For three months, we have had a steady increase in MBI sales. In March, we sold only 25 policies. In April, after our car forum with MBI training, sales jumped to 49 and reached a peak at 75 in May. Our goal for June is 100.

Seven branches reached or exceeded our 33% sales goal for life insurance sales. They were:

| | |
|---|---|
| Naval Supply Center | 52% |
| North Island | 46% |
| University | 41% |
| Cabrillo | 37% |
| Bonita | 36% |
| Imperial Beach | 34% |
| Information Center | 33% |

Congratulations to everyone who helped us achieve these improved results. We can do even better. Let's give it that extra push that I know you're all capable of doing.

## THE TELEPHONE DOCTOR'S FIVE FORBIDDEN PHRASES

1)  I don't know.

> It's better to tell callers "That's a good question. Let me find out for you."

2)  Use of "NO" at the beginning of a sentence.

> That's instant total rejection, and no member likes that. Always begin sentences with a positive, even if the eventual answer will be a negative.

3)  Hang on a second, I'll be right back.

> The speaker just lied to the caller.

4)  You'll have to . . .

> It's a no-no to tell callers what they "have" to do. We take orders, we don't give them.

5)  We can't do that.

> It shouldn't be in our vocabulary.

## Exhibit 9.7

St. Paul Federal Bank for Savings

### SALES EXTRA

---

## Four Individuals Go 4 for 4 in 1987 President's Club

| | | | |
|---|---|---|---|
| *Joseph Talanco* | *Ella Ghanem* | *Barbara Donato* | *Ann Neilsen* |
| *Mount Prospect* | *Elmwood Park* | *Harwood Heights* | *Franklin Park* |
| *$7,659,608* | *$7,125,149* | *$7,104,444* | *$5,721,845* |

The four individuals shown above achieved over $1 million in new funds in each quarter of 1987. Through their combined efforts they achieved a total of over $27.6 million in 1987. They each received a weekend for 2 in Cancun for their outstanding achievements.

### Buffalo Grove Top Sales Office 1987

**Buffalo Grove** achieved top sales office in 1987 by having consistent sales performance throughout the year. Their 1987 achievements are listed below:

* Over $13.8 million in New funds for 130.5% of their 1987 goal.
* A 1.47 cross-sell ratio for the year.
* Over $8.3 million in loan applications for 197.2% of goal.

Congratulations to Manager, **Lou Esposito**, and the entire Buffalo Grove staff. In recognition of this fine achievement, the entire office will be treated to "a day away" of their choice.

### Elmwood Park Top Office 1987 Customer Service

Lynda Goeb, Director of Customer Relations, presented Paula Settefrati of Elmwood Park with the award for Top Office in Customer Service for 1987.

Elmwood Park earned this distinction by consistently scoring high marks on our customer service surveys.

In recognition of their fine accomplishments, the Elmwood Park staff, including the drive-in staff, will receive a "branch night-out" of their choice.

Enjoy Elmwood Park, our customers assured us you've earned it!

### Elia Ghanem Finishes First in 1987

After finishing on top in the second, third, and fourth quarters of 1987, **Elia Ghanem** earned Top Salesperson honors for his overall performance in 1987. Elia's accomplishments are listed below: •

* Finished in Top 25 in new funds, cross sell, and loan applications all 4 quarters.
* Finished in the President's Club all 4 quarters.
* Acquired over $7.1 million in New Funds in 1987.
* Had a year to date cross-sell ratio of 1.77.
* Finished 1987 with nearly $2.6 million in loan applications.

Elia claims he had been working for this since early in the year, but said this is his second biggest accomplishment of 1987. "The first was my new baby daughter", he said. Stephanie was born in early February.

For his fine achievements Elia was awarded a cruise to the Carribean or the Mexican Riviera.

### Karen Heavner Top Teller 1987

Karen Heavner received the first annual award as the Top Teller in New Funds Referrals. During 1987 Karen achieved $1.18 million in referrals resulting in new accounts with new funds.

Karen is a Senior Customer Service Representative at the Westchester office. Karen received a Chicagoland weekend away of her choice for her sales achievement.

Congratulations to Karen and all those who participated in the Teller Referral program in 1987. Good luck in 1988!

## Exhibit 9.7 (cont.)

---

### SALES PERFORMANCE FOURTH QUARTER 1987

**BRANCHES ACHIEVING NEW FUNDS GOAL**

| Branch | % |
|---|---|
| Oak Park | 141.6% |
| Hanover Park | 133.5% |
| Buffalo Grove | 132.9% |
| Westchester | 128.1% |
| Addison | 124.1% |
| Downers Grove | 121.9% |
| North Avenue | 111.6% |
| Rolling Meadows | 109.9% |
| Franklin Park | 107.2% |
| Carol Stream | 104.6% |
| Morton Grove | 104.0% |
| Lombard | 102.5% |
| Oak Lawn | 100.8% |

**BRANCHES ACHIEVING 1.35 OR GREATER CROSS-SELL RATIO**

| Branch | Ratio |
|---|---|
| Oak Lawn | 1.61 |
| Elmwood Park | 1.57 |
| 22nd Street | 1.51 |
| Downers Grove | 1.47 |
| Berkeley | 1.47 |
| Mount Prospect | 1.45 |
| Buffalo Grove | 1.44 |
| Franklin Park | 1.44 |
| Westchester | 1.43 |
| Rolling Meadows | 1.42 |
| Blue Island | 1.41 |
| Lombard | 1.40 |
| Harwood Heights | 1.38 |
| Addison | 1.36 |
| Brickyard | 1.36 |
| Hanover Park | 1.35 |
| North Avenue | 1.35 |

**BRANCHES ACHIEVING LOAN APPLICATIONS GOAL**

| Branch | % |
|---|---|
| Rogers Park | 428.2% |
| Carol Stream | 414.0% |
| Morton Grove | 392.0% |
| Buffalo Grove | 287.9% |
| Oak Park | 265.4% |
| Hanover Park | 261.7% |
| 22nd Street | 212.7% |
| Blue Island | 203.6% |
| Mount Prospect | 185.0% |
| Westchester | 174.7% |
| Harwood Heights | 144.9% |
| Elmwood Park | 139.2% |
| Lombard | 128.7% |
| Addison | 126.8% |
| Franklin Park | 122.1% |
| North Avenue | 119.7% |
| Downers Grove | 118.7% |

**BRANCHES ACHIEVING BROKERAGE GOAL**

| Branch | % |
|---|---|
| Franklin Park | 287.5% |
| Westchester | 125.7% |
| Rolling Meadows | 120.3% |
| North Avenue | 119.2% |

**TOP CSR'S CROSS-SELL RATIO**

| Name | Branch | Ratio |
|---|---|---|
| Thomas Zwartz | OL | 2.06 |
| Ella Ghanem | EP | 1.78 |
| Diane Eckstein | RM | 1.76 |
| Martha Iachini | BK | 1.68 |
| Natalia Escarpita | 22 | 1.67 |
| Jeffrey Wrobel | OL | 1.66 |
| Joan Mentz | BI | 1.65 |
| Scott Clemetsen | BG | 1.65 |
| Beth Kubicki | BY | 1.63 |
| Susan Schaller | MP | 1.61 |
| Mary Fasolo | EP | 1.61 |
| Jennifer Yeh | OL | 1.61 |
| Ron Lambke | NA | 1.58 |
| Mark Kinsella | FP | 1.58 |
| Frances Blouin | BI | 1.57 |
| Gloria Rose | OL | 1.56 |
| Jay Militello | NA | 1.55 |
| Jennifer Finn | FP | 1.52 |

**4TH QUARTER PRESIDENT'S CLUB**

| Name | Branch | Total | Name | Branch | Total |
|---|---|---|---|---|---|
| Jeffrey Wrobel | OL | $4,745,704 | Jay Militello | NA | $1,493,429 |
| Gloria Rose | OL | 3,289,222 | Thomas Zwartz | OL | 1,477,056 |
| Jennifer Yeh | OL | 3,248,715 | Susan Schaller | MP | 1,435,462 |
| Ron Lambke | NA | 2,697,930 | Mary Fasolo | EP | 1,425,449 |
| Elaine Wiziecki | OL | 2,670,701 | Ilona Hood | AD | 1,424,296 |
| Christine Smith | MG | 2,230,239 | Josephine Clarke | LB | 1,381,814 |
| Joseph Talarico* | MP | 2,117,883 | Corinne Giammanco | HP | 1,327,443 |
| Carol Meyers | RM | 2,092,935 | Caroline Hyde | NA | 1,259,020 |
| Patricia Lepri | HH | 2,084,971 | Rebecca Paulson | DG | 1,173,041 |
| Susan Guevara | BY | 2,084,450 | Martha Iachini | BK | 1,168,088 |
| Ella Ghanem* | EP | 1,820,546 | Sheila Trimble | NA | 1,162,355 |
| Karen Rylander | OL | 1,815,117 | Karen Dvorak | CS | 1,151,480 |
| Barbara Donato* | HH | 1,782,833 | Paul Fischer | WC | 1,149,803 |
| Susan Plautz | RP | 1,664,241 | Jennifer Finn | FP | 1,149,338 |
| Ann Nielsen* | FP | 1,659,206 | James Pozdro | AD | 1,117,163 |
| Rochelle Sproviero | DG | 1,576,872 | Scott Backus | RM | 1,053,745 |
| Marianne Ahrweiler | WC | 1,571,993 | Wayne Jacob | FP | 1,021,278 |
| Helen Johnson | BG | 1,510,824 | Anna Giuliano | NA | 1,001,894 |

*Made President's Club all four quarters.

**TOP TELLER REFERRALS WITH NEW FUNDS**

| Name | Branch | Total |
|---|---|---|
| Martha Dykstra | OL | $856,060 |
| Karen Heavner | WC | 589,804 |
| Therese Harrigian | HH | 530,128 |
| Thomas Zwartz | OL | 486,907 |
| Christine De Chene | OL | 426,936 |
| Elisa Romeo | EP | 371,823 |
| John Fiore | HH | 359,524 |
| Karen Deal | BY | 337,760 |
| Kelly Swick | EP | 285,101 |
| Linda Lamonica | EP | 252,598 |
| Lisa Hable | WC | 227,215 |
| Rochelle Witt | EP | 224,712 |
| Marita Hanley | RP | 218,000 |
| Janet Higdon | RM | 217,201 |
| Marianne Mazzenga | HH | 204,704 |
| Fe Moore | BG | 190,838 |
| Louise Barkoff | OL | 187,116 |
| Rita Lintzens | BY | 175,481 |
| Jamie Guanci | BK | 162,385 |
| Sue Ames | DG | 152,040 |
| Irma Ramirez | EP | 159,692 |
| Jan Alten | FP | 150,000 |
| Carol Britten | NA | 147,370 |
| Thomas McNicholas | OL | 145,878 |
| Elaine Laux | DG | 139,980 |

**TOP INDIVIDUALS INVESTMENT NETWORK**

| Name | Branch | Total |
|---|---|---|
| Holly Sansone | WC | 125.7% |
| Nancy Quinn | RM | 120.3% |

**TOP INDIVIDUAL INSIDE LOAN ORIGINATION**

| Name | Branch | Total |
|---|---|---|
| Monica Meder | NA | $9,736,500 |

**TOP 25 CSR'S NEW FUNDS**

| Name | Branch | Total |
|---|---|---|
| Jeffrey Wrobel | OL | $4,745,704 |
| Gloria Rose | OL | 3,289,222 |
| Jennifer Yeh | OL | 3,248,715 |
| Ron Lambke | NA | 2,697,930 |
| Elaine Wiziecki | OL | 2,670,701 |
| Christine Smith | MG | 2,230,239 |
| Joseph Talarico | MP | 2,117,883 |
| Carol Meyers | RM | 2,092,935 |
| Patricia Lepri | HH | 2,084,971 |
| Susan Guevara | BY | 2,084,450 |
| Ella Ghanem | EP | 1,820,546 |
| Karen Rylander | OL | 1,815,117 |
| Barbara Donato | HH | 1,782,833 |
| Susan Plautz | RP | 1,664,241 |
| Ann Nielsen | FP | 1,659,206 |
| Rochelle Sproviero | DG | 1,576,872 |
| Marianne Ahrweiler | WC | 1,571,993 |
| Helen Johnson | BG | 1,510,824 |
| Jay Militello | NA | 1,493,429 |
| Thomas Zwartz | OL | 1,477,056 |
| Susan Schaller | MP | 1,435,462 |
| Mary Fasolo | EP | 1,425,449 |
| Ilona Hood | AD | 1,424,296 |
| Josephine Clarke | LB | 1,381,814 |
| Corinne Giammanco | HP | 1,327,443 |

**TOP 25 CSR'S LOAN APPLICATIONS**

| Name | Branch | Total |
|---|---|---|
| Christine Smith | MG | $1,094,700 |
| Dianne Sroka | OP | 1,039,800 |
| Helen Johnson | BG | 963,400 |
| Carol Meyers | RM | 910,000 |
| Nancy Quinn | RM | 891,900 |
| Frances Blouin | BI | 864,300 |
| Kristine Pokorny | LB | 829,500 |
| Karen Dvorak | CS | 632,800 |
| Marianne Ahrweiler | WC | 599,200 |
| Rochelle Sproviero | DG | 591,300 |
| Barbara Donato | HH | 581,800 |
| Angie Droulias | MG | 571,400 |
| Rebecca Paulson | DG | 548,800 |
| Diane Eckstein | RM | 525,000 |
| Susan Plautz | RP | 493,700 |
| Cheryl Culotta | HP | 482,200 |
| John Quinn | DG | 449,000 |
| Joseph Talarico | MP | 412,300 |
| Nadine Karpius | DG | 410,900 |
| Kathleen Statler | DG | 386,900 |
| Susan Schaller | MP | 378,000 |
| Ella Ghanem | EP | 357,700 |
| Yvonne Rutz | BI | 354,000 |
| Joan Mentz | BI | 319,900 |
| Jennifer Finn | FP | 294,000 |

**St Paul Federal Bank**
For Savings

196

If your newsletters mainly contain recipes, anniversary dates, and general information, consider spicing them up with reports about your employees' achievements.

## Five-Star Club

The hospitality industry has utilized the coveted five-star designation to recognize outstanding restaurants and hotels for sometime. Linda Bennett, assistant vice president of **First Interstate Bank,** Los Angeles North Division, shares their Five Star Award for Excellence program:

> Our Five Star Award for Excellence program sets standards in the areas of *Service, Sales, Spirit, Strength,* and *Surroundings.* All of our branches can compare themselves with these standards on a semiannual basis. A branch meeting or exceeding 90% of the standards is recognized and rewarded for achieving and maintaining outstanding performance by receiving the Five Star Award for Excellence.
>
> The heart of our Five Star program is the five Categories for Excellence: Service, Sales, Spirit, Strength, and Surroundings. Each category has subcategories, such as Fast, Friendly, and Responsible, which define the specific criteria. The categories are weighted as follows:

| | |
|---|---|
| Service | 30% |
| Sales | 30% |
| Spirit | 20% |
| Strength | 10% |
| Surroundings | 10% |

> Some of the tools we use for measuring a branch's qualifications are external mystery shopper results, internal mystery shopper results, in-branch customer surveys, internal reports, and District Manager/Division staff reports. All branches are evaluated based on their performance in the twelve months prior to the nomination.

Once a manager is confident that his/her branch has achieved Five Star status, the nomination checklist and a nomination summary with supporting materials are submitted to the District Manager to document the branch's accomplishments. Nominations are submitted in January and July.

The District Manager reviews the nomination package and discusses it with the Branch Manager. Where there is concurrence that the branch is a candidate for Five Star, the District Manager then recommends the branch to the nominating committee for approval.

A branch's certification remains in effect for one full year. Certified branches must nominate themselves again when their year is complete.

If the Five Star Award is not granted, the reasons and areas for improvement are explained to the Branch Manager by the District Manager. The branch is eligible to be nominated again during the next nomination period, six months later.

A complete overview of the Five Star awards and recognition program and the criteria for the five categories for excellence—service, sales, spirit, strength, and surroundings—are included in Exhibit 9.8.

## Service Achievement Clubs

Achievement clubs are an excellent way to reward top performers. However, it is important to be fair and create an equal opportunity for all to belong. An achievement club is a club to reward people who reach a specific level of performance or attain the necessary entrance criteria. Ideally, employees *earn* their membership in the club, as opposed to someone *choosing* them. However, many clubs allow members to be nominated.

The following is a list of criteria that could be used for entry into an exclusive service club:

★ Two perfect mystery shoppings within a quarter

★ Three complimentary letters or verbal comments from customers or members within a six-month period

## Exhibit 9.8

FIRST INTERSTATE BANK, Los Angeles, CA

# FIVE·STAR·AWARD

*for Excellence*

**Awards**

A branch which receives the Five Star Award for Excellence receives several awards and honors:

**Award
Announcement**

The branch is recognized in an awards ceremony at a Los Angeles North Division Managers Meeting. Typically, an officers' reception or network will follow the meeting in which the officers of the awarded branches can also be congratulated.

**Branch
Awards**

Each member of the branch staff receives a Five Star name badge and a customized letter of congratulations. These are presented along with two Five Star door decals for the branch to the branch manager at the time the awards are announced, at the L.A.N.D. Managers Meeting.

The branch receives a large wall plaque at an in-branch awards ceremony conducted by the Division Manager and the four District Managers.

A cash award of *$50.00 per staff member* is given to the Branch Employee Fund. The money can be used for a branch celebration or a branch project.

The branch staff receives special recognition at all Division meetings. including Managers Meetings, Calforum, and Sales Rallies.

Each officer of the branch receives a personalized desk plaque in honor of their achievement. In addition, they will be hosted at a luncheon on the 60th floor of the corporate offices in downtown Los Angeles by the Division Manager and the four District Managers.

The Branch Manager and spouse are hosted by the bank's President, the Division Manager and the four District Managers at a special Five Star Awards dinner, and receives a $250.00 cash award.

## Exhibit 9.8 (cont.)

 *Service*

There are three subcategories within Customer Service: Fast, Friendly, and Responsible. The Service Category represents **30%** of the weight in the Five Star Awards.

### *Fast*

★ Average response time (approval or denial) to the customer on consumer loan requests does not exceed 2 working days.

★ Meet customers needs and resolve their problems in a timely and efficient manner.

★ Telephone calls answered by the 3rd ring

★ Average telephone holding time does not exceed 1.5 minutes.

★ Customer average waiting time in teller lines does not exceed 5 minutes

### *Friendly*

★ Staff members acknowledge and greet every customer with a smile.

★ FSM's/FSR's and CSM's/CAR's identify themselves to all customers

★ FSM's/FSR's offer Welcome Folders or Business Cards to all customers served.

★ Staff members wear name badges and have current name plates. (Allowing time for new hires.)

★ Staff members thank all customers served

★ Staff members call every customer by name.

### *Responsible*

★ Staff members display problem ownership. (Listen: state regret and express empathy; clarify the facts; educate, correct the problem or refer; restore confidence.)

★ All phone calls are returned within 24 hours.

★ Customer complaints are effectively resolved at the branch level.

★ Branch holds productive service meetings regularly.

*Measurement Sources include:* External and internal Mystery Shopper results, in-branch survey mail survey results, and internal reports.

## Exhibit 9.8 (cont.)

 *Sales*

Within the "Sales" category there are 3 subcategories: Planning, Implementation and Results. The Sales Category represents **30%** of the weight in the Five Star Awards.

*Planning*

★ Branch has implemented a Marketing Plan that is tied to Branch Goals.

★ Branch holds productive Sales Meetings at least weekly.

★ Branch has established and is using a system to identify and develop preferred relationships.

*Implementation*

★ Branch has an on-going referral program and monitors results.

★ Sales results are charted weekly, and displayed in branch staff or lunch room.

★ Branch displays appropriate promotion and collateral materials, and removes such materials in a timely manner.

★ Branch has implemented a regular telemarketing program, including calling a new accounts within 15 working days of account opening (i.e. calling customers to thank them for their business, to probe for additional needs and cross-sell where applicable).

*Results*

★ Branch meets or exceeds sales goals in all promotions.

★ Branch meets or exceeds monthly Plu$Pay goals consistently.

★ Total loans and total core deposits meet or exceed budget.

*Measurement Sources include:* Plu$Pay reports, Bank promotion reports, external and internal Mystery Shopper results and Financial Reports.

201

## Exhibit 9.8 (cont.)

 *Spirit*

Within the "Spirit" category, there are three subcategories: Teamwork. Morale and Professionalism. The Spirit Category represents **20%** of the weight in the Five Star Awards.

*Teamwork*

★ 100% staff participation in promotions.

★ Fellow Bank employees treat each other with the same courtesy, efficiency and consideration as we treat our customers.

★ Branch demonstrates cooperation among staff members and with other units in the Division and in the bank.

*Morale*

★ Branch staff demonstrates a positive attitude.

★ Branch staff is aware of and committed to branch goals and proud of branch accomplishments.

★ Staff is recognized and rewarded for creativity, initiative and innovation.

★ Branch staff displays pride and ownership of branch activities and promotions.

★ Branch has an on-going recognition/ reward program in place for customer service and sales performance.

*Professionalism*

★ Staff members display a professional appearance.

★ Correspondence is professional and accurate.

★ Staff members answer every call by identifying themselves and using proper telephone etiquette.

★ Staff displays a professional attitude.

*Measurement Sources include:* External and internal Mystery Shopper results. District and Division staff visits and promotion results.

## Exhibit 9.8 (cont.)

 *Strength*

The "Strength" category has 2 subcategories: Leadership and Development. Within each, several performance standards are listed. The Strength Category represents **10%** of the weight in the Five Star Awards.

*Leadership*

★ Branch management consistently serves as a positive role model.

★ Branch actively provides assistance and training for other branches.

★ Branch Management uses positive reinforcement techniques (e.g. Service Grams and other recognition vehicles to motivate staff)

*Development*

★ Branch has implemented a plan for staff development.

★ Existing employees have completed Service Plus training, and for new employees, Service Plus Progress Charts are kept current and displayed in branch staff or lunch room.

★ Branch has a cross-training program, exhibited by having at least three people trained on each branch position.

★ Branch maintains and displays a current cross-training chart.

★ 100% of eligible staff participates in the Professional Teller Program, as stated in program rules.

★ Staff is utilized in an efficient manner.

*Measurement Sources include:* External and internal Mystery Shopper results, Professional Teller Program participation, participation in other training programs and Performance Evaluations.

---

## Exhibit 9.8 (cont.)

---

# *Surroundings*

Within the "Surroundings" category there are 2 subcategories: Clear & Effective Signage and Maintenance. The Surroundings Category represents **10%** of the weight in the Five Star Awards.

*Clear and Effective Signage*

---

★ Branch has clear directional signs.     ★ All signs are professional.

---

*Maintenance*

★ Branch maintains a clean appearance, including:
— Sales and Service Areas
— Staff room
— Stock room
— Vault
— Lobby
— Customer check stands
— ATM: trash containers in place and adequate supplies are maintained
— Parking Lot: area immediately adjacent to the branch is checked periodically for litter.

★ Records, forms and files are maintained to satisfy current needs and are stored neatly and in a proper place.

---

*Measurement Sources include:* External and internal Mystery Shopper results, mail-in survey results, District Manager and Division Staff visits and photos.

5

**204**

★ An average score of 9.5–10 on customer or employee comment cards

★ Nomination by a certain number of their peers

★ Five or more "praise" coupons from customers or members

Clubs also allow support and noncustomer-contact employees to participate. They can achieve entry by receiving a specific number of internal comment cards or "praise" coupons from other employees.

How you design a service club is limited only to your imagination. Club members may receive a letter from the president welcoming them; be named in the newsletter; receive a cash award, a memorable gift, or a half- or full-day off; or be invited to attend an exclusive event held at a lovely location. The following are examples of several service clubs.

## Pride
**Old Stone Bank,** Providence, Rhode Island, developed a comprehensive service club called PRIDE in April 1986. Robin Amaral, assistant treasurer and branch manager, shared the following details:

Old Stone has always had a unique corporate culture of pride which sets it apart from many financial services institutions. PRIDE stands for People Recognized In Demonstrating Excellence. Through this program, employees' extra efforts are recognized openly and awarded on-the-spot. This allows employees to share their awards with their peers as well as their customers.

We developed the program to encourage an atmosphere of outstanding customer service, innovation and sales by measuring employees' consistent performances. The program is designed to be an immediate and long-term recognition vehicle. On the individual level, it is meant to recognize performances which exceed normal job requirements and expectations.

The PRIDE program was developed from a committee that was given the goal of formulating a long-term recognition program.

This committee consisted of members from all areas of the bank's Retail Banking Group (RBG). Members included Mortgage officers, Consumer Credit officers, Retail Sales Support officers, as well as Bank Branch Managers and Regional Branch Managers.

The Retail Banking Group personnel are recognized by the awarding of bronze, silver and gold PRIDE awards, depending on the degree of excellence displayed.

A bronze award is a spot award given anytime with immediate work unit recognition. The criteria for this award is an *observable* demonstration of excellence in customer service and innovative action (i.e. positive resolution of complex customer situation, customer compliment letter, etc.).

A silver award may be awarded anytime, but should provide for immediate work unit recognition. The criteria for this award is an *exceptional* demonstration of excellence in customer service and innovative action (i.e. spotting and preventing a loss to the bank, innovative new ideas put into action, etc.).

Gold awards are awarded monthly in the work unit and announced again at the quarterly recognition celebration. Following this, the monthly corporate newsletter includes a PRIDE page which lists the gold award winners and a brief explanation of their accomplishments. The criteria for gold awards is an *outstanding* demonstration of excellence in customer service and innovative action (i.e. significant cost reduction idea, outstanding sales success, etc.).

The PRIDE committee meets monthly to approve gold award nominations. The nominator and decision-makers for all awards include branch managers, work unit supervisors, regional managers, department heads or senior management. Points are given for each award presented. A bronze award is worth two points, a silver award is six points, and a gold award is twelve points. All points provide eligibility for the quarterly and annual prizes.

When presenting the award, a small bronze, silver or gold "flat" and a certificate [Exhibit 9.9] are presented to the employee. The flat is displayed on the individual's nameplate and the certificate may be displayed in the office.

PRIDE points are continually monitored. At the PRIDE quarterly recognition celebration, the ten top point getters also receive cash awards. There is additional recognition for the two top point getters—one branch person and one department person. At the annual celebration, a PRIDE Person of the Year is recognized. This person is the employee who has accumulated the most points throughout the year. For the past three years, Old Stone has held the celebration at a local convention center. The annual celebration is filled with much excitement and "hoop-lah" and is enjoyed by all employees. It is the high point to a very exciting program!

As time goes on, with any program of this nature, the program becomes "routine" and needs new spice. To help find a solution, Old Stone organized a sub-committee consisting of non-exempt employee members. The committee was chaired by a PRIDE committee officer. This sub-committee had an open discussion and each person had previously spoken to coworkers in their departments and regions to get input for the discussion. The recommendations were then brought back to the PRIDE committee and new program ideas were developed.

### Quality Touch

Mike Trigg, senior vice president, and Rob Maddox, vice president of sales and service development, at **Society Corporation,** Cleveland, Ohio, have developed two recognition programs, Quality Touch and One of the Best, to reward frontline and operational and support staff members. Quality Touch is designed to reward employees in the retail and trust sectors. The following is an overview of their Quality Touch program:

Quality. That's what working at Society is all about. It is our unwavering commitment to provide personalized quality ser-

**Exhibit 9.9**

OLD STONE

Bronze Award

EXCELLENCE THROUGH
*PRIDE*

presented to

on

in recognition of an exceptional demonstration of excellence
in customer service and innovative action.

vice to our customers and coworkers. That makes Society one of the nation's top financial service companies.

At Society, recognition of this commitment to quality is important—we take great pride in the accomplishments and achievements of our fellow employees. Their efforts in improving and enhancing "the Society way of doing business" are recognized as the critical ingredient in Society's formula for success.

To demonstrate this commitment to employee excellence, Society has developed "Quality Touch." This is a comprehensive process designed to recognize and reward outstanding performers in Society's Retail and Trust sector.

The process is divided into four individual levels of recognition ranging from the "Red Jacket of Excellence" to the "Quality Touch" pen or calculator award. Society's "Quality Touch" assures that service excellence will never go unnoticed. [See the diagram of Quality Touch in Exhibit 9.10.]

*Levels of Recognition*   "Quality Touch" is an enhancement to the regionally based "Quality Touch" and "Star Quality" programs. This corporate process will continue to utilize key qualifying guidelines from the regional programs as its foundation. Additional levels of performance criteria have been added to provide greater recognition opportunities.

Level 1—At this level any employee can be recognized by a peer for demonstrating excellence in one or more of Society's six shared values. This peer nomination level will provide a choice of two awards: a "Quality Touch" pen or a "Quality Touch" calculator. Any employee may complete a nomination form for an employee that has demonstrated excellence in one or more of the six shared values.

Level 2—At this level any non-officer employee may be nominated who demonstrates consistent excellence in each of the

## Exhibit 9.10

Society Corporation, Cleveland, Ohio

**Quality Touch Award Program**
Recognition Process Overview
Retail and Trust Sector

**Who, When and Where**
*Awards are presented*

**Awards and**
**Performance Level**

**Officer Level**
*Semiannual*
Society Recognition Banquet

"Red Jacket
of Excellence"

**LEVEL IV**

**Red Jacket**
Distinguished Performance

**All Employees**
*Semiannual*
Officer/Regional-
District Meeting

"Quality Touch"

**LEVEL III**

**Lucite Statue and**
**$100.00 Net Check**
Quality Performance

**Non-Officer Level**
*Quarterly*
Department/Area
Meeting

"Quality Touch"

**LEVEL II**

**Lapel Pin and $50.00**
**Net Check**
Consistent
Performance

**All Employees**
*When*
*Appropriate*
Department/
Branch

"Quality Touch"

**LEVEL I**

**Pen or**
**Calculator**
Special
Performance

following areas:

★ Produces quality work.

★ Consistently maintains that "personal touch" in servicing all customers.

★ Demonstrates exceptional skill in meeting the customer's needs to their complete satisfaction.

★ Assists and teaches fellow workers.

Each reward recipient will receive a gold "Quality Touch" lapel pin and a $50 net check.

Level 3—Any employee is eligible to be nominated at this level who demonstrates a sincere commitment to service quality in each of the following areas:

★ Performs their service dependably.

★ Helps customers and provides prompt service.

★ Uses their abilities to convey trust and confidence.

★ Maintains a quality appearance of the facilities and/or the equipment that is used to provide service.

★ Has received a recognition award in the past.

The winners at this level will be awarded a contemporary lucite statue with the "Quality Touch" insignia and a $100 net check.

Level 4—At this level, any officer may be nominated for the "Red Jacket of Excellence" who demonstrates outstanding leadership in managing performance.

## One of the Best

**Society Corporation** also recognizes the value of its administrative and support area employees. The program "One of the Best" honors support staff who have demonstrated consistent excellence in customer service performance, both internally and externally.

"The One of the Best awards symbolize Society's highest formal recognition of employees in administrative and staff support areas", according to Mike Trigg, senior vice president of sales and service development. "The One of the Best program is Society's way of spotlighting employees with excellent track records and thanking them for a job well done."

Overall, One of the Best affects more than 2,300 key support members throughout the state. It is the brainchild of the Pride in Value-Added Performance Committee (P.I.V.A.P.), a group of key executives representing staff support teams throughout the corporation. Roger Noall, vice chairman and chief administration officer, who champions the recognition process, stated, "I feel it [is] absolutely paramount [that] we recognize those key performers who emulate excellence in everything they do."

Awards are distributed in four categories (see Exhibit 9.11) as follows:

★ Peer Awards: All administrative and staff support employees are permitted to nominate their coworkers and internal customers for excellence in performing individual activities. The nominations are reviewed by their respective award teams and the employees are presented with a mug or pen with the Society's Best award emblem. "The peer nomination gives employees an opportunity to applaud coworkers who have displayed outstanding service in a particular situation," said Mike Barger, senior vice president of bank operations, southern region, and chairman of the recognition subcommittee.

★ Society's Best Desk Award: Nonofficers commended for the program are given a desk award and a $50 check. These awards are presented quarterly at department meetings.

★ Society's Best Pin: Nonofficers and officers commended for the program are awarded a Society's Best lapel pin and receive a check for $100. These awards are presented at ceremonies conducted on a regional or divisional basis.

★ Pyramid-of-Excellence Clock: Officers commended for the program are awarded a quartz clock embedded in a clear

## Exhibit 9.11

Society Corporation, Cleveland, Ohio

"One of the Best"

Process Overview

**Who and When**                    **Awards and Performance Level**

| Who and When | | Awards and Performance Level |
|---|---|---|
| **Officer Level** *Semiannual* Corporate Recognition Banquet | "Pyramid of Excellence" **LEVEL IV** | **Pyramid Clock** Distinguished Performance |
| **Officers and Nonofficer Level** *Quarterly Department Meetings* | "Society's Best" **LEVEL III** | **Diamond Lapel Pin and $100 Check** Quality Performance |
| **Nonofficer Level** *Quarterly Department Meetings* | "Society's Best" **LEVEL II** | **Desk Award and $50 Check** Consistent Performance |
| **All Levels** *Department Meetings* | "Society's Best" **LEVEL I** | **Mug or Pen** Special Performance |

pyramid-shaped casing. These awards are presented semiannually in February and August at special recognition banquets. Robert W. Gillespie, society chairman and chief executive officer, hosted the 1990 banquet in Cleveland.

"This program recognizes the individuals in our corporation who represent the true sense of Society's corporate culture," said Gillespie in the bank's newsletter. "The culture represents an unwavering commitment to quality, initiative and innovation, and a dedication to providing superior service to the customer. Through the Society's Best award, employees who exemplify consistent excellence will never go unnoticed."

## Legend in the Making
In the July 1989 issue of *Bank Marketing*, **BayBanks'** program, Legend in the Making, was highlighted. Every four months BayBanks, Boston, Massachusetts, selects five outstanding "legend makers" from more than 2,000 branch employees throughout the company.

Designated as "corporate emissaries," these employees, along with their managers, traveled to organizations around the world that are noted for superior service, such as Disney World, the Hotel Bel-Air, Domino's Pizza, the Toronto Four Seasons Hotel, L. L. Bean, and Claridge's Hotel in London. They discussed the strategies, policies, and practices that have enhanced service in those organizations and brought the ideas back to BayBanks.

## Secret Service Agent
Joni Naugle, director of marketing for **Penn Savings Bank**, shared their Secret Service Agent internal recognition program (see Exhibit 9.12) in the January 1990 *Bank Marketing*. SECRET stands for: Smiles, Enthusiasm, Caring, Response, Ensured satisfaction, and Thanks. Being a Secret Service Agent at Penn is a high honor. And only the best qualify. All employees are eligible, except department, branch, or divisional managers. There are several ways to qualify.

When an employee receives a positive memorable experience from a fellow employee, a Secret Sleuth form is completed and forwarded to

## Exhibit 9.12

Begins Monday, May 1, 1989
& Ends Friday, July 31, 1989

# Be on the Lookout...
# a Secret Service Agent
# is Looking for You!

In our continuing efforts to reach the highest possible service levels, we are repeating our program which is designed to help management enhance, measure and recognize your service skills. During this special service awareness promotion. Secret Agents will be traveling around to your Department or Branch Office. They may contact you by telephone or in person. Their job is not to let you know who they are, but to find out how service minded you are, and you never know who the agent might be...a member or an employee! Put on your best smile and use all your service skills, because it can mean cash in your pocket!

**You could earn up to $50 for outstanding service! You will be scored by the specially trained Agent on the following service behavior:**

1. Your friendliness (remember a smile is the first way to set up a friendly experience)
2. Using the member's name at least once
3. Thorough knowledge of your job
4. Accuracy of the transaction or information you gave
5a. Giving one reference to another NIFCU product or service OR...
5b. Identifying yourself, by name, during your conversation

### Here's How You Will Be Scored:

| 1 | If you are below their expectations | $0 |
|---|---|---|
| 2 | If you meet their expectations | $5 FOR EACH CATEGORY ABOVE |
| 3 | If you exceed their expectations | $10 FOR EACH CATEGORY ABOVE |

Get ready...our Secret Service Agents are out there and that can mean up to $50 in your pocket!

215

marketing. A "You've Been Caught" certificate is validated and forwarded to the "caught" employee. Employees cannot "catch" coworkers in the same department or office. A qualified catch must be for someone who works elsewhere.

Providing positive memorable customer experiences (PMCE) to external customers can also get "You've Been Caught" certificates in three different ways. First, when a customer sends in a letter personally acknowledging a PMCE, two certificates will be issued. Second, a phone call from a customer to a divisional director or above will also get the noted employee a certificate. The third way to receive a "You've Been Caught" certificate is when a customer specifically acknowledges excellent service on a "Please Grade Me Card."

When 10 "You've Been Caught" certificates are received by one employee, he or she becomes an official Penn Secret Service Agent. In one month, almost 50 employees have been caught providing extraordinary service. Joni feels that if the Secret Service program does nothing more than close the gaps among departments, Penn will consider it extremely successful. This type of interdepartment acknowledgment can do a lot to build morale, and happy employees are more likely to provide better customer service.

I couldn't agree more—once again we see how employee morale can affect our levels of service. Don't hesitate—start designing a service club and recognizing your service stars.

## *Checkbook of Awards*

**Bridgeport Trust and Savings** in Connecticut developed a unique checkbook of awards. These awards, in the form of checks, include a disappearing act (a day off), dinner-for-two, tickets to a play, and a gift certificate.

Senior management uses these creative checks to give on-the-spot recognition to any frontline or support employee who contributes towards the sales and service culture. Getting senior midlevel managers involved in praising employees' successes will reinforce your service culture.

## Stars and Stickers

"Stars and Stickers" is a simple, low-cost idea that can be used in both frontline and operational departments. The philosophy is to encourage employees to reward the positive service behavior of fellow employees.

To implement this idea, purchase colorful stars and fun stickers and distribute them to your staff. Develop specific criteria and standards that you would like to reinforce. For example, answer calls in three rings or less, greet the customer and fellow employee by name, acknowledge all customers and employees within six seconds, thank the customer for his or her business, thank fellow employees for their call, and be responsive and friendly.

Review the criteria with your staff and announce that any time they notice a fellow employee delivering exceptional service, place a sticker on them. Can you imagine how pleased an employee would be if a coworker recognized his or her efforts? This program is a great way to create goodwill among your staff.

## Cash on the Spot

Employees getting a perfect shopping score for their service performance deserve a cash award on the spot. Awards can vary from $10 to $50, with $25 being the most common. If you are going to measure people, make sure you are rewarding those who do well. As you know, cash awards are appreciated by employees who do not earn a large salary.

**First National Bank of Chaska** in Minnesota pays $20 on the spot to any employee who gets a perfect shopping score by meeting all six elements of its "Secret" program—Smile, Eagerly greet customers, Call customers by name, Rapid, Accurate transactions, Eye contact, and Thank customer and ask them to return. Since starting this program, First National Bank of Chaska has expanded and modified the "Secret" standards to encompass its secretaries, bookkeepers, officers, and frontline and support staffs.

## Roving Trophy

Roving trophies are passed around to reward individual employees or departments for excellent service. For example, give a roving trophy to the branch or department with the highest service score, the highest average score for product knowledge, or the highest sales results; a frontline employee for receiving the most customer compliments; or a support department employee for exceptional service.

Consider designing a lovely trophy for service or sales excellence. Pass it around monthly to your top performers.

### Employee-of-the-Month Photos

I remember walking into a deck and patio furniture store several years ago and seeing an 8 x10 photo of an employee in the entrance area. The store owner told me he had been doing this for seven years to recognize his employees.

Display a picture of your "Employee of the Month" in a visible spot where your customers can see it. This is an old idea that needs to be dusted off and used more frequently.

### Customer Service Business Cards

**Penn Savings Bank**, gives all its employees business cards (Naugle, January 1990). Under their names is printed "Customer Service." Business cards tell what people are responsible for, and Penn Savings Bank wanted to be sure that each employee knew that customer service was his or her responsibility. Using business cards is an excellent way to make your employees feel important and to get the message across that service is everyone's responsibility.

### Split the Fees

To improve overall service in the home mortgage loan area, **First National Bank of Chicago** (*Products, Marketing, and Technology,* April 1988) instituted a simple guarantee: If for any reason customers were not completely satisfied with the service, they would get back their $300 application fee at the close of the loan. To encourage employees to "buy" into this plan, they would receive half of the fees that were not returned to customers. Customer-reported satisfaction rose from about 75 percent to 98.6 percent!

## *Nights on the Town and Trips*

Imagine the following scene. Your front doorbell rings and a chauffeur-driven limousine is waiting to take you and your spouse, or significant other, to a five-star restaurant, followed by dancing and a night at an elegant hotel. This is exactly how one bank rewards its managers for providing exceptional service and meeting their budgets. This same bank sent two customer service representatives to Hong Kong as a reward for their exceptional sales and service performance.

Whether it's a weekend-for-two at a bed and breakfast or a night-on-the-town, give awards that include spouses whenever possible (Smith, October 1989). Companies like IBM and Xerox have recognized, for a long time, the power of offering rewards that can be shared with someone special. After all, if spouses realize that they can share the awards and go on the weekend trips, they will be supportive and act as additional motivators.

**Bank of Montreal** in Toronto has a special club for its branch managers. At the beginning of each year, the criteria is announced regarding profits, sales performance, service standards, and so on. Managers who meet the criteria are treated to a first-class, dream vacation, with their spouses, at a spectacular resort in a foreign location. The winners all go together, along with the bank's president, to be acknowledged and pampered. Videos of the trip are taken and then used as motivation for the managers back home.

## *Radio and Newspaper Coverage*

**Champaign National Bank** in Illinois ran a full-page ad in its local paper, featuring its tellers at two branches. The ad invited customers to go to those branches for refreshments and to say "thanks" to their favorite tellers. Radio commercials were also used to promote the event (see Exhibit 9.13). Punch and cookies were served, and banners announcing Teller Appreciation Day were hung across the front of each branch. Each teller was presented with a flower and two theater tickets by Robert Wallace, the bank's president *(Measuring and Monitoring Service Quality)*.

219

## Exhibit 9.13

Champaign National Bank          June 26, 1987
Sandy Lyon, Dir. of Marketing
201 N. Randolph
Champaign, IL 61820

Job Name:   Teller Appreciation Radio Copy
Job No.:      87143/ :30 sec—Wednesday


Music:       (Up and under, CNB theme.)


Donna:      HELLO, I'M DONNA KOPMANN, TELLER SUPERVISOR
AT CHAMPAIGN NATIONAL BANK.


I'D LIKE YOU TO JOIN US FOR A STANDING
OVATION TO OUR TELLER STAFF ON "TELLER
APPRECIATION DAY," WEDNESDAY, JULY TWENTY-
SECOND!


CHAMPAIGN NATIONAL BANK EXTENDS ITS
"THANKS!" TO ALL OUR TELLERS FOR
OUTSTANDING PERFORMANCE. STOP BY, ENJOY
SOME FREE REFRESHMENTS, AND GIVE A NOTE OF
THANKS TO <u>YOUR</u> FAVORITE TELLER.


VISIT CHAMPAIGN NATIONAL BANK, BANKWEST,
OR BANKPARK ON "TELLER APPRECIATION DAY,"
WEDNESDAY JULY, TWENTY-SECOND


MEMBER F.D.I.C.

Music:       (Up and sing out.)

In January 1990, **Harleysville National Bank** of Harleysville, Pennsylvania, held a first-class Annual Awards Night, at which over 100 awards for sales and service were given out. A local paper covered the story and listed the many award-winning employees in an article (see Exhibit 9.14).

## Team Incentives

Besides acknowledging your individual stars, also recognize your high performance teams. For example, say, "If our branch or department reaches a 4.5 (5 is perfect) customer satisfaction score in the next service survey, we will get a catered dinner, tickets to a show, or $25 each." Or, "If we get our turnaround time down to three days, we're all going out for a special Italian dinner."

Superior service cannot be accomplished by any one person, it is the efforts of people working together toward a shared goal. Make sure you reward team performance.

## Domino's Pizza: A Case Study

The July 1988 issue of *Incentive* reported that Domino's Pizza spends $3 million annually on employee motivation campaigns to support its guarantee of "Delivery in 30 minutes or $3 off your pizza." Domino's conducts eight incentive programs annually. Aimed at all levels of employees—from drivers to managers—these motivation campaigns are designed to reward quality service, employee loyalty, and increased sales.

To encourage both speedy service and safe driving, the pizza chain created the "Safe Driver of the Month" award. Winners are selected by store managers when they have no traffic violations or accidents and are available for duty above and beyond their basic requirements. The winner receives a badge with his name and Safe Driver of the Month on it, as well as an engraved plaque for display in the store.

Thomas Monaghan, president and founder of Domino's, also owns the Detroit Tigers, which he uses as part of his award program for managers. In the Be My Guest program, 10 managers per region are

Exhibit 9.14

A2    Souderton Independent, Wednesday, January 31, 1990

# Harleysville National Holds Award Night

Covering a wide variety of performance excellence, Harleysville National Bank recently held its Annual Awards Night giving out over 100 awards. The bank's awards banquet has become an annual event culminating the bank's years of record earnings.

In the sales category, awards for outstanding performers in Harleysville National's commercial calling program were: Bob Kreamer, Ambler, manager of the North Penn Office; Kathryn Robertson, Schwenksville, manager of the Horsham Office; Shirley Shea, Hatfield, manager of the North Broad Office, and Richard Frain, Pottstown, manager of the Gilbertsville Office.

Honored for outstanding cross-selling efforts were Jean Wieder, Telford; Peg Linberger, Lansdale; Cheryl Detweiler, Stowe; Leeann Kovac, Sellersville; Kathy Giardina, Lansdale; Chris Schondelmaier, Boyertown, and Chris Groff, Obelisk.

Outstanding tellers cited were: Trudy Lynch, Horsham; Doris Stoltzfus, Douglassville; Sue Felbinger, Telford; Betsy Steen, Quakertown; Connie Benner, Pennsburg and Pam Yothers, Harleysville.

Awards for excellence in customer service went to Donna Bender, Perkiomenville; Annette Beyer, Harleysville; Carole Mondeaux, Souderton; Laney Hegh, Hatfield; Jennifer Erb, Harleysville; Donna Badman,

Pennsburg; Janine Shup, Red Hill; Karen Whitaker, Harleysville and Cathy Heckler, Harleysville.

The bank honored its entire Electronic Data Processing and Proof Departments for all their hard work during their recent conversions, both in hardware and software changes. Special mentions were made regarding the efforts of EDP manager Dennis Detwiler, Harleysville, and proof manager Laney Hegh, Hatfield.

The evening's celebration began with the final round of the bank's Quality Quest Product Knowledge Game Show. Developed by the bank as an innovative training method, Quality Quest Grand Prize Winners were Jennifer Erb, Harleysville; Tim Canfield, Quakertown; Rose Wentzel, Sellersville and Donna Barnicle, Harleysville. Runners-up included Ann Wilson, Harleysville; Tami Garber, Gilbertsville; Marie DeVoe, Lansdale and Lynette Rice, Telford.

The Grand Prize includes a day off and a chauffeured trip to New York City for lunch at Sardi's and seats to see "Phantom of the Opera."

222

selected by regional directors using such criteria as top sales and best delivery times. These managers are flown to Detroit to watch a game from Monaghan's private suite and to tour corporate headquarters.

Sales Levels, a program designed for all Domino's store managers, awards prizes for designated royalty sales levels achieved during a one-week period. The first time a manager earns $10,000 in royalty sales in one week, he or she gets a Hermes tie or scarf; the first $15,000 earned in one week yields a Schlessinger Brothers briefcase; $20,000, yields a Rolex stainless steel watch with the initials of Monaghan and the winner; and the manager who earns $25,000 in royalty sales in one week receives a trip to Domino's Lodge on Drummond Island, Michigan.

The Golden Challenge requires Domino's managers to increase their sales by 50 percent over the previous year if they want to win a special trip. That's hard to do. From 4,200 stores, only 60 managers and their spouses went to Bermuda in September 1988.

Some final words on incentives (Smith, October 1989). If you have put more emphasis on sales performance, consider paying sales commissions after service goals have been met. This may be difficult if your service goals can only be measured in group terms. Sales performance, however, is fairly easy to measure individually. Ideally, employees should be rewarded individually for meeting their sales or service goals. If you set goals and reward your employees who meet them, you can't go wrong.

# Chapter 10

# Attracting and Orienting New Employees

We have a philosophy in paying our personnel that says, "pay all you can." Every year, every month, every review date, figure out how to pay all you can, not what you have to pay to keep the people. That's a philosophy that works.

David D. Glass, CEO
Wal-Mart Stores, Inc.,
from an article in *Bank Marketing,* October 1987

This hotel is just one of several in the city with marble, chandeliers and beautiful carpets. The only thing that makes the difference is the staff. So I look for friendliness, a desire to serve, and that comes from the heart. You can teach somebody to put a plate down on the righthand side or how to pick up a water glass, but you can't teach them to be friendly.

Paul Limbert, General Manager
Park Hyatt Hotel, Washington, D.C.,
as quoted in *Service Quality* (Berry, Bennett, and Brown)

The task of transforming raw recruits into committed stars, able to cope with the pace of change that is becoming normal, begins with the recruiting process per se. The best follow three tenets, unfortunately ignored by most: 1. spend time, and lots of it, 2. insist that line people dominate the process, and 3. don't waffle about the qualities you are looking for in candidates.

Tom Peters,
Thriving on Chaos

Strong words of wisdom. Let's face it—we all have similar products and nice facilities. Even the most sophisticated service quality plan, measurement system, surveys, and standards will not necessarily yield a service culture. People deliver service. Therefore, the quality of the people you hire will directly affect your organization's service performance.

Many credit unions and banks have made quality service a strategic objective. Some have even identified revising their employee selection, orientation, and compensation practices as key issues. Few, however, have actually done anything about seriously upgrading the caliber of personnel. This chapter, therefore, offers you some suggestions on how to attract and orient new employees into your service environment.

## *Ask Your Customers or Members*

Don't make the mistake of assuming that you know what kind of service your customers or members are looking for from your personnel. Let them tell you what they want through one of your customer or member surveys. Once you have determined what they expect, develop a profile of the type of employees you wish to attract.

In *Service America*, Karl Albrecht and Ron Zemke indicate that British Airways, after conducting research, discovered the following four traits that customers wanted most in personnel:

1. Care and concern on the part of public contact people
2. Problem-solving capability in frontline personnel
3. Spontaneity or flexibility in the application of policies and procedures
4. The ability of frontline people to make things right when things have gone wrong

Armed with this wish list, British Airways proceeded to evaluate its hiring practices and conduct extensive training for its existing frontline people.

Are you certain you know exactly what your customers and members are looking for in your staff?

## Hire from Outside the Financial Industry

A small community bank in southern California hires many of its tellers and customer service representatives from Nordstrom's, the Seattle-based department store known for its high level of service. This bank has made a commitment to find the best and pay the most. As a result, it is profitable, and has happy customers and proud employees.

Turn your senior and midlevel managers into recruiters. Remind them to note whenever they receive excellent service in a restaurant, hotel, or any business. Watching someone in action is a better way of evaluating them, as opposed to their best interview behavior. Your managers should get the person's name, give him or her their business card, and thus build a file of hot recruits for the future.

Consider hiring your managers from retail environments such as department stores, or from McDonald's. These people have been trained to embrace the sales and service philosophy. **Bank of America** once hired a manager from a Pacific Stereo store, put him through a fast-paced training schedule, and had him selling products within four months. Soon thereafter he was placed as a branch sales manager of a troubled branch and completely turned it around. The man was a natural sales and service leader. Instead of rushing out for any warm body, groom your sales and service leaders from a retail environment.

## Super Teller Program

"How can I build an excellent sales and service team when my teller turnover is so high? I spend all of my time training new hires—it's like a revolving door." This is a comment I hear frequently in all parts of the country. Teller turnover is a serious problem and one that causes managers great frustration. I'd like to share a personal experience I had when I worked at **Bank of America** in 1985.

227

A vice president of operations at Bank of America wanted to reduce teller turnover in his region. This creative operations manager put together a "super teller" program that was designed to upgrade the position, improve service, and reduce turnover. First, the criteria for super tellers were developed. They had to sell more, serve better, and dress better—but were given more authority to serve the frontline customer. If they performed well after three months, they were made officers and given a substantial raise.

All branch employees were invited to apply, and ads attracted other qualified applicants. After training, these people were placed in high-potential branches. The customers felt the effect of this program immediately. Compliment-filled letters came pouring in to senior management. The tellers felt their role was important, and the negative associations of being a teller diminished.

Acknowledge the importance of your frontline employees and upgrade their positions. What's the use in investing in luxury facilities and the latest technology if we then hire mediocre employees? Investing in people is a profit strategy.

## *Personality Assessments*

As Paul Limbert mentioned in one of this chapter's opening quotes, you can teach someone technical skills, but you cannot teach them to like people and to be outgoing. Anyone can fake enthusiasm and eagerness for a short period of time. It is difficult to find people who genuinely care about others and have a high level of self-esteem. Rather than second guess yourself about interviewees, start giving all applicants and internal candidates personality assessments. The accuracy rate of personality assessments is high.

Personality traits such as extroversion and introversion can be measured along with the degree of empathy and the desire to serve others. I know of several institutions who use these profiles with great success.

## *New Employee Orientation*

Many leading service organizations like Xerox, IBM, and Hewlett-Packard have developed top-notch orientation programs to indoctrinate

228

new employees to their service philosophy and to instill a "customer-first" attitude.

Disneyland is famous for its employee orientation process. According to a March 1988 article in *Bank Marketing* by Barbara Duncan, manager of Disney University in California, "At Disneyland we promote a feeling of happiness. The people who work for us are 'cast members' not employees. On the very first day of employment, every cast member at Disneyland goes through an in-depth orientation process. This is where we tell our cast members who we are and explain what business we're in."

As I travel about the country, I hear many comments from managers and employees in banks and credit unions about their first day on the job:

"They had no desk or phone hooked up for me."

"No one came up to me to introduce themselves—I had to do it."

"The president is right down the hall and walked by me many times without saying hello. Finally, I introduced myself."

"I was there for three months before I even knew there was a mission statement that emphasized customer service and respect for the employees. The way people treat you here you'd never know it."

If I were to work in your organization, what would my first day be like? Let me take you to "fantasyland" where I am about to start my first day as a customer service representative for a bank or credit union.

As soon as I walk in, a fellow employee greets me by name, smiles, shakes my hand, and says, "Welcome, Barbara, we've been expecting you." My host or new supervisor greets me eagerly, and I am immediately given a copy of the mission statement and an overview of the organization's history and service philosophy. I then review an organization chart and see how all the support and operational departments interact. I see how my role fits into the bigger picture.

Next, I watch a professional video on customer service with a message from the CEO on his personal philosophy. Later in the day, my new manager takes me to lunch; and afterwards, I get a tour of all the key support departments. Everyone seems so friendly.

Finally, I am introduced to the president. While he warmly shakes my hand, I can't help but notice his friendly smile. He seems so eager to meet me. The customer bill of rights he is reviewing with me is impressive. I've never had anyone give me a customer bill of rights—let alone the president! Customer satisfaction ratings are very important to him, and he proudly shares the excellent survey from last year. What a professional and friendly group of people. I think I'm going to enjoy working here.

Does the above scenario sound like your new employee orientation? If not, this would be a good time to evaluate how you introduce employees into your service culture.

## Create Hiring Committees

I remember the time I was in a small community bank and the president was angry because an operations supervisor had just hired a shy, introverted teller without letting anyone else interview her. He said, "I'm sure she is qualified to do the basic job, Barbara, but I want our tellers to be comfortable interacting with our customers and actively generating referrals."

To upgrade the caliber of your staff, establish procedures so that any candidate must be interviewed by at least three other individuals, including senior management and a peer. A supervisor who is introverted and technically oriented would likely select an employee in his or her own likeness. This, of course, could sabotage your efforts to build a strong team of customer service professionals.

So what are you waiting for? Reevaluate your selection and orientation process and form your hiring committees. Make an investment in your greatest asset—your people.

# Chapter 11

## Being an Employee-focused Organization

The way your employees feel is the way your customers are going to feel.

Karl Albrecht

Isn't that the truth. Unhappy employees tend to deliver poor service. Happy employees tend to deliver good service. Sounds simple? Then why don't we have more happy employees?

Often when I listen to service presentations from many bank and credit union CEOs, the emphasis is on measurement, surveys, technology, and profitability. Occasionally, a comment is made about service recognition awards, such as Employee of the Month. These are wonderful ways to recognize people, but do they demonstrate our commitment to the well-being and development of our entire staff?

Most organizations are caught up with strategic planning, improving profitability and technology, and customer satisfaction. They lose sight of the fact that their employees are their most valuable asset. Without committed, loyal, and motivated employees, any service program is doomed to failure. I'm sure you'll agree that any new program is only as good as the people who execute it. In our rush to add more services and satisfy our customers and members, have we forgotten the importance of our staff?

We've all read fantastic mission statements that talk about respect and concern for the well-being of the employees. The problem is that few organizations really make employee satisfaction a priority. Often little is done to demonstrate to the employees that they are viewed as the greatest asset. It's easy to see why some managers and staff members may feel, Why should I care about them, they don't care about me.

Leslie R. Butler and Francis J. Dynan of **First Pennsylvania Bank,** in an article in the winter 1988 *Journal of Retail Banking,* said, "An enlightened company understands that every individual it employs seeks job satisfaction. Satisfaction is not restricted to the managers in the bonus pool. Communication becomes a key tool in letting people know where and how they stand within the company. Meetings, appraisals, and newsletters all contribute to informing the employee about what the company stands for and how business is conducted."

I have a theory that I am unable to prove at this point. Here it is: Organizations that are employee-focused and make the happiness of their employees a strategic priority have a significant competitive advantage. Are you skeptical? Let's listen to some words of wisdom from several well-known service leaders.

David Glass, president and CEO of Wal-Mart, explained in an October 1987 *Bank Marketing* article, "One of the basic principles at Wal-Mart is to establish a true partnership with our associates (employees). Wal-Mart is a family in which members work together and truly support each other. We simply want to develop people-supported systems because we believe that we are in a people-intensive business and they'll always be extremely important." Notice, David said *extremely* important.

In September of 1989, I had the pleasure of speaking at the Bank Marketing Association's National Marketing Conference. I was excited that Bill Marriott and Tom Leonard were also speaking on the program. Bill's topic was "Playing to Win: Marketing through More Effective Customer Service." Tom was speaking on "Playing to Win: Only Happy Customers Come Back."

Bill Marriott spent the majority of his time talking about how the Marriott Corporation believes in empowering its employees. I can sum up his entire presentation with his final comment, "As my father used to say, take care of your employees and they will take care of you." Recently I read in *USA Today* that when Bill Marriott is out visiting a hotel, he spends 10 percent of his time asking his managers about the occupancy rate and bottom line and 90 percent about how the employees feel.

Tom Leonard, president of Stew Leonards, spoke fondly of all his employees and the many benefits and educational programs available to them. He referred to them as part of the Leonard family. At least half of his presentation was devoted to employee satisfaction.

**Central Fidelity Bank** in McLean, Virginia, focuses on quality service as its top priority. The following excerpt from "Quality Service Ranks No. 1!" in the bank's February 1989 newsletter demonstrates Central Fidelity's commitment to its staff:

> Without a doubt, our people are our Bank's greatest asset, and we constantly improve the ways we treat and preserve this valuable resource. Employees are provided with the best possible rewards in terms of compensation, benefits and overall quality of "work life."
>
> An excellent medical insurance plan (during a time of tremendous upheaval in that industry), reducing the eligibility requirement for the Stock and Thrift Plan to only six months and developing a more progressive compensation program that upgrades crucial customer contact positions, further prove that commitment.

I hope we all see the need to be an employee-focused organization. This chapter presents several ideas that you can implement along the way.

## *Translating Employee Satisfaction into Member Satisfaction*

Mike Maslak became president and CEO of **North Island Federal Credit Union** in San Diego in July 1987. Since then, he has developed a fiercely loyal and dedicated management team that has lead to financial success. When I asked Mike to share his secret for leading the cultural change, he shared the following with me:

> Our rationale was to develop a people-based Management Team/ Employee Focused Organizational Culture in order to successfully compete in a deregulated financial services marketplace. Our primary objective included developing role models/leaders at all management levels at North Island. Secondary objectives included top-down/ bottom-up planning, decentralized decision making, implementation of measurement systems, and special emphasis on integrating the roles of Marketing and Human Resources into our corporate culture. Our formula is simple, but the process is complex:
>
> Employee Satisfaction = Member Satisfaction = Financial Success
>
> Championing the "new and improved" corporate culture had to start at the top with a commitment from the Board of Directors. Concurrent with the development of the new employee-focused organization culture, it was equally important to systematically develop a dedicated management team at all levels within the organization, starting at the top, eventually becoming pervasive and percolating down to staff levels to create teams within bigger teams, i.e., Branch and Department teams as sub-units within the corporate organization. This transition included the liberal use of the strategic planning committee process to facilitate a forum for participation in information exchange. Communication with a capital "C" at all levels of the organization is a key ingredient in our program.
>
> Focusing on employee satisfaction and developing a people-based management team has been very successful for us. All of our key financial ratios materially exceed industry peer

performance. By focus groups and surveys, member service and employee morale has been measured at an all time high. All these facts have been observed and confirmed by outside independent sources such as our CPA firm and NCUA as documented in their audit reports.

A caution about empowerment: Make certain that at all levels the corporate message is clear, the team is in place, and "everyone" has the "tools" to fulfill their roles prior to delegating responsibility and the authority to get the job done. Otherwise you run the risk of losing some control of day-to-day operations or negatively affecting the strategic direction of your organization.

Having worked with North Island, I can personally attest to the fact that Mike's priority is the happiness of his managers and employees. His managers and employees exude energy that says, "I love working at North Island."

## *Mission Statements Emphasizing Employee Satisfaction*

When you read your mission statement where is the emphasis put? When your employees review your mission statement, do they get the impression that their job satisfaction and well-being are priorities in your company? As indicated earlier, many top-quality service organizations have identified their employees' happiness as a priority and back this up with action steps in their strategic plans. Perhaps you should consider reevaluating your mission statement and your strategic plan. If you have references to employee well-being in your mission statement also include objectives for implementing them.

**Comerica Bank** in Detroit, Michigan, is committed to its employees as shown by the annual report for 1988:

The people of Comerica, collectively, were the critical factor in the company's success in 1988. They achieved new levels of efficiency and productivity and endeavored to conduct themselves according to a new definition of quality as a commitment "to always understand and meet the expectations of our customers." In this spirit, the people of Comerica serviced businesses, consumers, and internal departments, which also were brought into the definitional framework of "customer."

Comerica's human resources programs and policies are designed to attract, motivate and reward success-oriented people. Comerica provides a competitive compensation program and a benefits package that allows employees to choose options that fit their individual needs. The Comerica employee has the opportunity for extensive internal training in job skills and management development, and for undergraduate or graduate level studies with the help of Comerica's tuition reimbursement program. Five hundred sixty-one employees advanced in their careers during 1988 by securing higher level positions through Comerica's Mobility Program.

Comerica also cares about the well-being of its employees. Through our corporate wellness program, the company in 1989 will offer for the first time, employee medical screening for blood pressure, cholesterol levels and other measures of wellness, together with recommendations for improving fitness. The company's caring also includes support for other kinds of circumstances that employees might encounter in their personal lives. The company provides, at no expense to the employee, private and confidential counseling by outside professionals to help employees and members of their families cope with the stresses of today's world, including such things as financial pressures, marital difficulties, and substance abuse. Comerica offers these programs because we want our employees to be their best, for themselves and when they come to work. We believe this gives us a competitive advantage in the marketplace and solidifies Comerica's position as "preferred employer," a place where people want to work.

## Listen to Your Employees

Listening to your employees is a major step in the direction of having an employee-focused organization. Use Mike Maslak's "fireside chats," mentioned in Chapter 1, to gather employees from different departments and different positions. Ask them to honestly share ideas on what they feel needs to be changed and on what could be done to improve the relations between management and employees.

Now act on their ideas—and quickly. There is nothing worse than soliciting feedback and not following through on the information.

## *Climate Surveys*

We use surveys and questionnaires to determine the perceptions and expectations of our customers. It is equally important that we have a clear picture of our employees' perceptions and expectations. Climate surveys or "employee report cards" are a key factor in developing an employee-focused company. How can we implement a sales and service culture if we are not addressing a problem that might be spreading throughout our organization—employee dissatisfaction. In *The Service Advantage,* Albrecht and Bradford discuss the importance of addressing "quality of work life" issues for employees.

The following example is summarized from *Personal Selling Power,* January-February 1990. Once a year Federal Express asks each of its employees a carefully developed set of questions to determine how they view the company. The program, called Survey—Feedback—Action, fleshes out unexpressed needs, pinpoints problems with their immediate managers, and addresses specific aspects of their careers.

These surveys are strictly anonymous and managers are told never to ask for, or review, the responses of an individual. Doing so violates the guarantee of an individual's anonymity and any manager violating this guarantee will be terminated. Federal Express managers receive a composite score of all findings and are expected to sit down with their team to develop a specific action plan for ongoing improvement. As a result of this survey, managers display a high sense of urgency toward solving and preventing problems.

A climate survey allows all staff members to anonymously express their opinions in writing on areas such as awareness of the company's goals, feedback and recognition, opportunity for advancement, positive social climate, justice and fair play, performance, commitment to the organization, how they view management, how they feel about communication, and many other aspects.

In a service organization, people operate on the philosophy that "everyone has a customer to please." If ill-feelings, turf wars and dissatisfactions are brewing, no one is interested in pleasing anybody, internally or externally. It is imperative, therefore, that we find out exactly how our employees feel and act on it. Even if we totally disagree with their perceptions, the fact is they exist.

## *Encourage Self-Management*

Employee-focused organizations instill an attitude in every employee that says, "I manage myself and I can make decisions." To encourage self-managed employees requires confident management that is open to delegating decisions downward. Midlevel managers need training in how to be effective leaders. Leaders delegate for results and unleash energy. They give responsibility and support and then get out of the way.

I interviewed a fascinating CEO, John Paul Jones DeJoria of John Paul Mitchell Systems (JPMS), a highly profitable and service-driven hair products manufacturer. Profits are high, employee morale is high, and turnover is low. I asked him, "What is your philosophy for keeping your employees happy and making them feel important." John Paul gave me a big smile and said, "I hire the best people I can find— qualified and happy people. I pay them way more than the industry average. Then I give them total responsibility, my support, and get out of the way. I don't believe in supervisors who manage supervisors. Banks tend to do that—it's inefficient. All of my staff work for themselves."

Having interviewed many of John Paul's employees, I can attest to the fact that they absolutely love working for JPMS. Nearly everyone of his staff said the main reason they enjoy working for him is, "He lets me run the show—I feel like I'm important."

## *Frequent Praise and Recognition*

Concentrate on building a culture where praise and recognition is given frequently and the focus is on noticing what is done right. Most organizations take the *right* things for granted and only give feedback when something goes wrong. Again, recognition techniques such as on-the-spot checkbooks of awards and praising coupons are easy to implement. These and many other ideas for recognizing employees are described in Chapter 9.

## *Opportunities for Career Advancement*

Regardless of your size, your people need a clear picture of what opportunities exist for promotions and advancement, and of what they need to do to be considered for them. Managers and supervisors need training in how to conduct one-on-one, career-pathing sessions with their employees. Employees should also be encouraged to visit other departments and to talk with coworkers to find mentors within the company.

In a small bank, mortgage company, or credit union, it is important to let employees know they have options outside your organization. While you want to keep your top performers, it is unrealistic to assume that you can offer advancement to all unless you are growing at a significant rate.

Providing education and training is another way of opening opportunities for your employees. Federal Express, for example, sends its employees, even part-timers, to educational seminars and workshops and pays for their tuition. Even though Federal Express knows that many of these people will leave and move on, it provides these opportunities nonetheless. This strategy has paid off in developing a proud, loyal, and highly motivated work force for Federal Express.

Stew Leonard and John Paul Jones DeJoria also believe in investing dollars by providing training for their staffs. Leonard sends many of his employees through the Dale Carnegie course. John Paul Jones sends his staff to Zig Ziglar's workshops. They both believe the money is well spent.

## *Social Activities and Team Spirit*

I remember being served by an enthusiastic waitress at a hotel one evening. She told me about the fun social activities the hotel sponsored for the staff. Earlier in the day she, along with her coworkers, had competed in several team events against other hotels in the area. Pride was evident in her voice.

For people to work as a team, they must feel comfortable with one another and share a familylike spirit. Employee events, whether they be fundraisers, picnics, softball games, or contests, create esprit de corps.

## *Removing Class Barriers*

If we want to create motivated, committed sales and service teams, our employees must be treated as equals—no class barriers. Eliminate the idea of officer versus nonofficer or exempt versus nonexempt. Pick titles that apply to everyone, such as associate, partner, or personal banker.

When moving into new office space, or buying new furniture, avoid having different desk sizes for managers, officers, and clerical personnel. This sends out a message that says, "We are not equals, and you are not important until you get a bigger desk."

Some organizations have executive dining rooms and only allow executives to dine in them. Somehow this does not seem to fit in with the idea of an employee-focused organization.

Remember, our frontline employees are important because they are closest to our customers or members. Anything we can do to make them feel important and equal is absolutely critical.

## *Employee Appreciation Days*

If you truly appreciate your employees and believe they are your greatest asset, why not have an Employee Appreciation Day? The key to making this event successful is getting the CEO and all senior management actively involved in its preparation and implementation.

Have your senior managers spend the day praising employees, delivering gifts, hosting parties, and filling in at work stations. CEOs must become involved, too. I know a CEO who sent each employee a gigantic chocolate kiss with a personal note of thanks on employee appreciation day.

## *Special Perks*

Today's shrinking labor pool of qualified applicants and our diverse work force is making recruiting a hot issue. Independent employees are demanding flexibility to accommodate their family's needs and personal commitments. Those organizations who are creative in providing special perks and flexible work options will have a distinct competitive advantage in attracting and retaining quality people.

**North Carolina National Bank's** overall labor force was 75 percent female in 1986. By surveying their staff in Charlotte, North Carolina, they discovered that flexible work schedules to accommodate child-care arrangements were of great interest. In response, NCNB offers a child-care resource and referral service, free of charge, and is planning to develop a day-care center. In addition, they developed a "Phase In" program that allows an employee to work a reduced number of hours at full benefits with a prorated salary during the maternity leave that has been extended from four months to six months. Their pretax, child-care reimbursement fund allows employees to set aside pretax dollars to pay child-care expenses (McColl, August 1988).

Employee-focused companies provide special benefits to improve the quality of work life. Some perks you can consider are:

- ★ Providing on-site aerobic classes and exercise equipment
- ★ Paying for attendance at special industry conferences
- ★ Setting up job sharing, flexible hours, and compressed work weeks
- ★ Instituting "Work-at-Home" projects
- ★ Allowing extended, unpaid time off
- ★ Getting spouses involved in activities
- ★ Arranging for child care and for referral services

## *Encouraging Employees to Dream and Set Goals*

If we value our employees, why not encourage them to dream, to set goals—to be the best they can be? It's possible that at least half of our employees would rather be doing something else if they could. They work for a paycheck. It is sad, but many managers and employees are just burned out. They have no genuine joy for their work because it is not their true passion in life; therefore, they feel trapped. The other half are quite pleased working in our organization, and some of these hope to advance. It is far easier to motivate employees who have goals and dreams than those who do not.

Does your organization encourage managers and employees to write out their business and personal goals? Find out what your employees want to do in the future. Employees who seek advancement in your organization need guidance on how to proceed. Employees who have an entrepreneurial bent also need to be encouraged. I know of a credit union employee, for example, who wants to be an illustrator for children's books. Her manager is encouraging her to take classes and to use her artistic talents at work.

John Paul Jones DeJoria truly believes that if his employees want to pursue something else in their lives, and he helps them, all parties benefit. He believes in paying his people better than any other company in his industry; in empowering them to make decisions; in encouraging them to move on; and in creating an environment of trust, compassion, and excellence. This gentleman is genuinely focused on his employees' happiness. But what are the benefits?

In John Paul's case, his company has become one of the most profitable hair product manufacturers in the United States. John Paul believes his secret to success is, "Hire happy people, and encourage them to go for their dreams." Several of his staff told me they had discussed some of their goals with him. One woman said, "He knows I want my own business in three years, and he is helping me."

## *Be One of the Best*

How would you like your organization to be listed as one of the best companies to work for? **VanCity Savings Credit Union**, Vancouver, British Columbia, has achieved that distinction. In addition, VanCity also made the list for the best companies for "spirit" and for "women" (see Exhibits 11.1 and 11.2). As a result, they have no shortage of qualified applicants and an unusually happy, loyal, and dedicated staff.

VanCity is truly a fine example of how a company can thrive by focusing on the well-being of its employees. The following summary is excerpted from *The Financial Post: 100 Best Companies to Work for in Canada*, by Eva Innes, Jim Lyon, and Jim Harris.

> VanCity has an enviable corporate culture and climate as follows:
>
> Pay: **Good**          Atmosphere: **Very Good**
>
> Benefits: **Very Good**          Job Satisfaction: **Very Good**
>
> Promotion: **Good**          Communications: **Very Good**
>
> Job Security: **Very Good**          Personal Development: **Very Good**

*VanCity is the third largest credit union in the world (after those of the U.S. Navy and United Airlines). It has assets of $2.2 billion (Canadian) and functions essentially as a retail bank for about 180,000 owner-members. There are about 740 employees, 165 at head office, the remainder spread among 24 branches throughout Greater Vancouver.*

**VanCity Management** recognizes that employees are the key in the financial services industry. They are dealing with a product (money) that is undifferentiated except for the service that employees add to it. And employees at VanCity believe in having fun.

There are not many financial institutions where a branch manager will dress up as Frankenstein at Halloween and sling a cheeky sign across her back saying: "I work for the Bank of Montreal." Rather than frowning on such frivolity, senior management

## Exhibit 11.1

### From the *Financial Post: 100 Best Companies to Work for in Canada*

### THE BEST COMPANIES FOR SPIRIT

Apple
B.C. Tel
CAE Electronics
Canada Trust
Canadian Hunter
Canadian Pacific Hotels
Four Seasons Hotels
Hongkong Bank
J. W. Lindsay

MacDonald Dettwiler
McDonald's Restaurants
NovAtel
Parkridge Centre
The Personal
Shoppers Drug Mart
Steelcase
VanCity

Each of these companies has what can best be described as a superior esprit de corps — a working atmosphere of enthusiasm, enjoyment, amiability, co-operation and fun. This spirit permeates all ranks, not management alone.

In some cases, this spirit can be linked to the physical working environment. Some company offices, such as those at Steelcase (office experts), are ergonomically superior, clearly designed to enhance employee enjoyment and productivity.

Clearly, though, a good physical working environment alone cannot create a team spirit. Some of the most enthusiastic employees we met work in average, undistinguished factory environments.

Spirit stems from a complicated blend of excellent up-down communications, a sense of purpose and a genuine involvement in decision making. Good companies define a clear mission. They convince employees to share the vision and help to implement it.

Workers who feel they're putting a part of themselves into their jobs on a daily basis are the most likely to develop emthusiasm and a sense of well-being.

## Exhibit 11.2

### From the *Financial Post: 100 Best Companies to Work for in Canada*

#### THE BEST COMPANIES FOR WOMEN

| | |
|---|---|
| B. C. Telephone | Procter & Gamble |
| Federal Express | Royal Trust |
| Manufacturers Life | VanCity |
| Pillsbury | Warner Lambert |

#### RUNNERS-UP

| | |
|---|---|
| Four Seasons Hotels | Great-West Life |
| The Personal | Royal Bank |

Companies that offer superior opportunities for women to advance into management appear in the upper list. In them, remarkable numbers of women are in managerial positions and executive ranks. Federal Express, recognized as one of the top employers for women in the U.S., leads the pack with a remarkable 50% women managers and 35% female executives.

Companies in the runners-up list have strong numbers of women in managerial positions, but fewer in executive posts. These companies have the potential to make dramatic strides.

But numbers alone are not the only criterion for judging good companies for women. Attitudes toward women juggling careers and motherhood also play an important role. Many of these companies make life easier for their women employees through a variety of programs, such as flex-time, job sharing and day-care assistance. Others create new career paths to the top, or provide career counseling to help women advance upward. These are all factors we have taken in account when judging which companies are best for women.

In spite of the significant advances in overall numbers since the first edition of this book, there are still disappointingly few women presidents and vice-presidents. And the route to senior positions still seems to be stereotyped: either through human resources or public affairs.

joins in and dons fancy dress for Halloween visits to branches. Some members complained it was too much, though, when one branch brought in rabbits at Easter.

There are other friendly touches. Management sees to it that all employees get cards on their birthdays and the anniversaries of joining the organization, and handwritten notes from the personnel department or the vice-president of marketing are penned to staff meriting special recognition.

There are awards for people who lose weight, quit smoking or jog 1,000 miles a year. (Somewhat counterproductively, the prize for the latter feat includes dinner at one of Vancouver's finest restaurants.) There are also prizes for branches that write the most business or persuade the most members to switch their registered retirement savings plans to VanCity.

If the organization's management style is light, it has also been sure. VanCity's growth has been remarkable. Founded in 1946 by 22 members, it has grown rapidly, especially in the past decade or so.

Employees rate their job satisfaction as high, and they agree that VanCity actively encourages personal growth and provides the means for this to be achieved. A woman employee comments: "If you want to move ahead, everything is on a silver platter for you if you want to take it. They want you to know as much as you can about everything."

The credit union places great emphasis on training, running its own courses and paying the cost of outside tuition, including university courses.

Many VanCity members bank with the credit union because they feel pride in a thriving home-grown financial institution. They also say it is friendlier than the chartered banks.

New employees, especially, are struck by the pleasant atmosphere. One woman, meeting a senior executive for the first time in a group of about 20 people, was amazed that he later remembered her by her first name.

A woman employee said she feels good about the intensive training she gets at VanCity. "If the competition don't really know about their products and we do, well, that is one up for us." Among VanCity's more unusual products is the popular Ethical Growth Fund, which permits conscientious investors to put their money into companies that don't make military products, are not in the nuclear industry and don't trade with South Africa.

VanCity's roots go deep in its community, and it makes special efforts to support local organizations financially. Each year, it adopts a theme for corporate donations. In 1989, it was multiculturalism, and all requests for donations had to be linked to that theme. Employees also may ask for cash grants (typically $100 to $500) to help support nonprofit community organizations they are involved in.

More than 80% of VanCity employees are women. They occupy 38% of the management jobs, 20% of the executive posts and comprise 35% of the board of directors.

Because it is reluctant to lose the skills and experience of expensively trained employees wanting to take an extended break to care for a young family, VanCity in 1989 introduced a return-to-work program based on European models.

Linda Crompton, vice-president of human resources, explains: "There's a continuing worry about how to get a job when they want to get back into the workforce. We say, 'If you elect you can take two or three years off. We will keep you on the books.' "

Jobs are guaranteed. Employees stay on the staff mailing list and are invited to attend social functions. Twice a year, they are expected to work for a week or two to stay on top of new technology. When the program was announced, 80 women asked to take advantage of it.

Employees sit on a committee that compares VanCity salaries and benefits to those of other financial institutions and makes recommendations to management. Since the committee was started in 1977, its ideas have been accepted without exception.

VanCity does little recruiting outside, except for specialized skills, preferring to promote from within and train staff to handle extra responsibility. In 1989, it was getting about 120 unsolicited applications a month. However, in common with most financial institutions, it was experiencing difficulty in attracting well-qualified people for its more junior positions.

To make the jobs more interesting and justify higher pay rates, VanCity has begun training new entrants for greater immediate responsibility. Rather than simply placing new employees in lowly teller positions where they learn on the job, it began putting newcomers through a month-long training course to acquire the skills for a variety of jobs. This way, it hopes employees will stick around longer in an industry with notoriously high turnover.

Employees are so enthusiastic about VanCity they admit they occasionally sound "corny." When the credit union asked workers to suggest an advertising slogan, 122 of them replied with repeated references to such concepts as "happiness, pride, friendship and family."

An employee social club, whose directors are elected from among the branches, meets monthly and organizes a Christmas party, a dinner dance, a casino night, a golf tournament, a baseball league, a curling bonspiel and a boat cruise. All are well attended.

As an additional benefit, VanCity also pays the costs (up to $500 a year) for visits to a clinical psychologist. Counseling sessions include advice on problems with alcohol or drugs, marriage breakdown, kids in difficulties. A brochure advertising the confidential employee assistance program says: "You're our most valuable resource. It stands to reason that if we can help you solve outside problems which may be affecting your work, everyone benefits."

Other benefits are low-cost loans for employees. Senior staff, for example, can obtain a mortgage amounting to double their annual salary at half the conventional interest rate.

A woman employee said: "We are not all perfect, obviously, but when there is bad service given, or we feel it is not up to par, I feel very hurt. At VanCity, a piece of it is mine."

For employees, VanCity has made the usually staid banking business sparkle.

Let Van City's shining example be a lesson to all of us. Without our staff members, there *is* no business. The work force of the '90s will be much more difficult to attract, motivate, and retain. Those organizations that focus on the happiness of their employees will have an edge in the service arena.

# Chapter 12

## Developing a Branch, Quality Service Plan

Those of you managing in a branch environment have the greatest challenge in implementing a service program. With turnover, limited staff, increased paperwork, new products, and demanding customers or members, maintaining a superior level of service is not easy. Do not despair! With your enthusiasm, you can develop a branch quality service plan to achieve success.

Let's use some of the key concepts and ideas mentioned in the previous chapters to develop the plan. First, we'll lay out some simple strategies, phase-by-phase, in order of priority, and with a brief explanation. If you would like more detailed information on any one idea, simply flip back to the appropriate chapter.

### *Phase I—Leading by Example*
### Developing a Mission Statement
If you have a bank or credit union mission statement, review it with your staff and make sure they understand what it means. Next, it is critical

that you and your staff develop a mission statement for your branch that spells out clearly what your branch stands for and why you exist.

One branch manager and his staff came up with the following statement:

> The Ninth Street Branch's mission is to ensure that every customer leaves satisfied, with a smile on their face. We value our fellow workers and seek to create a fun and rewarding environment for all.

Now you are ready to ask your employees to develop their own personal mission statements or pledges of how they intend to contribute to the branch's mission as individuals.

### Greet Employees as if They Were Customers
Make sure you are greeting your staff members each morning by name in a friendly and responsive manner.

### Include Service on Meeting Agendas
Hold regular service meetings and make sure that service quality and sales are always the first items on the agenda. Review your goals and service scores with your team and never let the topic fade away.

### Fill In for Your Staff
Roll up your sleeves, pitch in, and let them see you serving the customers or members with a big smile. Be a role model for them to follow.

## Phase II—Improving Internal Service and Cooperation
### Develop a Branch Employee Survey
Develop a simple questionnaire to determine your team's feelings about the existing levels of service, the policies that hinder them, their decision-making ability, and frequent customer complaints. The survey should also ask for your employees' ideas for improving service and team spirit.

### On-Site Visits to Support Departments

To promote team work and empathy among support departments, arrange for your people to visit the main office's operational areas and observe how those jobs are done. Likewise, invite supervisors from support departments to visit your branch and speak at a meeting.

### Praising Coupons

Encourage your team members to use praising coupons to recognize fellow branch employees who give them superior service.

## Phase III—Empowering and Listening to Your Employees

### Employee Surveys and Focus Groups

From the survey mentioned in Phase III and through employee focus groups, determine how often employees say, "I can't do that, I have to ask my manager." Empower your staff to begin taking more responsibility and to make decisions. Let them know when it is appropriate to make exceptions to policies. Give them a specific dollar limit to work with each month for waiving fees, offering free checks, or sending flowers.

### Reward Risk Takers

Develop a certificate or special award for the "Risk Taker of the Month." Give it to any staff member who wisely broke a rule in an effort to save or satisfy a customer or member.

## Phase IV—Retaining Your Customers or Members

### Thank-You Note Contests

With your staff's commitment, develop a thank-you note contest. Challenge each staff member to send out his or her own handwritten notes each day for a month to *existing* customers and members. Give awards to the three who send out the most notes at the end of a month.

### Customer or Member Appreciation Weeks

Get your staff involved in planning a week-long appreciation event for your good customers or members. Create ambiance with music and balloons, have greeters at the door from all areas of the bank, give flowers to adults and candy to children, raffle some prizes, and thank each and every person for his or her business.

## Opinion Surveys and Focus Groups

Send out a survey to all your branch customers or members to find out how they feel about your existing service and products. Leave room on the survey for any other comments they wish to share.

Invite several of your customers or members from a variety of market segments to a focus group at your branch or an off-site location. Prepare specific questions and let them respond in an informal manner.

## Distinctive Touches

Meet with your staff and come up with a list of ideas that have a personal touch, and that will make your customers or members feel important and set you apart from your competition. Some examples of distinctive touches are customer of the week, a courtesy telephone, toys to occupy children, and selling postage stamps.

## *Phase V—Developing Standards for Service*

### Conduct Research

Visit bookstores and libraries, talk to business owners, and use the Bank Marketing Association library to find out what kinds of standards other organizations use. Also study Exhibits 5.1 through 5.8 in Chapter 5.

### Develop Standards for Your Branch and Each Team Member

In a meeting, ask your staff to agree on which areas need more defined standards. Some areas to consider are telephone use, error reduction, written correspondence, turnaround time, courtesy, waiting time, and complaint resolution. Once you have group standards, display them in a visible area. Now you can ask each individual in your branch to draft measurable standards that they are willing to carry out.

## *Phase VI—Providing Creative Training*
### Field Trips for Training
To heighten the awareness of service and stimulate creativity among your staff, arrange for fun and informative field trips to service-driven organizations in your area. For example, send some of your customer service representatives or tellers to a Marriott or a Nordstrom's. Have them meet with some employees, and make a report about the experience at your next service meeting.

### Product Knowledge Games and Tests
To reinforce product knowledge, plan a fun game or give your staff members a written test. Get them involved in making up the questions and planning the game. Be consistent and test regularly. Publish the scores and offer incentives for those who receive perfect scores.

### Utilize Guest Speakers
At your next meeting, get one of your good customers or members to talk to your staff about what good service means to them, what they like and do not like, and how the competition is approaching them.

In addition, find a retail employee from a high-quality hotel or department store to speak to your staff about how they are trained and to give tips for handling customers.

### Provide Cross Training
Improving the responsiveness and service levels in your branch requires a well-trained staff that can easily fill in for one another. Develop a cross-training plan for your team and get their input.

## *Phase VII—Monitoring Complaints and Measuring Service*
### Comment Cards
Once your staff is ready, give your customers or members the opportunity to comment on your service by utilizing comment cards. You can distribute these the first week of each month, or quarter, to a sampling of customers. Also keep them on display at all times. Make sure every card gets a response in a timely

manner. Use a numerical rating from 1 to 5 or 1 to 10 and set a minimum level of performance that you expect for your branch and each team member. Chapter 7 has more information about customer comment cards.

### New Account and Closed Account Survey
Randomly select new customer or members who recently opened an account with your branch and ask them, either by telephone or in writing, to rate the service they received. Likewise, have your customers fill out closed account surveys to find out exactly why they left your bank or credit union. Share all results with your staff.

### Mystery Shoppers
To improve the professionalism of your staff have customers or members, coworkers from another branch, friends, or trained shoppers shop your branch in person and by phone. Tally up the scores and reward those employees who received a perfect score.

## *Phase VIII—Holding Your People Accountable for Service*
### Include Service Goals and Standards in All Performance Appraisals
Take the standards you developed for each person on your team and include them in performance appraisals. Ask them to achieve a specific rating, based on the comment cards and mystery shopper scores. Decide how important service is in their overall review and assign a weighted value to it. For example, 25 percent of a teller's review will be based on achieving a specific service score.

### Product Knowledge Accountability
If you test your employees for product knowledge, then it is fairly easy to ask them to achieve a minimum score, such as 80 percent, which will be included in their appraisal. By being held accountable at review time, your employees will accept responsibility for learning about your branch's products.

### Phase IX—Rewarding and Recognizing Service Excellence

#### Involve Customers or Members in Employee Recognition

Give coupons to your customers or members to allow them to recognize your employees for exceptional service. Each coupon can equal a particular point value. Create tiers for different levels of performance, and give awards for specific numbers of coupons or points. Display the awards in the staff room, and acknowledge the winners in your newsletter or at a special awards program.

#### Special Breakfasts or Dinners

Hold a special event to reward your top service performers in front of their peers. Invite your senior management and the top performers' spouses. Make it as much fun as possible—with music, decorations, prizes, and lots of applause.

#### Checkbook of Awards

Create a unique "checkbook" to provide on-the-spot recognition whenever you see someone going the extra mile. Awards in the form of checks can be lunch, gift certificates, time off, cookies, or theater tickets.

### Phase X—Attracting and Orienting New Employees

#### Hire from Outside the Financial Industry

Always be on the lookout for good service-oriented people when you are out and about. The next time you get exceptional service in a restaurant or department store, get the name and telephone number of that individual. When you have an opening at your branch, give that person a call. Hire for personality first, not technical expertise. New employees can learn the technical skills through training.

#### Personality Assessments

If possible, give every internal and external candidate a personality assessment to determine his or her suitability for sales and service.

### New Employee Orientation

Make sure that you share your branch's, as well as the organization's, mission statement and service philosophy with each new team member. Show them your branch's service plan, comment cards, survey results, and any communications that will give them the big picture. Make them feel welcome and introduce them, in a special way, to the rest of the staff. Take new employees to lunch during their first week and share your vision with them.

### Form a Hiring Committee

Create a committee of at least three people to make the final selection on all candidates. One committee member should be a senior person; one, a peer; and one, the candidate's immediate manager. Don't let just one person make the hiring decisions. Get a group consensus.

## *Phase XI—Focusing on Employee Satisfaction*

### Encourage Self-management

Delegate responsibility and decision-making whenever possible. Ask your staff what they need to be happy in their job, and listen to their ideas. Conduct one-on-one sessions, ask for their input, and carry out their suggestions.

### Praise and Recognize

Build a culture in your branch where praise and recognition for doing things *right* is the norm. Let employees know you appreciate their efforts.

### Encourage Goal Setting

Ask your team members to write down their individual goals for the future. What do they want to be doing in one, three, and five years? Whether they want to advance in your organization or open their own business, help them map out a plan of action. You cannot motivate an employee who feels stuck. Show them they have options and inspire them to go for their dreams. Review each employees' goals one-on-one. But do not force them to share their goals—make it voluntary. If you are genuinely concerned with your employees' happiness, you will win their loyalty.

You should be able to implement this quality service plan at your branch. Be careful though. Rather than being overly aggressive and trying to do everything at once, be realistic and start with one phase at a time. For those of you who are well past the basics, you can pick some of the more complex service strategies from chapters 1 through 10 and work them into your plan.

The only thing left to do now is to come up with a timetable for your service plan and to assign tasks to your team members. Get everyone on your team involved and excited about the quality service plan—it's their plan, too.

# Chapter 13

## Developing a Comprehensive Service Plan

Building a permanent, quality service culture requires a comprehensive written action plan. If you have a successful service program in place, you can complement your existing program by selecting some of the ideas outlined earlier in this book. If you are just beginning a quality service program or are not satisfied with your existing one, consider developing a long-term plan of action.

Chris Lamb, senior vice president of operations at **North Island Federal Credit Union** in San Diego, developed a comprehensive business plan for service. Her plan included service training, focus groups, member surveys, a monthly comment box, an incentive committee, an employee-of-the-month program, and much more. To date, all phases of the program have been implemented in preparation for the sales culture.

When I asked Chris about the results they had achieved to date, she said, "All our CAMEL ratios are excellent, all our ESP [Excellence in Service Program] goals have been achieved, and our monthly member survey shows a 97 percent satisfaction rate in employee knowledge, friendliness, and problem solving."

By sticking to a long-term service strategy, North Island has happy members, a happy board of directors, and, most of all, a happy group of satisfied employees. These are all key elements leading to their financial success. Plus, they now have a strong base from which to begin working on their sales culture.

The previous chapters offered many ideas for reinforcing service throughout your organization. So many ideas, in fact, that they can be overwhelming. This brief chapter simplifies the process by outlining a step-by-step plan for achieving service quality. The strategies mentioned in the plan are explained in detail in previous chapters. Simply refer to the index to locate additional information on the topic of interest.

**Step 1: Senior Management Demonstrates a Commitment to a Service Quality Program**

   A. CEO Arrange a Management Retreat

      1. Create or redefine your mission statement to reflect commitment to service and your employees

      2. Get your support and operational department managers to "buy" into the program

      3. Make service a priority in your strategic plan

      4. Build service objectives into your operating plan for all departments

      5. End the retreat with initial action steps for each manager to implement

      6. Set a date for a follow-up meeting

   B. Conduct an Employee Climate Survey

      1. Survey your employees to determine how they feel about your organization and the service you presently provide

2.  Begin addressing concerns and obstacles that surface from your survey, prior to moving forward

## Step 2:   Begin Sharing the Vision

A.  Communicate Vision and Service Mission at Employee Kickoff Meeting

1.  Organize a fun service celebration
2.  Have CEO share the service vision and mission statement
3.  Share the results of the employee climate survey with the staff
4.  Explain the "big picture," how employees fit in, what they can expect, and your overall service strategy
5.  Allow for questions and feedback

B.  Senior Management Serves as Role Models for Service Champions

1.  CEO includes service as an item on the agenda at every executive meeting
2.  Each manager develops a department or branch mission statement
3.  Senior management goes out in the field by adopting a branch or department
4.  CEO begins "fireside chats"
5.  CEO writes a service column in the employee paper and recognizes star employees

## Step 3:   Define Service Internally and Externally

A.  Focus on Internal Service First

1.  Have each department head ask his or her internal customers (employees) what they expect from the department
2.  Survey employees to rate the existing service received by internal support departments

3. Share survey results with department managers and staff

4. Develop quality teams in each branch or department to review internal procedures, forms, policies, and obstacles to service quality

5. Create praising coupons for employees to recognize excellent internal service

B. Determine Your Customers or Members Expectations and Perceptions

1. Conduct an opinion survey of your existing members or customers to determine their expectations and how they perceive your existing service

2. Conduct focus groups with your existing customers and noncustomers as well

3. Evaluate results and define the service expectations of your members or customers

4. Share all survey and focus group results with your staff

C. Empower Your Employees to Make Decisions and Listen to Their Ideas

1. Conduct a survey asking your employees for ideas to improve service, about perceived obstacles, and how their authority should be expanded

2. Ask quality service teams for recommendations

3. Act on recommendations and communicate with your staff

4. Empower employees with authority to be responsive to customers or members

5. Attempt to remove operational and procedural obstacles

6. Create a "Risk-Taker Award" for those who appropriately bend the rules to serve a member or customer

## Step 4: Set Standards for Service and Provide Training

A. Set Standards for Service Quality. Using information from internal and external surveys and focus groups, develop

1. A customer or member bill of rights

2. Telephone standards for the entire organization

3. Complaint resolution standards for all departments

4. Customized department and branch quality service standards, based on primary focus; for example, turnaround time, accuracy, or responsiveness

5. Personal quality service standards for each employee

B. Provide Top-down Training

1. Deliver quality service and sales leadership training for CEO, managers, and supervisors

2. Deliver customer service and telephone skills training for all frontline staff, officers, and senior management

3. Deliver internal service and telephone skills training for all support and operational staff and managers

4. Develop product knowledge testing or certification programs for the entire staff

**Step 5: Measure and Reward Service Performance Against Expectations**

A. Monitor Complaints and Measure Service

1. Develop an error- and complaint-resolution program

2. Utilize new account and closed account surveys

3. Mail and distribute comment cards with numerical ratings to customers or members, or conduct random-sampling surveys by phone or mail

4. Create a mystery shopper program to monitor employee service performance

5. Mail opinion surveys to customers or members twice a year to measure progress

6. Distribute comment cards or surveys periodically to all employees to measure the internal service received by support and operational departments

B. Reward and Recognize Your Service Stars

1. Develop on-the-spot rewards to be used by management to recognize service excellence

2. Create a service award club for frontline and support and operational staff

3. Profile service heroes in your sales and service newsletter

4. Have customers or members give praising coupons to your staff

5. Hold a service awards banquet to recognize your star employees in front of their peers

6. Distribute team and individual cash incentives if annual service and sales goals were achieved

### Step 6: Hold People Accountable for Service Performance

A. Revise All Job Descriptions to Include Service and/or Sales

1. Revise job descriptions, where appropriate, to emphasize the importance of service quality and/or sales

2. Revise job descriptions, where appropriate, to emphasize the importance of product knowledge

B. Revise Performance Appraisals

1. Add specific service scores and sales goals in all managers' performance appraisals for either internal or external service, and assign a weighted value

2. Add measurable service standards, sales goals, and product knowledge scores in employees' performance appraisals, where appropriate, and weigh according to priority

3. Coach all managers and employees not meeting standards

### Step 7: Develop a Customer or Member Retention Program

A. Customer-centered Programs

1. Develop a customer or member advisory council

2. Hold customer or member luncheons

3. Hold customer or member appreciation weeks

4. Develop a service guarantee program

B. Employee-centered Programs

1. Develop a sales advisory council

2. Increase penetration by paying employees incentives for selling packaged accounts

3. Ask employees for ideas on distinctive service programs

## Step 8:   Invest in Quality People

A. Revise Your Selection Process and Orientation Program

1. Establish a profile for ideal candidates and communicate it to all

2. Set up hiring committees to screen candidates

3. Use personality profiles and screening devices whenever possible

4. Upgrade your entry-level salary structure to attract top-quality talent

5. Hire service-oriented people from retail environments

6. Revise your new employee orientation to include a service and sales philosophy

B. Make a Commitment to Be an Employee-focused Company

1. Revise your mission statement to include emphasis on employee satisfaction

2. Conduct regular climate surveys to measure employee satisfaction and to address key issues

3. Make praise and recognition a part of your culture

4. Pay a bit more than your competitors

5. Develop special perks, such as tuition reimbursement, flexible hours, and child-care assistance

6.  Communicate with your staff, and include the staff in all decisions

7.  Incorporate personal growth, goal setting, and self-esteem workshops into your training schedule

8.  Allow for extra time off without pay

9.  Encourage and challenge employees to pursue business and personal goals

To make your service program, as just outlined, come alive, assign action steps and completion dates for each item to individuals, branches, or departments. Use the worksheet in Exhibit 13.1 as an example for writing your own customized service action plan. It shows how to implement a plan for one service objective. You now have a detailed plan to follow and from which to measure your progress.

### Exhibit 13.1

#### Quality Service Action Plan

Objective:   Measure Internal and External Service

| Strategy | Assigned To | Target Date | Status |
|---|---|---|---|
| Survey all employees to measure internal service | Operations & Marketing | Jan. & June | |
| Utilize new account and closed account surveys | Branch Mgrs. & Marketing | Begin in Feb. | & ongoing monthly |
| Develop error and complaint resolution program with marketing | Operations & Branch Mgrs. | 2nd quarter | |
| Mail and/or distribute comment cards to customers or members | Branch Mgrs., Mortgage & Marketing | 3rd quarter | quarterly |
| Utilize mystery shoppers | Marketing | Begin 3rd quarter | & ongoing |
| Mail opinion surveys to customers or members | Marketing | Once a year | Jan. |

By mapping out each step of your quality service plan with a specific strategy, assigned group, and target date, you are laying a foundation for success. If this document is referred to and used by your CEO in every meeting, your chances for success are excellent.

Take your action plan, add some enthusiasm, commitment, and perseverance and you're ready to embark on your service journey. Don't forget to have some fun along the way, and when you fall down, just pick yourself up and try again.

Be patient. A service program does not have a beginning and an end, it is constantly being refined. Depending on your size and number of employees, it can easily take from one to three years before you complete the initial action plan and see significant progress. Rather than using the Band-Aid, quick-fix approach, complete one step at a time. When you are confident that progress has been made in one area, then proceed to the next step. Remember, it is the "quality" of your efforts that count, not the "quantity."

**"The only certain means of success is
to render more and better service
than is expected of you,
no matter what
your task may be."**

**Og Mandino**

## *One Last Note*

I designed this book to be simple and practical. Hopefully, you can use several of the ideas to complement your quality service program. Now, may I ask you for some input? If you experience success in any areas of your service program and would like to have your ideas included in a future book or article, please send me an outline of your program, with samples, to the address on the next page. In particular, I would like solid examples of how you designed standards, measured internal service, revised performance appraisals, and developed employee-focused programs. Thanks for your ideas in advance.

## *For Additional Information*

Based in Oakland, California, Romano & Sanfilippo is a full-service consulting, training, and speaking organization committed to assisting financial institutions develop a sales and customer service culture. Romano & Sanfilippo takes a "total approach" to organizational change and believes that all departments and staff members must understand how they contribute to the overall mission.

Barbara Sanfilippo and her husband and business partner, Bob Romano (formerly with Xerox Corporation), provide many services, including:

★ Assessing the existing culture

★ Conducting employee climate surveys

★ Leading senior management service awareness retreats

★ Developing customized sales and service action plans

★ Delivering sales, customer service, and sales leadership training

★ RENT-A-SALES COACH

In addition, Barbara is a popular guest speaker at management, sales, and awards conferences. She also conducts special strategy sessions and workshops for senior management, branch manager, and board of director retreats. A promotional package is available on request.

For information about consulting services, available speaking dates, or books, tapes, and videos, please call or write:

Barbara Sanfilippo
Romano & Sanfilippo
73 Buckeye Avenue
Oakland, CA 94618

(415) 547-6683

# Bibliography

"Advisory Boards Glue Banks to Communities." *Community Bank Marketing Newsletter*, 16, no. 1 (January 1989), pp. 1, 2.

Albrecht, Karl, and Lawrence J. Bradford. *The Service Advantage: How to Identify and Fulfill Customer Needs*. Homewood, Illinois: Dow Jones-Irwin, 1990.

Albrecht, Karl, and Ron Zemke. *Service America!: Doing Business in the New Economy*. Homewood, Illinois: Dow Jones-Irwin, 1985.

"BayBanks Creates Employees 'Legends' as Emissaries." *Bank Marketing* 21, no. 7 (July 1989), p.6.

Bennett, David R. "Monthly Strategy Session: Service Quality as a Profit Strategy—You Can Become A Service Leader." *Retail Banking Strategist* 2, no. 1 (December 1988), pp. 10–12.

Berry, Leonard L. "Approaches to Measuring Quality of Service." *American Banker*, pp. 6, 39.

Berry, Leonard. "Banks, Retailers Share Customer Service Priority." *American Banker* (November 6, 1985), pp. 4, 8, 9.

Berry, Leonard L. "Society Corp. Staff Uses Teamwork to Improve Service." *American Banker* (April 6, 1989), p. 4.

Berry, Leonard L., David R. Bennett, and Carter W. Brown. *Service Quality: A Profit Strategy for Financial Institutions.* Homewood, Illinois: Dow Jones-Irwin, 1989.

Berry, Leonard L., and George Rieder, "A Grocery List for Bankers— Lessons from Randall's Stores." *American Banker* (December 24, 1985), pp. 4,11.

Blume, Eric R. "Customer Service: Giving Companies the Competitive Edge." *Training & Development Journal* 42, no. 9 (September 1988), pp. 24–28, 30, 32.

Browning, D. Dale. "Put Up or Pay Up." *Bank Marketing* (September 1989), pp. 53–55.

Butler, Leslie R. and Francis J. Dynan. "Putting Service Quality into Practice: A Case Study." *Journal of Retail Banking* 10, no. 4 (Winter 1988), pp. 5–13.

Carlzon, Jan. "Moments of Truth: Seize These Golden Opportunities to Serve Your Customers." *Success!* (May 1987), pp. 52, 53.

"Customer Satisfaction Is Key to Service Sector." *Western Banker* (Sandy Corporation) 81, no. 4 (April 1989), pp. 26, 27.

Desatnick, Robert L. "Service: A CEO's Perspective." *Management Review* (October 1987), pp. 41–43.

"Domino's Pizza Delivering the Marketing Promise." *Incentive* 162, no. 7 (July 1988), pp. 48, 69.

Dow, Roger J. "At Marriott, the 'Little Things' Add Up to Better Service." *Bank Marketing* 20, no. 6 (June 1988), pp. 70.

Duncan, Barbara. "At Disneyland, Customer Service Is Not a 'Fantasy'." *Bank Marketing* (March 1988), p. 68.

Glass, David D. "Sales Culture at Wal-Mart Means Thinking like Customers." *Bank Marketing* (October 1987), p. 78.

Gschwandtner, Gerhard. "Secrets of Sales Success at Federal Express." *Personal Selling Power* (Fredricksburg, Virginia) 10, no. 1, (January-February 1990), pp. 12–20.